Carol Reed

D0993184

Manchester University Press

BRIAN MCFARLANE, NEIL SINYARD *series editors*

ALLEN EYLES, PHILIP FRENCH, SUE HARPER,
TIM PULLEINE, JEFFREY RICHARDS, TOM RYALL
series advisers

already published

Roy Ward Baker   GEOFF MAYER

Jack Clayton   NEIL SINYARD

Lance Comfort   BRIAN MCFARLANE

Terence Davies   WENDY EVERETT

Terence Fisher   PETER HUTCHINGS

Launder and Gilliat   BRUCE BABINGTON

Joseph Losey   COLIN GARDNER

Michael Reeves   BENJAMIN HALLIGAN

J. Lee Thompson   STEVE CHIBNALL

Carol Reed

BRITISH FILM MAKERS

PETER WILLIAM EVANS

Manchester University Press

MANCHESTER AND NEW YORK

distributed exclusively in the USA by Palgrave

Copyright © Peter William Evans 2005

The right of Peter William Evans to be identified as the author of this work has been asserted by him in accordance with the Copyright, Designs and Patents Act 1988.

Published by Manchester University Press
Oxford Road, Manchester M13 9NR, UK
and Room 400, 175 Fifth Avenue, New York, NY 10010, USA
www.manchesteruniversitypress.co.uk

Distributed exclusively in the USA by
Palgrave, 175 Fifth Avenue, New York, NY 10010, USA

Distributed exclusively in Canada by
UBC Press, University of British Columbia, 2029 West Mall, Vancouver, BC, Canada V6T 1Z2

British Library Cataloguing-in-Publication Data
A catalogue record for this book is available from the British Library

Library of Congress Cataloging-in-Publication Data applied for

ISBN 0 7190 6366 3 *hardback*
EAN 978 0 7190 6366 4
ISBN 0 7190 6367 1 *paperback*
EAN 978 0 7190 6367 1

First published 2005

14 13 12 11 10 09 08 07 06 05   10 9 8 7 6 5 4 3 2 1

Typeset in Scala with Meta display
by Koinonia, Manchester
Printed in Great Britain
by Bell & Bain Limited, Glasgow

Contents

List of plates

The author gratefully acknowledges the following for permission of the use of the stills: Optimum Releasing (*The Third Man*); Canal+Image UK (*The Fallen Idol*); Columbia TriStar (*Our Man in Havana, The Key, Oliver!*); TVAI (*Night Train to Munich*); MGM Plaza (*Trapeze*); Carlton International (*Climbing High, The Way Ahead, Odd Man Out*). All stills supplied by BFI Films: Stills, Posters and Designs

Series editors' foreword

The aim of this series is to present in lively, authoritative volumes a guide to those film-makers who have made British cinema a rewarding but still under-researched branch of world cinema. The intention is to provide books which are up-to-date in terms of information and critical approach, but not bound to any one theoretical methodology. Though all books in the series will have certain elements in common – comprehensive filmographies, annotated bibliographies, appropriate illustration – the actual critical tools employed will be the responsibility of the individual authors.

Nevertheless, an important recurring element will be a concern for how the oeuvre of each film-maker does or does not fit certain critical and industrial contexts, as well as for the wider social contexts which helped to shape not just that particular film-maker but the course of British cinema at large.

Although the series is director-orientated, the editors believe that reference to a variety of stances and contexts is more likely to reconceptualise and reappraise the phenomenon of British cinema as a complex, shifting field of production. All the texts in the series will engage in detailed discussion of major works of the film-makers involved, but they all consider as well the importance of other key collaborators, of studio organisation, of audience reception, of recurring themes and structures: all those other aspects which go towards the construction of a national cinema.

The series explores and charts a field which is more than ripe for serious excavation. The acknowledged leaders of the field will be reappraised; just as important, though, will be the bringing to light of those who have not so far received any serious attention. They are all part of the very rich texture of British cinema, and it will be the work of this series to give them all their due.

Acknowledgements

I would like to thank John Box and Oswald Morris for illuminating conversations with me on their work with Carol Reed; Charles Barr for lending me *Penny Paradise*; Sue Harris for lending me her copies of Marcel Carné films; Consuelo Sanmateu for sending me some cuttings on *The Third Man*; the Filmoteca Nacional, Madrid, Roehampton University, College Library, Queen Mary, University of London, Senate House, University of London library, the Oratory School, the BFI library, special collections (Janet Moat and Claire Thomas), the film and stills viewing sections, and Michael Brooke, the British Library (especially Ian Rawes), for allowing me to consult material on Carol Reed; Ian Christie for introducing me to John Box; Andrea Sabbadini, my co-organiser of the Institute of Psychoanalysis sessions at the Riverside and ICA on film and psychoanalysis, and Christopher Cordess and Miguel Angel Ramón for unfailingly illuminating comments on aspects of psychoanalysis and film; Michael Brearley for introducing me to *Psychoanalysis and Culture*, edited by David Bell; my brother Michael Evans for discussion on Graham Greene; Patricia D'Allemand, Omar García, Michael Brick, Michael Kalischer, Simon Harvey and Elisabetta Girelli, for forwarding or lending me material related to the writing of this book; Neil Sinyard for inviting me to write this volume; Matthew Frost for his support at Manchester University Press; Bruce Babington for our enduring friendship and many years of happy collaboration on various projects (and, with specific reference to Carol Reed, our involvement in launching the film degrees at Newcastle University, where it fell to me to teach *The Third Man*); my colleagues who teach on the various BA and MA film courses at Queen Mary, University of London, among them Mark Glancy who invited me to read a paper on *Our Man in Havana* at the Seminar on British Cinema, at the Institute of Historical Research, University of London.

I would like to thank my son Tom and daughter Jenny for sharing my film enthusiasms, and Isabel Santaolalla for her constant support and encouragement, for reading and making many suggestions on earlier drafts. Without her, my own 'way ahead' would have been infinitely less clear.

Stills from *The Fallen Idol* courtesy of Canal+Image UK; *The Third Man*, Optimum Releasing; *Our Man in Havana, The Key, Oliver!*, Columbia TriStar Films UK; *Night Train to Munich*, TVAI; *Trapeze*, MGM Plaza; *Climbing High, The Way Ahead, Odd Man Out*, Carlton International

To my mother, Rose-Marie Evans

Introduction

My interest in Reed began, perhaps predictably, with *The Third Man* (1949). At school, films were shown every other Sunday evening. Over a period of five years my film education – already at a respectable level thanks to supervision by my mother – was further developed by screenings of a wide range of films, some wonderful, like *The 3.10 to Yuma* (1957), *Shane* (1953) and *Julius Caesar* (1953), and some only slightly less wonderful, like *Expresso Bongo* (1959). The film that left an enduring impression was *The Third Man*. I had already been prepared for its splendours by one of the masters, who described the first appearance of Harry Lime in the doorway in a way that made me impatient to see the rest of the film the following Sunday. That viewing led to a journey through the remainder of Reed's films and, finally, many years later, to the writing of this volume. The landmarks along the way have been many and varied, exhilarating and disappointing, surprising and predictable. I hope at the very least to have shown by the end that the films under discussion here were made by someone who deserves to be remembered for many more than the trio of 1940s masterpieces (*Odd Man Out* (1946), *The Fallen Idol* (1948), *The Third Man*) that spring to most people's minds when his name is mentioned.

Detailed commentary on all of Reed's films would have been impossible in a volume of this size. I have therefore opted for combining mainly chronological coverage of all major stages of Reed's career with special attention not only to the acknowledged masterpieces but also to films that deserve re-appraisal (e.g. *Outcast of the Islands* (1952), *Trapeze* (1958), *Oliver!* (1968)). Each of the decades is allotted a general introduction, with commentary on all the films from the period, followed by detailed analysis of those I consider significant both in their own right and as important stages in the development of Reed's career. Chronology is disrupted in two ways: first, by concentration out of sequence in each of their sections on *Climbing High* (1938) and *Trapeze*, largely to allow greater room for discussion of two undeservedly neglected films; and second, in the section devoted to Graham Greene, whose work with Carol Reed led to one of the most significant partnerships in the history of film and literature, by grouping together *Our Man in Havana* (1959) with *The Fallen Idol* and *The Third Man*.

I have relied on a variety of theoretical and critical models, allowing the films themselves as far as possible to dictate the approach. In discussion of form and content I have also been mindful of historical, aesthetic and biographical contexts, noting the parallels and overlaps with contemporary film-makers, hoping to avoid crude associations between these frames of reference. Reed's illegitimacy – as the natural son of the famous actor-manager Sir Herbert Beerbohm Tree, who died in 1917, when Reed was ten years old – has been offered by Robert Moss and others as an explanation for the recurrence of father/son narratives. The stress on this issue in the overall patterns of Reed's films has, though, underplayed the importance of the mother/son and mother/daughter relationships. Even where a film like *Outcast* is clearly about a young man's search for his father in the figure of an admired bene-factor, the importance of mother-related desires quickly becomes apparent. Where the protagonist is female, especially in the 1930s films, characters like Catherine in *Bank Holiday* (1938) measure themselves against a maternal ideal. But elsewhere, as in *The Fallen Idol* or even as late as in *Oliver!* the adult relationships of women with lovers or husbands are ultimately intelligible in the light of maternal bonds, even where the film includes no characters who are mothers. Without wishing to offer a psychopathology of Reed's work, I have nevertheless sometimes relied on psychoanalytical models in the belief that these would help further elucidate Reed's interest in character, behaviour, and human relations in films that are repeatedly concerned with parent/child relations. Psychoanalysis has of course been one of the dominant tendencies in film theory at least as far back as the work of Commoli and Narboni in the 1960s, and their readings against the grain. My own readings here often follow this pattern but, as well as relying on post-Freudian approaches, I have returned to Freud for clarity, whenever necessary or appropriate.

According to Morris, Reed was, in comparison, say, with David Lean, a more spontaneous director. Where Lean prepared every last detail before shooting began, Reed welcomed improvisation on the set. In full control of proceedings, he seemed willing nevertheless to alter his view of a character through suggestions from others. His early work as an actor clearly also instilled in him a respect for the views of the stars in his own films. Morris's comparison with Lean fits in, additionally, with my attempts to consider the further links or discrepancies between Reed, Lean and Hitchcock, at one time considered Britain's foremost directors. There even often appears to be an element of playful intertextuality, something clearly in evidence, above all, in *Night Train to Munich* (1940) which, also written by Launder and Gilliat, gestures to *The Lady Vanishes* (1938). Reed's films, though, refer not only to British directors like Lean or Hitchcock, but also to the wider traditions of film (e.g. Ford, Wyler, Clair, or the German Expressionists). Beyond noting these narrowly cinematic links, I have also attempted to place Reed's films within the broader contexts of cultural trends, especially in literature, and, avoiding overstatement, within their historical and social backgrounds. Besides the obvious and direct associations between, say, Reed and Greene, or the various other writers (e.g. Wells or Priestley) on whose work Reed based his films, the less obvious but equally significant influence of, say, feminist writing in the 1930s, or the work of the 'Angry Young Men' in the 1950s and 1960s are important references for awareness of the ways in which these currents animate the behaviour of Reed's characters. Given the constraints of space, the organization of the book has made it regretfully necessary to make no more than passing reference to two outstanding films, *The Girl in the News* (1941) and *The Young Mr Pitt* (1942). As the former was one of the seven films Reed made with Margaret Lockwood, I have felt that her contribution is adequately covered in detailed discussion of three other major films (*Bank Holiday, A Girl Must Live* (1939) and *Night Train to Munich*). *The Young Mr Pitt* is not wholly neglected: in the section on *The Way Ahead* (1944) in Chapter 3 comparisons are made between Robert Donat and David Niven as models of heroic masculinity.

Born in Putney (30 December 1906), one of five brothers and one sister in a family run by an efficient and devoted single parent (Beatrice May Pinney), Reed (an imperfect anagram of his father's name 'Tree'), was educated at King's School, Canterbury. According to Wapshott (1990: 55), he sought to distance himself from the memory of his father, and was clearly very attached to his mother, a devoted but also determined woman. After leaving school at sixteen, and following an abortive career in the USA as a prospective chicken-farmer, he took to acting, soon joining Edgar Wallace's company, first on stage, and then in films, when Wallace became chairman of British Lion Pictures. On Wallace's death, he teamed up with Basil Dean as dialogue director at Ealing, thereafter progressing to assistant director. An especially influential figure in those early days appears to have been Jack Ruben, with whom he worked as assistant director on *Java Head* (1934). Reed's credits as assistant director include *The Constant Nymph* (1934), *Sing as*

We Go (1934), and *Lorna Doone* (1935). His first solo directorial film, *Midshipman Easy* (1935), followed his contribution to the romantic comedy *It Happened in Paris* (1935) directed by Robert Wyler. *Midshipman Easy* was the first of many films to explore the maturing process of the male, and the difficulties of measuring up to a masculine ideal. Clearly, as many of Reed's films, like *Midshipman Easy*, were commissioned, and as he moved from one production company to another (e.g. Columbia, London Films, Hecht-Lancaster), and from one genre to another, questions of authorship, of seeing in the films he directed a clear pattern of authorial intention, become hugely problematic. When one takes into account not only the usual questions of collaboration with, say, screenwriters like Launder and Gilliat, directors of cinematography like Robert Krasker (*Odd Man Out*, *The Third Man*, *Trapeze*), and Oswald Morris (*The Key* (1958), *Our Man in Havana*, *Oliver!*) or of art directors like John Box (*Our Man in Havana*, *Oliver!*), whose extremely influential work adds to the distinctiveness of Reed's films, the matter of authorship becomes, as ever, extremely complicated. Reed himself was modestly sceptical about attempts to bracket his work with that of European *auteurs* like Visconti and Bergman: 'I know that there are great directors, like Visconti and Bergman, who have a certain view of life, but I don't think that a director who knows how to put a film together need impose his ideas on the world' (Samuels, 1972: 166), and dismissed the notion of a coherent pattern in his own work: 'I tend to look for something exactly opposite from what I've just done' (Samuels, 1972: 166).

But even if, in turn, one dismisses these self-effacing remarks as those of a naturally modest man, significant patterns emerge. Beyond the measure of consistency achieved through his role as producer on nine of his own films, Reed's work sometimes either wholly or in part allows self-conscious reflection on the film-maker's art. *The Agony and the Ecstasy* (1965) is largely about the place of art in a turbulent world; the writer of pulp fiction, Holly Martins, in *The Third Man*, or the manic painter, Lukey, in *Odd Man Out*, are also, in this respect, the precursors of *The Agony and the Ecstasy's* Michelangelo, like Reed himself (creating art against a background of war), attempting to make sense through art of a world ruled by violence and chaos. Although Reed's most overtly self-conscious film, *The Agony and the Ecstasy*, is readable via Freud's discussion of Leonardo da Vinci as in some ways an autobiography of absent fatherhood, his output as a whole, with its repetitive focus on mothers and maternal figures, a prolonged act, in a Kleinian sense, of reparation, given a characteristically melancholy tone born of illegitimacy.

Beyond such meditations on the relations between art and life,

Reed's films clearly show a tendency for certain kinds of narrative, character and situation. The marked patterns of his films – crime, foreign settings, parent–child relationships – seem to indicate, consciously or unconsciously, either a search for or a willingness to accept commissions for films concerned with loss, destabilised or marginalised characters, and difference and otherness, tendencies that led Raymond Durgnat to classify Reed as 'the most imposing pessimist' of the British cinema (1971: 166). Threaded into these larger patterns is his added fondness for loose ends, folly, and the condemnation of characters who refuse to respect the point of view of others. Reed's endings are often, if not unambiguously tragic, hardly optimistic: Harry Lime (in *The Third Man*), Rex Black (in *The Running Man* (1963)), Ivo (in *The Man Between* (1953)), Johnny McQueen (in *Odd Man Out*), and Mrs Baines (in *The Fallen Idol*) all die; David and Stella are separated at the end of *The Key*, Ribble and Lola in *Trapeze* are set for a stormy ride together, ever mindful of the missing partner, Tino, in their broken triangle of love; Willems and Aissa in *Outcast of the Islands* are condemned to a life of bitterness; the platoon heads for an uncertain future in *The Way Ahead*; and who knows what lies in wait for the fugitive family in *Laburnum Grove* (1936), perhaps only momentarily free from the clutches of the law. In all of these films, and elsewhere, folly is a theme that Reed explores through two sets of opposed characters. Some, like Willems in *Outcast*, Jenny in *The Stars Look Down* (1939), or Rex in *The Running Man* are prepared to wreck things in pursuit of their goals, in the process provoking a mixed response from the audience: condemnation and sympathy for their disruption of the social order; others have an aura of innocence, behaving childishly, producing chaos even when not seeking it. Wormold in *Our Man in Havana* or Baines in *The Fallen Idol* exemplify the type and, in so doing, are sometimes identified with children. These characters highlight Reed's perennial interest not only in parent/child relations but also in questions of loss, innocence and experience, often in ways that seem designed to prompt reflection on socio-historical as well as on more psychological determinants.

The transgressive characters are often twinned with conformists – for instance, Holly Martins and Harry Lime in *The Third Man*, or Hawthorne and Wormold in *Our Man in Havana* – whose accommodations with convention lead not only to understandable reconciliation with the social law but also to betrayals of self and others. Reed reserved his truest aim for the egotists, those characters like Joe Gowlan in *The Stars Look Down*, Segura, the chief of police, in *Our Man in Havana*, Bill Sikes in *Oliver!* or Charles Sidley in *Follow Me* (1972), so blinkered by their own needs and interests they fail to appreciate those of others, treating them either as adjuncts to their own selves or as individuals whose reality is inseparable from their perception of it. The divisions, though, are blurred, as Reed, like Hitchcock, confuses the boundaries between innocence and guilt. A remark made by the policeman to the priest in *Odd Man Out* could serve as an epigraph for all Reed's films: 'In my profession, Father, there is neither good nor bad. There is only innocence and guilt. That's all.' Though Reed is concerned to show the processes of the social construction of the self, the destructive forces of nature are also acknowledged. Many characters are caught in the grip of inexplicable desires, urges that undercut the audience's temptation to attach blame to their behaviour. Baines, Willems, Kipps, Catherine (in *Bank Holiday*), are all to some extent governed by uncontrollable forces that spring up inside them, beyond their own reality, often leading to trouble or even catastrophe. As Kathy remarks in *Odd Man Out*, 'What I feel is stronger than my religion, stronger than myself.' Reed's films carry an assumption that in human nature there is potential for the eruption of discord and disharmony. Human society attempts to anticipate or to control this potential with mixed results. Love, for instance, is usually envisaged more as an avoidable imprisonment than an emancipation of the self: Anna in *The Third Man*, Nancy in *Oliver!*, Willems in *Outcast*, Kathleen in *Odd Man Out*, are all, driven by the Furies of desire, drawn to lovers identified with loss or death, their *amour fou* born more of tendencies towards self-destruction than renewal.

These splits or doubles in characterisation are often matched by patterns of space or narrative that provide rival perspectives on observed realities: for instance, England and Spain in *The Running Man*, the numbers and narrative in *Oliver!*, the memories of the Chelsea Pensioners and the experiences of the soldiers in the battlefields of the Second World War in *The Way Ahead*. These themes are relayed through Reed's undisputed brilliance of form: the realism developed while making wartime documentaries; the editing, already celebrated by Karel Reisz, of *Odd Man Out*; the expressionistic compositions of *The Third Man*; the attention to visual detail like the jangling coat hangers announcing tragedy in *The Key* in the *mise-en-scène*; the colour-coded patterns of virtue and vice in *Oliver!*; the talent for suspense, observable, for instance, in the incriminating letter inviting discovery by the police in *The Fallen Idol*; the non-diegetic use of music in *Trapeze*, with its reliance on the waltz of the 'Blue Danube'; the knack of selecting expressive faces for close-ups and interiority in, say, the motley band of holiday-makers in *Bank Holiday*. Two of Reed's most significant collaborators, John Box and Oswald Morris, have stressed to me in conversation the great importance he attached to character, the care with which he treated his actors and actresses in teasing out the nuances of personality. Reed's exploitation of the resources of film language, as well as his handling of actors and actresses to draw out extraordinary performances from major stars like Margaret Lockwood, Michael Redgrave, Alec Guinness, as well as minor ones (for instance, F. J. McCormick, as the would-be betrayer in *Odd Man Out*) and all the many children he relied on, such as, Bobby Henrey in *The Fallen Idol*, the nameless native boy in *Outcast*, the accusing Viennese child in *The Third Man*, Mark Lester and Jack Wild in *Oliver!*, and the boy (Jonathan Ashmore) pining for his father in *A Kid for Two Farthings* (1955), make him one of the British cinema's outstanding directors, whose films either in part or in whole deserve far greater recognition than has recently been their due.

Married twice, first to Diana Wynyard and then to Penelope Dudley Ward, his services to British cinema were recognised through the conferment of a knighthood in 1952. He died on 25 April 1976.

Early days: girls in the news

2

As Carol Reed began to make his way in films the British cinema in the 1930s was already characterised, on the one hand, by the rise of the documentary tradition epitomised by Grierson and Cavalcanti and, on the other, by popular genre-based, star-studded films and studio production headed by moghuls like Alexander Korda. Reed's films, like those directed by Victor Saville, Alfred Hitchcock, Michael Powell and David Lean, are indebted to both tendencies. The 1930s saw great upheavals in the social, economic and political life of the country (e.g. the effects of the Wall Street Crash, high unemployment, the rise of Nazism), and Reed's films do not fail to reflect the vicissitudes of the times.

The first decade of Carol Reed's career as a film director reveals in embryo the characteristics of the later masterpieces, especially the films of the 1940s. Often directing films for which he was commissioned, he nevertheless managed to stamp on each what would come to be recognised as his trademark: ironic, underplayed narratives often concerned with parent/child relationships, divided selves, class and crime.

Reed's interest in the parent–child relationship, an interminable inquest across all the films into the origins of the self, is remarkable from the outset. Based on Captain Maryatt's boys' adventure novel, *Mr Midshipman Easy*, Reed's *Midshipman Easy* is the story of the developing maturity of a young man. Easy begins his career at sea, with his precociousness a constant irritant to comrades and superiors. His catchphrase, 'I should like to argue the point,' may be the pretentious mannerism of the school debating society maestro but, more significantly, it draws attention to the father's forming influence over the son. The lessons of reason and equality which Easy attributes to parental guidance serve him well at sea and elsewhere. His fair-mindedness is an inspiration to others, for instance when he intervenes to prevent prisoners of war being made to walk the plank.

The father–son relationship yields to those between fathers and daughters in *Laburnum Grove* and *Penny Paradise* (1938). Both films – made for ATP at Ealing – star Edmund Gwenn as the *pater familias* whose calm, benign demeanour sets a fine example to his children. While in *Penny Paradise* the daughter is motherless, in *Laburnum Grove* the mother is a key character, available to point out to her daughter and others the father's admirable qualities. The film was based on the J. B. Priestley play, first performed on 28 November 1933 in London at the Duchess theatre. As George, Edmund Gwenn perfectly incarnates Priestley's description of him as a man of 'quiet assurance and authority beneath his easy manner' (1935: 11) who early on in the film confesses to his family that they have all been living off his dishonest income: 'Every penny that's come into the house over the last few years has been dishonestly earned!'.

Delivered casually and light-heartedly, the remark seems designed above all to scare away the scroungers both inside and outside the family: Lucy (Ethel Coleridge), George's sister-in-law, and Bernard (Cedric Hardwicke), her husband, a failed businessman with endless fabrications of exploits in the Far East, residents in the Redfern household ever since their return from overseas; and especially, Elsie Redfern's fiancé, Harold (Francis James), whose cooling passion betrays his mercenary designs. Significantly, when after initial dismissals of his pretensions to criminality are made, further suspicions are aroused about George's activities, Elsie is persuaded by her mother to go along with these in order to test Harold's devotion.

In this film the parent–child relationship focuses on the parent, especially the benevolent father, more than the child. *Laburnum Grove* highlights two of Reed's perennial themes: class and the divided self. As in *Penny Paradise, Bank Holiday, A Girl Must Live* (1939), and then, later on, in *Kipps* (1941) and many other films, Reed depicts the cultural background as well as the lifestyle and aspirations of driven characters. The almost documentary attention to the customs and manners of different classes allows him to explain to some extent his characters' actions and desires through appeals to social as well as psychological conditioning. Documentary footage used in fiction films was to become a standard feature of his later films, leading critics such as Andrew Sarris (1957a: 10) to bracket him with other directors in the social realist tradition.

Concentrating on working-class manners in Liverpool, and in a way that recalls the films of René Clair, *Penny Paradise* uses the dream of a win on the football pools to explore the vicissitudes of proletarian life in the north of England. *Bank Holiday* offers glimpses of various social *milieux*: the working-class family whose boorish father thinks more of the pub than of his children or long-suffering wife; the lower-middle-class Beauty contestants, whose most engaging representative, 'Miss Fulham', eventually prefers to the tarnished glory of glamour competition the promise of true romance with the middle-class man (Hugh Williams) abandoned by his unresponsive partner (Margaret Lockwood). In *A Girl Must Live* the struggles of actors and actresses to make a living bring them into contact with the aristocracy, a class with ambivalent attitudes to theatricals. Here, while the Earl of Pangbourne (Hugh Sinclair) is smitten by 'Leslie James' (Margaret Lockwood), the prejudices of his aunt (Kathleen Boutall) almost succeed in disrupting the marriage between her blue-blooded nephew and the woman she regards as no better than an adventuress.

In all of these films the main character is presented as a divided, sometimes alienated, individual. Joe (Edmund Gwenn) in *Penny Paradise* is provoked by circumstances into denying his philanthropic instincts, suddenly released by his belief that he has won the pools. George in *Laburnum Grove* leads a double life: on the surface he is a happily married family man living inconspicuously a drab existence of slippers, pipes and traditional Sunday dinners in a suburban terrace; secretly, though, he is the brains behind a counterfeit racket, almost exposed by a dogged policeman before, in the nick of time, he and his still unsuspecting family manage to make their escape. Since Reed often prefers an unhappy ending, this variant – a celebration of the little man's triumph over the law – is significant. In its defence of ingenuity and daring, and in its ironic commentary on the smug cosiness of suburban Shooters Green, the film is not all that remote from the depiction of an alienating world in which the hero-villain Harry Lime plies his lethal trade. The line between sainthood and villainy even when not drawn, as in the Graham Greene scripts, from a theological standpoint, remains blurred in a narrative driven by only secular impulse.

Laburnum Grove's interest in divided selves is developed, as in *Talk of the Devil* (1937), in a crime narrative, a format to which Reed was repeatedly attracted. Even *A Girl Must Live*, a sort of British equivalent of the Hollywood backstage musical, allows room for this fascination with crime. The combination of music and crime in Reed's work is most remarkable in *The Third Man*, where the mixed jauntiness and disturbing intensity of Karas's zither provide suitable commentary on the seediness of the Vienna-based racketeers. There are similar effects elsewhere. In *Oliver!*, for instance, where the lyrics and melodies of Lionel Bart's score convey the violence as well as the deprivation of the underclass. In *A Girl Must Live* the protagonist, 'Leslie James', is not guilty of criminality, only of deception. She is another of Reed's characters whose assumption of a false identity provides release from heritage and circumstance. Criminality, however, can be said to define the ambitions of Hugo (Naunton Wayne), a classier pimp who preys on the weaknesses of wealthy patrons for the charms of available chorines. The film's emphasis, though, is not on Hugo but 'Leslie James'. Reed is often accused of being more of a man's man, in whose films the male point of view takes precedence. And, indeed, it is remarkable how many of his films either have the word 'man' in the title, or else refer to a man either by name or profession: *Odd Man Out*, *The Third Man*, *The Man Between* (1953), *Our Man in Havana*, *The Running Man*, *Midshipman Easy*, *Kipps*, *The Young Mr Pitt*, *The Fallen Idol*, *An Outcast of the Islands*. Yet Reed's films, always interesting in their treatment of women, even when they are relegated to secondary importance in the narrative, sometimes prioritised female protagonists, especially in the 1930s, in remarkable ways. Two films in particular are worthy of more than passing attention, starring Margaret Lockwood, *Bank Holiday* and *A Girl Must Live*, and in both of which conventional notions of femininity are called into question. Margaret Lockwood appeared in five more Reed films: *Midshipman Easy*, *Who's Your Lady Friend?* (1937), *The Stars Look Down*, *Night Train to Munich* and *Girl in the News*. Reed met Lockwood when he was a dialogue director first at Ealing and then Gainsborough, an acquaintance that prepared the ground for their later collaboration. Sue Harper (2000: 24) includes Lockwood in a group of emerging actresses whose 'wholesome, sensible' appearance and manner challenged the dominance of ladylike actresses like Evelyn Laye and Florence Desmond. These girls were characterised by uncompromising attitudes and straight talking. Unlike the mannish women of the period, such as Flora Robson and Cicely Courtneidge, they were attractive, less head-strong than the so-called 'Madcap Girls' (Harper 2000: 26) like Jessie Matthews, but equally suitable for casting in romantic comedies.

Bank Holiday (1938)

Referring to *Bank Holiday*, where as Nurse Catherine, Margaret Lockwood is caught between the competing attributes of two men, the conventional Geoff (Hugh Williams) and the more romantic Stephen (John Lodge), Bruce Babington defines her as a woman 'moving between two men, one of them prosaically embodying her own class restrictions, the other higher-classed and romantic' (Babington 2001:

99). *Bank Holiday*, on Lockwood's own admission her first really big film (Lockwood 1955: 54), is remarkable for its uncompromising attitude even in sexual matters towards female self-determination, even if her modern outlook risks outraging convention. Lockwood's Nurse Catherine is a blend of submissiveness and emancipation, her obliging nature no guarantee of conformity. A glamorous star, Lockwood nevertheless plays a character who at one point in a swimming pool scene resists the controlling gaze of her insipid partner Geoff by refusing to dive into the water to stimulate even further his visual pleasure. The film is the story of Nurse Catherine's August Bank Holiday tryst with Geoff at a seaside resort. The holiday makes her realise she is not really in love with Geoff, whose tetchy and somewhat immature personality – he is pointedly referred to by her as 'Little Geoff' – suffers by comparison with her romantic fantasy of Stephen, whose wife (Linden Travers) she has nursed in fatal childbirth. Catherine realises almost telepathically that after his wife's death in labour Stephen becomes suicidal, and rushes to him just in time to rescue him from tragedy. At one point, when Catherine is roused from sleep on the crowded beach where, like thousands of others who have found no room at the fully booked hotels, she and Geoff have had to spend the night, she approaches the water's edge. Reflections of moonbeam-grazed ripples of water flicker on her body; the film cuts to Stephen, who is also near water, standing on a London bridge many miles away. The clairvoyant link between them recalls the extra-sensory relations in dreams between the lucid-dream lovers in *Peter Ibbetson* (Hathaway, 1935), or the *amour fou* passionate pilgrims of many a Surrealist film. In its expression of the intensity of feeling between two distant but also linked soul-mates, the film comes closest in Reed's work to the genius of David Lean, in some ways a more romantic director, in a film like *The Passionate Friends* (1948), where Ann Todd and Trevor Howard play out a notion of desire as an endless impulse to recapture an irrecoverable primal unity.

Catherine's undisguised indifference to conventional sexual morality, expressed through willingness to spend a weekend away with a man to whom she is not married, places Margaret Lockwood on the borderline of the list of clean-cut stars identified by Sue Harper, though of course her wholesomeness is what makes her transgression all the more shocking. The film constantly provokes the viewer into moral judgement. As Catherine stands on the tube escalator, heading for the train that will take her to a seaside destination of forbidden delights, a film poster comes into view: 'Sinners: love was their only crime'; 'Sinners: they sacrificed everything for love'. Love is indeed, as ever in art, identified with transgression – here, though, not the prospect of a libidinal weekend with Geoff, but the more enduring romance with Stephen – its criminality defined not only as an outrage against social convention but also as a psychologically disruptive force. In being more attracted to Stephen, the recently widowed but far more romantic figure, Catherine, like Wells's Ann Veronica, earns the audience's admiration for initiative while arousing its concern over the destiny of a romance that is largely a figment of her over-heated imagination.

Catherine, the maternally defined nurse, but as yet childless spinster, is enchanted by the fantasy of the caring father-figure painted by Stephen's wife. The mature man, not his immature version, 'little Geoff', is the nurse's object of desire; his dying wife, the mother of his child becomes the screen on which is projected her own maternal fantasy. And yet, this is a man so upset by his wife's death he refuses to take home his baby, and attempts suicide as his mourning turns into melancholia. His mind, perhaps, even after rescue by Catherine, will be forever filled with the memories, seen in flashback throughout the film, of his wife.

The risks of Catherine's fantasy are relayed through Reed's characteristic attention to lighting and composition. When Stephen is informed of his wife's death he refuses to see their baby, desperate only to go to his wife. Once he enters the room, the frame is split, showing to the left a room bathed in shadow, in which Stephen himself appears as a silhouette; to the right, fully lit, in a doorway stands Catherine, her nurse's snowy white uniform adding to the luminosity, an ironic portrayal of the darker forces that illuminate her fantasy. The shadows theme is given comic expression later on in the film at the seaside resort when two inebriated middle-aged women emerge from a pub singing a popular song of the day, 'Two shadows in the moonlight'. Stephen's recourse to Shelley's *Adonais*, ' No more let life divide what death can join together', seemingly applies not only to his relationship with his wife but also to Catherine's pursuit of a lover who, in some senses, is also dead. In a circular pattern, dressed again as a nurse, Catherine leans over the bed-ridden hospitalised figure of Stephen recovering from his failed suicide attempt, and declares, 'Everybody comes back. The holiday is over.' The scene invites comparison with the closures of texts like *Jane Eyre* (Stevenson, 1943) or *All that Heaven Allows* (Sirk, 1954) where optimism is undermined by dependency, trauma and control. The fantasy of romantic love, the 'holiday', turns out after all to be no more than a desire for convention and all the constraints that social heavens allow. The lighter treatment of such matters, again as carried by the Margaret Lockwood persona, appears in *A Girl Must Live*.

A Girl Must Live (1939)

As has been noted by Moss (1987), Wapshott (1990) and Babington (2002), *A Girl Must Live* is a British version of the Hollywood backstage musical. But whereas, say, a film like *Gold Diggers of 1933* (Leroy, 1933) and, to a lesser extent, other 1930s Busby Berkeley musicals made at Warners refer either directly or indirectly to historical realities (Roth 1981; Babington and Evans 1985), *A Girl Must Live* avoids unambiguous allusion of this type. Nevertheless, made towards the end of 1938, and released on 19 April 1939, it inevitably picks up on the mood of anxiety spreading across Europe, transmitted partly through denial – there are no direct references to events on the continent – and partly through characteristically phlegmatic British understatement. The direct address of social or political issues, such as in the 'Forgotten Man' number in *Gold Diggers of 1933*, finds no favour here. Even so, the eventual union between a chorine and a lord of the realm seems inspired both by generic traditions of social transgression in romantic comedy (*Pretty Woman* (Marshall, 1990)) is an interesting relatively recent adherent to this tradition), and a spirit of togetherness in times of crisis. The reviews were largely negative, justifying detraction through adverse comparisons with the verve and inventiveness of the Hollywood prototype. The producer of the show in *A Girl Must Live* is Joe Gold, an American whose efforts to instil American production values and standards into his motley chorines is pitiful, even if the numbers do have a certain bathetic fascination. After the girls sing and dance their first number, 'Who's your love, tell me who, who's your love? / Could it be little me who's your love?', Joe derides their efforts by comparing the troupe to the Chelsea Pensioners, probably the retired servicemen and not the famous London football team nicknamed after them.

It is not only the singing and dancing that seem geriatric; the choreography is woeful, and the camerawork, perhaps intent on rivalling its poverty of invention, limited to medium and close shots of the chorines. Nevertheless, the lyrics pack a punch, rising from bathos to incisiveness, focusing on themes of ruthless materialism, identity and desire. As 'Leslie James', Margaret Lockwood is an escapee from a Swiss finishing school, pretends to be the daughter of a famous actress, takes up residence in a Bloomsbury boarding house, and joins the 'Midnight Frolics', a musical production that plays at first in a London night club and then at the baronial mansion of the Earl of Pangborough, a significant change of setting that, especially when the Earl himself accompanies the chorines on his ancestral organ, consolidates the classless togetherness of the group. Two other chorines vie for the Earl of Pangborough's attention. Through these three demotic backstage Graces the film offers contrasting pursuits of happiness. Gloria (Renee Houston) and Clytie (Lilli Palmer), the ruthless self-seekers, are punished for cynically using sex to plunder the wallets of prosperous men. Nevertheless, as with other Reed characters who arouse a mixed response of disapproval and admiration of their dubious enterprises, Gloria and Clytie are partially redeemed by their verve and dynamism, qualities relayed through wit as well as through decisive action: once these two sniff a part or the availability of a benefactor, their efforts to outflank a rival know no limits. Verbal wit complements inventive manoeuvre: for instance, when Gloria informs Lilli she is the first white woman the Earl of Pangborough has seen in seven years, the latter replies, 'What did he do? Take the next boat back?'.

The witty screenplay was by Frank Launder, who also wrote *Girl in the News* and, with Sidney Gilliat, *Night Train to Munich* and *The Young Mr Pitt*. Launder's work, characterised by a blend of sharp analysis and comedy, focuses here on the clash between pleasure and reality principles. Once they appear in their first number, the chorines seem like inferior Marlene Dietrich look-alikes. The plumage on the hair, the plunging neckline, black stockings and suspenders, combine with the bawdy lyrics, as each girl flaunts her special talent (e.g. 'I can't sing or romance, but I can dance', or 'I'm a well-read girl, give me a second look / I can tell you a story you won't find in any book'), to project the girls' desperate attempts to exchange sexual favours for material security. Gloria and Lilli unashamedly press their bodies into profitable service. When Lilli manages to tempt the Earl of Pangborough back to her room in order to change out of the cheap dress on which she has accidentally-on-purpose spilled her drink, she undresses in a way that, through her carefully positioned table lamp, allows the silhouette of her disrobed body to fall within sight of her gullible prey. The scene visually prefigures the witty exchange in the baronial mansion when in reply to the Earl's remark, 'For sheer down to earth humanity they'd outstrip the lot of them' (he is referring to women of his own class), his aunt retorts, 'Outstrip certainly!'.

Margaret Lockwood's Leslie James shares the drive and ingenuity, but not the cupidity of Gloria and Lilli. To her, acting means living, not an opportunity for reeling in a benefactor. It is the antidote to the cloistered world of the Swiss finishing school, an opportunity to participate in the glamorous dramas of life, playing a role that releases her creativity and liberates her from a more conventional, socially defined self. Not just, as defined by Christine Gledhill and Gillian Swanson (1996: 10), a 'social arriviste', she is the incarnation of changing attitudes to femininity in 1930s Britain, like many women no longer satisfied by predominantly domestic labelling even though not yet, since Britain is still not at war, colonising the male-occupied public spaces of factory or office made necessary by home front requirements.

A Girl Must Live, with its significantly ambiguous title referring to liberation as much as to survival, is a film that, following Gledhill's and Swanson's argument, reflects the kinds of transformation in women's lives in Britain in the 1930s, and that became much more clearly expressed in films, like *Millions Like Us* (Launder and Gilliat, 1943), made during the war. Margaret Lockwood, a good girl with a potential for wickedness (drawn out in the 1940s in her Gainsborough melo-dramas), the English suburban beauty with chocolate-brown eyes and the dark aura of exoticism (she is a Spaniard in *Midshipman Easy*), internalised through her persona this transitional phase of femininity. Her Reed films seem almost to chart the development of women's changing status in Britain, progressing from the *ingénues* of *Midshipman Easy* and *Who's Your Lady Friend?* to the affirmative, independently minded heroines of *Bank Holiday* and *A Girl Must Live* to the more suspicious, but still innocent protagonist in *Girl in the News,* to Reed's own version of the Wicked Lady in *The Stars Look Down.* That film, and *Night Train to Munich,* which sees Lockwood reduced to a more conventional role, her submissiveness complementary to the re-asserted male (Rex Harrison), dramatises – like Hollywood Noir – the reactionary hysteria towards women who have overstepped the mark by casting them in more conformist roles as daughters or *femmes fatales.* The complex issues raised through *Bank Holiday* and *A Girl Must Live,* two of the most remarkable 'feminist' films of 1930s British cinema, are also aired in *Climbing High,* a film routinely condemned by everyone, including Reed himself (Samuels 1972: 168), where Jessie Matthews, not Margaret Lockwood, advances the feminist theme.

Climbing High (1938)

MGM's British distribution arm, Gaumont-British, along with British International Pictures, one of the most important British film companies in the 1930s, followed up its enormous success of *The Lady Vanishes* (Hitchcock, 1938) with *Climbing High,* a film that Jessie Matthews made in fulfilment of her contract obligations at the studio. She agreed to appear in *Climbing High* provided she was not expected to sing or dance. She was partnered Michael Redgrave, fresh from his triumph in *The Lady Vanishes,* and a string of other roles on the West End stage. As the ideal lover, Michael Redgrave was appearing here in the first of three films, followed by *The Stars Look Down* and *Kipps,* he made with Reed. Already a rising star as a stage actor, Redgrave, tall, regular-featured, fit and athletic was beginning to acquire a reputation as a cinematic romantic leading man with a sense of humour, above all in *The Lady Vanishes.* As the *News Chronicle* reviewer put it, 'Michael Redgrave is certainly digging himself in as a romantic hero with a sense of fun ... (Anon 1939b).

This was Jessie Matthews's last appearance as a major box office star in a film that did not start auspiciously. In her autobiography, *Over My Shoulder* she recalls her unease and sense of disloyalty when her husband's (Sonnie Hale) script suffered radical revision. Moreover, relations between Matthews and Redgrave were initially difficult. Having just met her co-star, she writes, 'five minutes later I found myself lying on the studio floor making love to a handsome young man who was billed as "The wonder boy of modern film land"' (Matthews 1974: 154). She refers to Redgrave's contempt for the dialogue (condemned by Redgrave, along with the film as a whole, in his own autobiography, *In My Mind's Eye. An Autobiography* (1983)), which she informs him had been written by her husband. Relations between Matthews and Redgrave improved (Strachan 2004: 167), and after early clashes, the collaboration became intimate enough for her to consider ending her marriage. Professionally, too, she was able to offer helpful advice to a relative novice as a film director.

A romantic comedy, *Climbing High* owed much not only to English stage comedy (for instance, to farces by Frederick Lonsdale or Ben Travers) but also to Hollywood screwball (such as *It Happened One Night* (Capra, 1934)) and its British musical or non-musical variants (e.g. Korda's *Wedding Rehearsal* (1932), and *Girl from Maxim's* (1933)). The prototype of all romantic comedies, *As You Like It* (Czinner), a British film version of the play, had appeared only two years previously, in 1936. Like most of Reed's films, though, the focus of *Climbing High* is wide enough to allow reflection on the wider social issues of the day. So, as well as being a story about the eventual union of ideal romantic partners, the film gently satirises English class and character, its depiction of the mercenary upper-classes recalling the satirical milieu of Evelyn Waugh's novels. The hedonistic cynicism of the penniless aristocrats is a slightly seedier version of the self-indulgent idlers in *Decline and Fall* (1928) or *Vile Bodies* (1930), the representatives of a class in decline. Like its American counterpart, the English form of screwball emerges against a backdrop of economic and political upheaval. Unemployment soared in the 1930s in a country that suffered as much as anywhere else in the aftermath of the Wall Street Crash of 1929. Attempts to revive the country by Lloyd George on the same basis as Roosevelt's New deal politics in the USA were unsuccessful. His National Government gave way to Chamberlain's Conservative administration as the political turmoil engulfing continental Europe finally reached Britain, and a decade that had successfully withstood challenges to the country's political structure – unlike, say, the rise of fascism in Spain, Italy and Germany – closed with seemingly inevitable uncertainty. Released in 1938, just as Britain was heading for war, *Climbing High* seems like a last Utopian gesture before Reed turned his thoughts and talents to graver matters. As regards its social ambience, the film is far removed from the hugely popular working-class comedies and musicals starring George Formby and Gracie Fields (on one of which, *Sing As We Go* (Dean, 1934), Reed had worked as assistant director), and a little nearer the more middle-class musicals and comedies, and comedies with songs, starring the likes of Jack Buchanan, Jack Hulbert and Tom Walls, or the Aldwych farces of Ben Travers, many of which were screened in the 1930s.

Hollywood romantic comedy (a genre that up to the 1930s was distinguished by Griffith, Chaplin, Lubitsch and Hawks), relies, as has often been remarked, on a couple-centred narrative that includes other minor characters whose roles either set in relief the lustrous nature of the ideal pairing, or else draw attention through their antic or otherwise eccentric behaviour to the wild desires released through their unexpected courtship. Though many such comedies have an urban setting, others vary the location to include often temporary migration to a 'place apart', commonly a pastoral *mise-en-scène* – sometimes literally the countryside, at other times a foreign land – in line with what Northrop Frye (1969) has termed the 'Green World' of Shakespearean comedy. Various obstacles are initially placed in the paths of the ideal lovers but, in obedience to the demands of the higher law of the happy ending, these are eventually overcome. The difficulties are usually driven by external pressures as well as by internal blockages or misunderstandings, often provoked by the designs of unsuitable partners who must be defeated so that the true partnership can be formed. These features are prominent in *It Happened in Paris* (1935), a film that inevitably recalls through its title one of the great Hollywood romantic comedies, *It Happened One Night*. Directed by Robert Wyler, with assistance from Reed, the film traces the attempts of the lovers, Paul (John Loder) and Jacqueline (Nancy Burne), to overcome difficulties of class and nationality, as well as the predatory designs of unsuitable rivals, as they strive to form the ideal couple. Paul begins by inadvertently appropriating Jacqueline's knickers, but by the end he has also stolen her heart. The pattern is followed even in a jaundiced version of the genre, Hitchcock's *The Farmer's Wife* (1928), where the farmer, not deterred by another character's remark that love is worse than whooping cough, and marriage a steamroller that flattens the life out of an individual, must negotiate four eligible but unsuitable partners before finding his other self, Aminta, the uxorious ideal.

The courtship, as opposed to the marriage or re-marriage (Cavell, 1981) narrative usually passes through three stages: meeting, complication, resolution. The meeting is typically accidental (e.g. on board ship in *The Lady Eve* (Sturges, 1941), a taxi in *One Hour with You* (Lubitsch, 1932), a golf course in *Bringing Up Baby* (Hawks, 1938), or a Parisian street in *It Happened in Paris*), a tradition respected by *Climbing High,* where the eventual lovers come across each other following Nicky's (Redgrave) accidental knocking over of Diana (Matthews) while driving his friend Reggie's (Basil Radford) car. The incident is repeated a few minutes later after Diana's exit from the advertising agency where she has found employment: 'Eight million! Eight million! ... Eight million people in London, and you have to pick on me!' she protests, re-affirming a generic law that the lovers' destiny is to discover that ideal partner, something in turn re-affirmed by Nicky's intuitive platonism: 'I hardly know you, and yet I'm probably on the verge of falling in love with you. It's happening even as we're standing here. It's not our doing. It's just a matter of chemistry. We're playthings of science. Couple of test tubes.' The early stages of courtship necessitate equal measures of thrust and counter thrust by the lovers, so, unsurprisingly, Diana's revenge is taken when, following repeated attempts to pick up the modern Cinderella's shoe, Nicky is himself knocked over to become the object of his lady's ridicule as she limps away, only temporarily irate.

These preliminary skirmishes, inevitable stages of courtship strategy, testing the lovers' mettle and resolve, nevertheless go beyond compliance with the formal demands of the genre in pointing to a truth of love. The pratfalls comically enact what in *Bringing up Baby* the psychiatrist defines as the conflictive nature of desire. In both cases the refusals of the disdainful, moonlike Diana and the gallant ardour of Nicky, a 1930s Actaeon whose dedication to the chase will not falter, are readable, in the case of the former, as an intuitive understanding of denial, a fear of facing up to strong drives and, in the latter, an urge to control and possess the object desirable, as psychoanalysts contend, precisely because of its elusiveness.

The mixed emotions and motives that initially govern the actions of the lovers are readable socially as well as psychologically. As in *It*

Happened in Paris, where Jacqueline is a struggling dress designer, and Paul a millionaire who has come to Paris 'to get away from the life I hated', Diana's background is poorer and socially inferior to Nicky's. While, in line with romantic love's indifference to social barriers, Nicky has fallen in love beneath him, her surrender to his overtures is in this sense an example of 'climbing high'. In falling for each other the lovers fulfil the social promise of an ideal society based on merit, virtue or compatibility, not class. Or does it? While Diana's role is socially inferior to Nicky's, Jessie Matthews's fake accent and comportment are hardly common. The exaggeratedly upper-class pronunciation, an attempt to cover up her own humble origins, point to the class-consciousness of 1930s British society which the film's generic couple-centred democracy of love does little to dispel. Nicky Brooke, too – though disingenuously attempting to pass himself off as 'lower middle class' – is in flight from his aristocratic milieu, above all from the pushy Gold-Digger Lady Constance, the nubile hope of a family on its uppers, who see in him the solution to their economic predicament. His pretence to be plain 'John Smith', the *nom de plume* of the classless, un-class-conscious Everyman, in his courtship of Diana, like Paul Knight, the millionaire pretending to be 'Paul Jones' the painter in *It Happened in Paris*, is as much an escape from the meanings of 'Nicky Brooke', of what through social advantage Nicky Brooke has become, as a necessary stratagem of love. To the comment, 'Anyone would think this Nicholas Brooke was an enemy of yours,' Nicky significantly replies: 'He is in a way.'

In denouncing class-consciousness the film does not of course go as far as to champion the Marxism espoused by Max (Alastair Sim), the comically morose and ineffectual parasite who sets himself up as a radical voice in a conservative society. In a discussion of conservatism and its alignment with certain women writers who came to prominence between the wars, Alison Light (1991) draws attention to changing attitudes towards nationality, self and society occasioned to a large extent by the consequences of the First World War. As on the continent, where, for instance Dadaism and Surrealism had carried through art a politicised response to the triumphalist values of the old social order that had led to the outbreak of war, so too in Britain, even in work where Dada and Surrealism had not left their mark, women writers, as Alison Light convincingly argues, like Ivy Compton-Burnett, Agatha Christie or Daphne Du Maurier questioned venerable truths, placing in crisis norms of subjectivity, class, patriotism, redefining the very essence of Englishness. This inquest was mirrored in film in the inter-war years in the work of Hitchcock, Lean and Reed. Hitchcock for instance, in *The Thirty Nine Steps* (1935), handcuffs his hero to a woman for the greater part of the film in the interests not only of creating narrative opportunities for suspense but also of compelling the male to acknowledge the female, and through enforced union, to modify a concept of hegemony developed in an atmosphere of misogyny (first suggested in the film through the milkman's song).

Romantic comedy, as film historians have argued (Cavell (1981); Britton (1983); Babington and Evans (1989)) is perhaps the genre that most naturally finds room for the hero's *éducation sentimentale*, a schooling that leads to a love, or understanding, of an other as much as of the self. In its own minor way, *Climbing High* contributes to this pattern. Elsewhere, Reed seemed more in tune with the more conservative tendencies of the British cinema – such as in his war films – but romantic comedy encouraged greater dissidence. *Climbing High* is of a piece with the work of other inter-war artists, its very title an ironic commentary on social climbing and classless love. As the film was made while the country prepared for war, its dismissal of communism (the USSR had not yet joined the allies), its satire of the penniless upper classes, and, as in *A Girl Must Live*, its celebration of classless love, are all readable through romantic comedy's traditions of plot and character, and as an appeal for pulling together, ignoring divisions of class in uncertain times. Furthermore, the accent on youth, and on the couple's rejection of outmoded form, the witty repartee and light-hearted treatment of the lovers' japes and ordeals, adapt comedy's traditional alliance with the young lovers against the *senex* establishment to the film's championing of modernity and youthful energy as the nation prepared for the worst.

In this sense, Nicky's flight from Lady Constance is a retreat from the past as well as from domineering forms of femininity. The aristocrats are not only, as sticklers for form, enemies of social mobility, but also materialistic and deceitful. The past, as represented by the impoverished Lady Constance's family and hangers-on, is a sham out of place in modern times. Constance and her mother put on an act where, in contrast to its attached aura of meanings in Nicky's wooing of Diana, theatricality confirms the hollowness of their lives. 'John Smith' in one sense allows Nicky to rise to the lofty romantic heights of his moon goddess Diana but, in another, it humbles him, pulls him down socially to ground level, Diana's mundane and classless world, one where in contrast to Constance's fake illness contracted to earn the sympathy of a wealthy catch, she is stricken only by the disease of love. Where Constance is a study in vanity, Diana ends up modelling by accident, her self-display and submission to the rigours of being 'made over' in the cosmetics scene driven by economic need.

The film's contrasts of rival forms of femininity are mirrored by variants of masculinity. *Climbing High's* ideal of the Englishman avoids the rugged manliness of Diana's Canadian brother (Torin Thatcher), the wild unpredictability of the escaped lunatic (Francis L. Sullivan), the prissiness of the advertising agency owner (Noel Maddison), the Marxist eccentricities of Max (Alastair Sim), and even the Old School conservatism of Reggie, though none of these, as befits comedy, lacks saving graces. Nevertheless, the primary function of these subsidiary male characters is to offset the lustrous qualities of the romantic male ideal. All in some ways contribute to the film's construction of national identity: Diana's brother lives and works in Canada, a country once derided by Voltaire as being no more than 'des arpents de neige', a land not only frozen but also identified with Neanderthal woodcutters or Mountie He-men. When Jim, Diana's brother remarks in the film's opening Canadian forest scene, as lumberjacks fell trees all around him, 'There's no place like Canada ... Imagine anyone preferring London to this,' few in the audience were expected to agree with him.

The director of the fashion photography agency is American; not, however, the representative of the rugged West, or the intellectual East, but the more sexually ambiguous world of New York fashion-houses, whose prissiness recalls in Hollywood romantic comedies the mannerisms of a legion of minor actors like Edward Everett Horton, Charlie Ruggles, and Eric Blore. Finally, Reggie is too much the old school tie type who, for all his loyalty and generosity, represents the kind of Englishman who fails on the grounds of attitude and looks to measure up to the ideal, and also perhaps because his Gentleman's Club aura has taught him little of women. All of these characters are further linked through the theme of desire, and draw attention to the film's enquiry into sexuality, sexual orientation and romantic love.

The sexually indeterminate director of the advertising agency, the brutish asylum fugitive, the primitive brother, and the probably sexually inept Reggie, are negative models against which may be measured the ideal embodied in Nicky. His English romantic hero has a *soupçon* of each of these – the reticence or ineptitude of Reggie, the manliness of the Canadian, the ease in women's company of the advertising agency owner, and even, when one recalls Shakespeare's comment about lunatics, lovers and poets, the brutishness of the escapee. While approving of the film in general, reviewers of the day took a flatly literal approach to the treatment of the lunatic, overlooking the functional and metaphorical significance of madness as an element of desire (Anon 1939a; Anon 1939b; Anon 1939c).

Nicky/John's place of definition is Switzerland, though the association is wreathed in irony, a sort of bloodless Utopia, which even Diana refers to as a 'neutral country; it's the home of the Red Cross and the League of Nations.' Even so, it is, after all, not just – in Harry Lime's later sneer – a nation of cuckoo clocks, but the setting for love's triumph, where Jim accepts his sister's independence and love for Nicky/John. The caring (Red Cross), democratic (League of Nations), purity and wholesomeness (the snow-covered mountains) of the country that draw the lovers to it serve as parts of an elaborate metaphor of love. The stereotype of Switzerland as a dull, if sanitary, place is turned on its head, so that not only does it become the *mise-en-scène* of desire for the successful conclusion of its ideal couple's courtship, but also the place where a Swiss citizen, the hotel receptionist, can ridicule the English: 'The English! They make such a joke of dying and such a dreary business of living.' The encomium of the stiff upper lip is mixed with satirical reference to the drabness of the English. Whatever the truth of the second part of the aphorism, Nicky/John's behaviour demonstrates that there are exceptions, which may, of course, only help prove the rule. Romantic comedy demands of its lovers a capacity for playfulness and risk as well as beauty, and, in the gallant's relations with women, egalitarianism as well as chivalry and manliness. The ideal couple will return to their habitat, London; Switzerland, though, that haven of neutrality, where conflict is abolished, is a place that, like Connecticut in *Bringing up Baby*, or Venice in *Trouble in Paradise*, has finally united them, and also provided the setting for romantic comedy's Utopian solution to all problems of nationality, class, gender and family.

1 *Climbing High.* Nicky (Michael Redgrave) and Diana (Jessie Matthews) in the *locus amoenus* of British Screwball Comedy

2 *Night Train to Munich.* Gus/Dickie Randall (Rex Harrison), Charters (Basil Redford) and Caldicott (Naunton Wayne) as Gentlemen or Players in times of love and war?

3 *The Way Ahead*. Perry (David Niven) defending 'England, my England'

4 *Odd Man Out*. Johnny (James Mason) and Kathleen (Kathleen Ryan) torn between love and duty

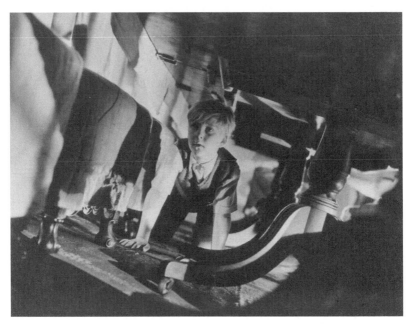

5 *The Fallen Idol*. The disturbed eye view of the child (Bobby Henrey)

6 *The Third Man*. Me and my shadow: the naïve hero (Joseph Cotten) and his double (Orson Welles)

7 *Our Man in Havana.* The exotic Englishman abroad (Noel Coward) serenaded with *Domitila*

8 *The Key.* Fatal attraction: David (William Holden) in the arms of a modern Circe (Sophia Loren)

9 *Trapeze*. The triangle of desire: Mike (Burt Lancaster), Lola (Gina Lollobrigida) and Tino (Tony Curtis)

10 *Oliver!* Where is love? Oliver (Mark Lester), Nancy (Shani Wallis) and Sikes (Oliver Reed)

The 1940s: love and death

3

The Stars Look Down (1940)

The film that followed *Climbing High, A Girl Must Live*, had been made while Reed was under contract at Gainsborough, so when the opportunity arose for him to direct *The Stars Look Down* permission was needed to work for another studio to direct the film that many regard as his first major work. Pauline Kael even went so far as to claim that it was 'possibly his best' (1968: 439–41). Both this judgement and Robert Moss's view that the earlier films were little more than the first fruits of a young director feeling his way do justice neither to early films like *Laburnum Grove, A Girl Must Live, Bank Holiday* or even *Climbing High* nor to the masterpieces of the late 1940s. A newly formed film company, Grand National, acquired the rights to *The Stars Look Down* (first published 1935) and hoped to emulate the success of another film based on a novel by A. J. Cronin, King Vidor's Hollywood version of *The Citadel* (1938). An initially hesitant Margaret Lockwood, also temporarily released from Gainsborough, was signed up with Reed, a huge budget for the day of £100,000 was allotted to the film, and shooting began in March 1939, on location at the St Helen's Siddick colliery in Workington, at Twickenham, and at Shepperton studios. Robert Moss (1987: 107) emphasises the lessons learnt from British documentaries, especially *Industrial Britain* (Grierson, 1933), *Coalface* (Cavalcanti, 1936), and *The Face of Britain* (Rotha, 1939), that Reed put into practice in later years both in his own documentaries and in *The Stars Look Down*, where his quest for an authentic representation of the miners' plight in northern England left Paul Rotha distinctly unimpressed (in Whitehall 1962: 23). *The Stars Look Down* was one of three films on coal mining themes – including *The Proud Valley* (Tennyson, 1939) and *How Green Was My Valley* (Ford, 1941) – made, at the end of a troubled decade, in Britain and Hollywood. Its release was held back in America until after the opening of *How Green Was My Valley*.

In their attention to the struggles of a mining community – Wales in the case of *How Green Was My Valley*, Northumberland in *The Stars Look Down* – these films reveal key divergences between Hollywood and Britain, as well as between John Ford and Carol Reed. While *Stars*, for instance, has been read by Graham Greene (1980: 265) as a film about the class struggle between miners and mine-owners, it also surveys, not always to Greene's liking (though he finds much, here as elsewhere in Reed's work, that is admirable), the family, its relationship to the wider community, religion, class conflict and romance, all topics also covered by *How Green Was My Valley*. More separates than unites these two films.

In *How Green Was My Valley* the family, as represented by the Morgans, is idealised, its members paragons of unblemished nobility, the *mise-en-scène* of family home and pit village a projection of their inhabitants' fundamental wholesomeness, order and decency. These virtues characterise even the treatment of the frustrated romance between Mr Griffith (Walter Pidgeon), the lofty preacher, and the pit beauty Angharad (Mauren O'Hara), its demise accepted as a necessary sacrifice to higher ideals. That this extreme act of self-effacement should be identified with a minister comes as no surprise in a film where religion is regarded as an important unifying and uplifiting force in the life of the community. In a voice-over Hugh comments, 'Respect for Chapel was the first thing my father taught me.' Ford's lyricism blends into the film's sentimentality, here as elsewhere matching the almost bucolic radiance of pictorial composition with the patterned intervention of full-throated hymn or emblematic music, such as the opening 'Men of Harlech', or later 'Cym Ran', that all but turn the film, like the later *Wagonmaster* (Ford, 1950), into a variant of the Hollywood musical. At Angharad's wedding, her father's complaint about the absence of hymns emphasises the importance of sacred melody in the community. Clearly, music is intrinsic to Welsh culture, for as Hugh puts it, 'singing is in my people as sight in the eye.' Ford's Celtic heritage – to the point where three Irish actors, Sarah Allgood as the family matriarch, Maureen O'Hara as Mr Griffith's disappointed lover, Angharad, and Barry Fitzgerald as the boxer Dai Bando's sponge man – sabotages the distinctiveness of Welsh culture, a heresy presumably encouraged by awareness that failure to respect such nuances would be unlikely to unsettle American audiences.

To British audiences the *pot pourri* of Irish, American, fake Welsh and unfathomable 'ethnic' accents in *How Green Was My Valley* is only capped by attempts to affect regional accents in *The Stars Look Down*. When asked by the reporter on the Newcastle *Evening Chronicle* (Anon 1940b) about this, Carol Reed replied: 'it was decided that as the film was to have such a wide public, only the hint of a North-country accent was required.' The interviewer charitably comments to his readers: 'Remember this when you see *The Stars Look Down* – as you must – and forgive director Carol Reed for putting a dialect which has more of Yorkshire and Lancashire than Tyneside into the mouths of his "Tynecastle" folk, because the wider the public the better for this epic of the men and women of our North-country coalfields.' A Geordie reviewer now, listening to those accents that have more of the unknown than of the North-country would not, one suspects, be so forgiving.

Admittedly, as Richard Whitehall points out (1962), the working-class characters are, unusually, not here portrayed as buffoons in a film that treats seriously the hardships of the poor. But Whitehall's comments on the film as a whole are mixed, though his misgivings are not always warranted. Two objections in particular deserve scrutiny: first, his comments on Margaret Lockwood's miscasting as Jenny, David's unfaithful wife, and second, his criticism of the film's mixture of styles. The casting of Lockwood and the darker expressionistic tones vary the documentary mode and contribute to the film's engagement, beyond social realism, with melodrama. Reed has little intention of producing an apologia for the miners, and even remarked that he could equally well have made a film on those events from the opposite point of view (Samuels 1972: 174). Reed's Tynecastle, and Sleescale, a confection of studio and location settings, are clearly meant to be Newcastle and its environs. He chose not to alter these curious equivalents, inherited from the novel, for the real locations, determined to preserve the wider relevance of the story to more than local or regional interests. As in the Cronin original, there are references to actual Newcastle landmarks: for instance, Westgate Road and Jesmond Dene. At one point, too, the 'Blaydon Races' – so identified with the North East capital – is sung, and the youngest member of the Fenwick family (Desmond Tester) has been signed up to play football for 'Tynecastle United', a clear reference to the region's premier (*pace* Sunderland followers) professional team. The boy's name, Hughie, would have undoubtedly brought to mind to football cognoscenti in the audience the Scottish footballer, Hughie Gallacher, a star at Newcastle (1925–30) and Chelsea (1930–34).

But even though, as Jeffrey Richards argues (1997: 255–6), the same elements of commonality and comradeship appear in *The Proud Valley*, the idyllic south Walian proletarian setting of *How Green Was My Valley*, with its implausible white picket fences protecting equally improbable spacious miners' houses, is replaced in *The Stars Look Down* by an ambience of grimness, pinched faces, bare interiors and unrelieved poverty. Reed's characteristic fondness for low angle shots intensifies the atmosphere of doom from which none of the characters ever ultimately finds relief. After the credits and commentary over the initial shots of the beleaguered community, the film maintains its despondent tone by setting up the confrontation between striking miners and an alliance of corrupt union officials and the mine's owner, Mr Barrass. Led by Fenwick, the miners suspect that Barrass knows of the dangers of flooding to a pit – Scupper Flats – he intends to re-open. He risks the men's lives, the water comes crashing through, and causes the deaths of Fenwick and several others who are trapped in the mine. But for all Barrass's profit-motivated blindness – which leads to his suicide – the film avoids simplistic divisions between virtuous workers and villainous bosses. It is more interested in the portrayal of an entire community's subjection, regardless of class, to external pressure. Circumstances create an atmosphere of entangled desires that corrodes the will, brutalising men and women, owners and employees, in equal measure. The scene of the attack by the striking mob on the butcher's shop recalls, though less shockingly, the assault on the shop-keeper Maigrat in another mine-narrative, Zola's *Germinal* (1885), where the savagery, which culminates in the women's ripping out of Maigrat's private parts, that are then attached to a pole and raised aloft in triumph, is provoked by Maigrat's provision of goods from his shop in return for sexual favours. In *The Stars Look Down* the raid on the butcher's shop is driven not by sexual revenge but by the sheer instinct for survival by starving men and women, whose hunger ultimately over-rides calls for restraint. Fenwick, the strike leader, alone attempts to halt the looting, but to no avail. For all its rhetoric of sympathy on behalf of men and women who have reached the limits of human endurance, the scene nevertheless characteristically offers a balanced and unsentimental account of the situation, recording not only the despair that drives individuals to primitive and brutish regression but also to the villainy of some, like Joe Gowlam, a 'born capitalist', as David contemptuously calls him, who seizes the opportunity during the raid on the butcher's to rob the till. Fenwick, horrified by the action of the mob, and Joe Gowlam, preferring to line his pocket more than his belly, are at opposite ends of humanity.

Emlyn Williams's jaunty, wide-boy manner made him a natural choice for the suspicious, shady and even villainous characters he played in Reed's films, twice opposite Margaret Lockwood, both here and later on, as an adulterer. In *Girl in the News* he compounds adultery with murder. Gowlam's stripe-suited, straw-hatted charm lies not in any saving moral grace or secret admiration for the élan of his egotistic schemes; rather it derives precisely from his self-assurance, the refusal to be identified with the fake romance of working-class life of the kind celebrated in *How Green Was My Valley*, and a determination to rise from the squalor of his birthright. Barrass, too, is no mere stage villain. Both Whitehall and Basil Wright, quoted approvingly by Whitehall, consider him (in Wright's words) 'a compound of melodramatic clichés' (1962: 45). In the early stages he does seem a little rudimentary, but he gradually acquires complexity especially when joining the hunt for the missing men in the flooded mine, and when, eventually, as all hope for the men's rescue is dashed, guilt leads to suicide. He does not die at the hands of another, having shown no remorse, even though the sentiment belongs more to the inner torment of a Judas – here a betrayer of a whole community – than to that of a Simon Peter. In this the film differs from the novel, which spares Barass the pricks of conscience and allows him to live on unmoved by the plight of his workers.

The outer milieu of social injustice soon gives way to the interior melodramatic world of private struggle. The torments of the former are reflected in the tensions of the latter. Imprisoned by the gloomy, threadbare walls of the Fenwick household, sits David at his desk by a window: were they only to acknowledge it, he is the family's hope for the future – as Huw was the Morgans's in *How Green Was My Valley* – the scholar whose university education would prepare him for a career in politics and the opportunity to improve the condition of exploited miners and other workers. Very quickly the film draws attention to family tension as David's mother Martha (Nancy Price) appears, in the form of a shadow, as if to forewarn the audience of her darker influence over her son. The effects of what might loosely be called expressionistic lighting, seen at first in the Fenwick household, are repeated throughout the film, most notably towards the end when David discovers his wife's adultery with Joe Gowlam. David's mother remains a stony presence in the room, refusing to return her son's greeting, 'Morning, mother!'. She exits from the room, and heads for the local butcher's to beg for scraps. Turned away empty-handed, she returns home and, finding David still buried in his books, addresses him contemptuously: 'You and your scholarships!.'

This crossing of documentary – the harsh realities of mining life – and expressionism – the chiaroscuro photography – belongs, despite Whitehall's strictures, to the film's patterns of creative energy. *The Stars Look Down* makes no apology for blending genre and style. The documentary effects anchor the narrative in a plausible setting: many of the exteriors, including shots of real coal mines, city streets, miserable back lanes crammed with back-to-back terrace houses where the strikers congregate, provide the necessary grainy realism that would have been lost in studio sets. The more melodramatic aspects of the film – the dynamics of family and social relationships – are accommodated more comfortably in the artifice of studio *mise-en-scènes*. The interior of the mine, as well as interiors elsewhere, were shot in the studio, mainly at Twickenham, and here the documentary style – of natural lighting and establishing shots – is often sacrificed for more 'expressionistic' effects emphasising character and psychology.

In this as in other Reed films, characters require understanding not only in their own right but also in relation to family structures. For every solitary character such as Johnny McQueen, Harry Lime or Pope Julius there is an Oliver Twist, a Philippe (*The Fallen Idol*) or an Elsie (*Laburnum Grove*). Even where no blood ties link them together, surrogate family relationships, as in *Trapeze, The Fallen Idol,* or *An Outcast of the Islands,* sometimes do so. In *The Stars Look Down* the key parent/child relationships are these: Barras and son; the Fenwicks; Jenny and her mother; Joe Gowlam and Slogger, his father. In all cases the behaviour of the offspring is virtually incomprehensible without reference to the parent(s). The Barras father/son relationship is sketchy, but, significantly, the son seems temperamentally the antithesis of his domineering father. The son's inadequacy, in the eyes of his father, reaches its most humiliating point when David is hired to act as Richard's tutor. The film abandons interest in an earlier script's fidelity to the novel, where Barras's daughter Hilda plays an increasingly prominent role, precisely in order to concentrate on the father/son relationship. The case of Joe Gowlam's relationship to Slogger is even more striking. Here, Joe's eager dissociation from his mining heritage represents the desire to find a more fulfilling, less demanding way of earning a living than coking for coal. But Joe's determination to leave Sleescale also implies a rejection of his father, Slogger, a miner who finds no shame in scrounging from his son. First seen draped across the coalhouse roof of one of the back-to-backs, Joe distances himself from the other men at the outset, his jokey detachment presaging early retirement from the pit. When he returns it is as an entrepreneur, ready to betray former friends and colleagues by teaming up with Barras. His initial career, following retirement from mining, as a bookie, his affair with a married woman, his ill-treatment of Jenny, and his identification with the city – Tynecastle – are all features at odds with the values of decent miners. Where other Reed characters go in search of fathers, in *The Stars Look Down* the Joe/Slogger and Barras/Richard relationships highlight the son's efforts to disown the patriarch.

The father/son relationships are complemented by those between offspring and their mothers, the most important of whom are Jenny's, Mrs Sunley, and David's, Martha. Like the mother who rages at David for attempting to lure her son Pat away from mining to education, Martha belongs to a tradition of working-class women whose hostility to learning springs not only from an instinct for survival and the need for the hard cash of today rather than the promised wealth of tomorrow, but also, according to the screenplay, from an ingrained British suspicion of Bolshevism.

The film's anti-Marxism is especially pronounced in Martha. The manuscript of the treatment reads:

> Martha, this lively character – who is disgusted at her son having left the Pit and not carrying on in the family tradition – would never appreciate her son has done good – to her he is a Bolshi – Remember Cronin – 'When Barras says work, the men should work' she remembers when her father used to go down the Pit when conditions were much worse. Now the men have luxury compared to those days – so she thinks – this is the most definate [sic] character in the Picture. (Williams and Reed 1939: 21)

The novel's emphasis is slightly different, stressing the manliness of the miner, equating education and politics with unmanliness. When David returns to the mine, the narrator observes, referring to Martha's substitution of demonstrative affection to the coolness shown to her son all the time he was studying, teaching or pursuing a political career: 'Through all those years of study, of schoolmastering, of the Federation, yes, even of Parliament, she had sealed her heart against him. But now that he had been driven to return to the Neptune she saw him truly her son, following the tradition of his father, a reality, a man at last' (Cronin 1997: 600).

Both of these prejudices lie behind Martha's attitude to her son, but there are other causes. Living up to the New Testament significance of her name as the more domesticated of Lazarus's sisters, Martha is both victim and victimiser. Victimised by her heritage, by a recognisable but ultimately incomprehensible desire to maintain the family's traditions, she is a portrait of defiance, shaped by a history of pride and inherited, unrelieved family poverty. Martha's victimisation inhibits expression of finer emotions. When David sets off from home to the university, his words 'Well, I'm off', are met with silence until he is finally about to go out of the door. Eventually, his mother sends him on his way with the cheerless words, 'Here, you'll want a bite to eat on the train.' Once he is out of the house, she approaches the window, releasing her emotions in the safe knowledge that they are not being witnessed by her son. Constrained by economic misery, Martha even finds difficulty in relating to her daughter-in-law. Suspicions of the motives and behaviour of others seem justified when, after finally agreeing to visit her newly wed son's home, she is rewarded by Jenny's impatience to be rid of her parents-in-law in order not to miss a date at the theatre.

The pathos of this scene fails to eradicate the impression of Martha as victimiser. Her enslavement to tradition, her unwillingness to place her faith – through her son – in the value of education, and the baleful expression that casts a gloom over her family, turn her home into a kind of prison, after the fashion of those patriarchalised inter-war literary female characters referred to by Alison Light (1991), creating an authoritarian mental space from which David seeks release, at first through education and subsequently through marriage to a woman who seems in every way the antithesis of his mother.

David's interest in education and in Jenny is the return of the repressed and, with respect to the latter, in somewhat monstrous form. Significantly, Jenny is an outsider, the mark of difference, an affirmation of femininity and a disruption of the patriarchal order internalised by Martha, not a Sleescale native, but an urbanite, someone identified with an admittedly low-order, common form of excitement, revelry and fun. Her job as an usherette, where the film being shown is *I Killed the Count* (Zelnick, 1939), is an augury perhaps, though less tragically, of her future destruction of David through adultery with Joe Gowlam. Jenny represents David's affront to the introjected patriarchal values identified with his mother.

While some reviewers approved of the film's treatment of the mining theme, others were less complimentary about the role of Jenny. The anonymous *Manchester Guardian* reviewer, for instance, wrote: 'Another defect ... is that David's marriage to the shallow and nasty Jenny ... is given from the beginning no emotional basis; in consequence the failure of the marriage is merely tedious and sordid' (Anon 1940a). The reviewer appears to have underestimated her significance as both a representation of femininity in revolt and as a screen perhaps for the projection of a son's resentful feelings toward his mother. His attraction to Jenny is eventually overshadowed by hostility after the discovery of the resumption of her affair with Joe Gowlam. Additionally, when through Jenny's insensitivity David's anger is given violent expression, there is the suggestion that his rage has been conditioned not only by resentment towards men like Barras who have made the lives of miners everywhere a misery, but also by the entanglements of family life. In the workplace David's anger, controlled and articulate, is uninhibited; at his parental home, David seems constrained to the point of submission, forced to speak in hushed tones, his reasonableness in the face of his mother's reserve an image of unnatural self-effacement. At their marital home Jenny finally incites David into violence through a steady flow of provocative remarks, beginning with a prohibition on eating with his fingers, followed by the command to excuse himself on leaving the table, and finally with a reference to his father as a 'jailbird'. David strikes Jenny, a gesture that seems to aim as much at the imposition of a regime of domestic tyranny as at the insult to his father. This streak of violence, ever ready to re-surface, even though in this scene Jenny's self-awareness leads her to seek forgiveness – 'David, it was wicked of me, wicked; oh but I deserved it!' – indicates a latent hostility of which David himself seems unaware. When Joe Gowlam visits the couple a little later in the film, David greets his old friend, knife in hand, with the savage words, delivered straight from his troubled unconscious: 'I hope you don't think I was trying to cut Jenny's throat.' He is already, in a sense, undoing the violence he has committed against his wife, displacing on to her the guilt in reality shared by her two suitors, the devoted husband too blind to his own failings, and the faithless lover too lost to ambition.

David's violence reaches its most extreme form after he returns home one night to find Joe Gowlam leaving the house. The confrontation between cuckolded husband and wife is lit expressionistically. For a moment, the audience is uncertain how the scene will end. There can be no sure way of telling whether it will conclude fatally or uneventfully, and the ultimate triumph of self-control is a victory that might easily have ended in tragic defeat.

Like David, Jenny continues to play out the unfinished dramas of family life, especially the relationship with her mother. As David is bound to his mother, so Jenny is dominated by hers. Mrs Sunley exemplifies Karen Horney's notion of maternal narcissism, in which the boundary between mother and daughter is abolished, a process in which as Estela Welldon also argues, the daughter is regarded by the mother as at some level not an individual but an extension of the self (1980). In her efforts on behalf of Joe Gowlam, Jenny's mother almost seems to be wooing him for herself. Mrs Sunley's displeasure at Joe's decision to stop lodging at the Sunley residence indicates over-investment in her daughter's affairs. When, on the rebound, Jenny traps David into marriage, her decision seems conditioned as much by a wish to appease her mother as by revenge against a faithless lover. Jenny's emotional enslavement by her mother's Munchausen by Proxy syndrome is given vivid visual expression at one point when she appears at David's home, determined to seduce a man for whom she feels no passion into a proposal of marriage. She storms out of her own house at night, before the film cuts to a shot of David working at home, by the window. Rain falls on the window pane, and before long Jenny is glimpsed through it, standing in the rain, as if framed by the window, in another portrayal by Reed of the child's captivity by the parent.

The parent–child relationships of *The Stars Look Down* complement the theme of social unrest in the mining community and illustrate melodrama's blend of personal and social themes. The strife in the outer frame of the miners' dispute mirrors the turbulence of domestic life. The squalid picture of private lives damaged by family relationships mirrors the grimy geographical landscape in which it finds expression. The film ends with the disaster in the mine, and the entombment of the men. As the people outside kneel, the priest recites the Lord's Prayer, and the camera shifts its aim upwards from the mine to the heavens. The voice-over intones, more in despair than in hope or optimism: 'And so out of the darkness of the world that could be and must be, a world purged of its ancient greeds, a world in which dreams are not empty and sacrificed in vain, a world of infinite promise which the unconquerable spirit of man will some day fall into fulfilment.' The sentiment seems to relate to the miseries of both personal and social worlds, embodying an almost Schopenhaurian view of existence as struggle, where good fortune, happiness and tranquillity are seen not as the norm but as the exception to life's general rule of disintegration, misfortune and affliction. Where W. G. Pabst's great film, *Kameradschaft* (1931), with which *The Stars Look Down* is sometimes compared, was far more upbeat, celebrating the solidarity and camaraderie of miners across the borders of nationality, as the German miners rushed to the aid of their trapped French colleagues, *The Stars Look Down* offers no parallel consolation in the affairs of men and women, justifiably earning its reputation as one of Reed's bleakest films. From the injustices of the social system in *The Stars Look Down*, Reed turned to the gathering storm clouds of war in *Night Train to Munich*.

Night Train to Munich (1940)

'Munich' for contemporary audiences would inevitably have called to mind the Munich crisis of 1938 and Chamberlain's attempts to keep Britain out of the Second World War. The crisis to which the night train in this film (the first of five projects Reed made for Fox) leads refers to attempts by a British agent to rescue a Czech scientist from the hands of the Nazis, but other less politically motivated matters are aired in what is one of the most brilliant thrillers of the British cinema. As Gilliat points out, the film – based on the original magazine serial by Gordon Wellesley – began as a story set in the mythical state of Ironia: 'Our script, or rather the treatment, began the same way, but the outbreak of war enabled the country to be properly identified. We virtually used up Gordon's story in the first ten minutes and invented most of the rest' (Brown 1977: 96).

Direct comparisons with Hitchcock, in the 1930s and 1940s Reed's only rival as Britain's leading film-maker, can be made through *Night Train to Munich* and *The Lady Vanishes* (1938). Both are comedy thrillers ('not a propaganda picture but a great comedy-drama of today' claimed the original poster for *Night Train*); both concern the outbreak of the Second World War, were written by Launder and Gilliat, featured Charters and Caldicott, and starred Margaret Lockwood. Clearly *Night Train* was made in the hope of repeating the success of *The Lady Vanishes*, and yet, though the similarities are striking, the differences are perhaps even more significant. If less had been made of similarity and more of difference, the *New Statesman* reviewer might have been more forgiving: 'The chief fault of *Night Train to Munich* is that it tries to join two worlds: Hitler's Europe as we began to see it unrolled in black and white last September and the jaunty return of those two brilliant cricket-talking buffoons, Naunton Wayne and Basil Radford ... With more speed, and a less threatening background to be blotted out by thrills, this might have been as good a film as *The Lady Vanishes*' (Whitebate 1940).

Night Train clearly winks knowingly at *The Lady Vanishes*. It exploits the commercial success of its precursor, and enters into a game of playful allusion to Hitchcock, acknowledging the merits of the earlier film but also decrying them, in line with the contradictory tendencies of intertextuality defined by Julia Kristeva (1969), Barthes (1970), Harold Bloom (1973) and other cultural theorists. *Night Train* is thus simultaneously commentary on *The Lady Vanishes* and a development of areas ignored by the earlier film. These allusions exploit a successful formula but are also an acknowledgement of love-hatred for Hitchcock, a characteristically ironic *homage* which, in recognising the earlier film's brilliance, also notes and addresses its deficiencies and differences.

The most striking difference between the two films lies in the shift of emphasis in relations between the couple – here played by Margaret Lockwood and Rex Harrison (instead of *The Lady Vanishes*'s Michael Redgrave) – so that the male, not the female, becomes the driving force. Lockwood's Iris in *The Vanishing Lady* is another, in Tania Modleski's phrase, of Hitchcock's 'women who knew too much' (1988). Convinced of Miss Foy's suspicious disappearance, she refuses to be distracted by unsatisfactory explanations, and persuades first Gilbert and then Charters and Caldicott that her anxieties are justified. As Anna in *Night Train to Munich*, a film more concerned with British masculinities and father/daughter relations, Margaret Lockwood plays more of a support role, allowing her partner to take the initiative. In *The Lady Vanishes* Iris embarks on an emotional as well as a literal journey, heading for London and, characteristically for Hitchcock, reluctantly for matrimony. Significantly, Iris is accompanied by two female friends at the beginning of the film, and has no father (unlike Anna in *Night Train*). The female trio forms a secular version of the three Graces, modern women at ease in one another's company, independent spirits enjoying the carefree pleasures of sisterhood. True, Iris becomes attached to Gilbert, but this seems more in the tradition of liaisons formed by screwball lovers, a sort of union of kindred playmates, where gender-specific roles have little meaning, as Redgrave's unmasculine devotion to folk dancing complements Iris's unfeminine talent for spying and investigation, a capacity shared with another transgressive woman, Miss Foy. The dancing and music theme recalls H. G. Wells's remark in *Ann Veronica* that 'by dancing men ... come to feel and think of their bodies' (1995: 121). The early scenes also invoke the first meeting between Astaire and Rogers in *Top Hat* (Sandrich, 1935) where Ginger's slumber is disturbed by Fred's tap dancing in the hotel room above. *The Lady Vanishes*'s borrowing of *Top Hat*'s romantic musical comedy ambience is further stressed through Gilbert's supervision of folk dancing in the room above the one occupied by Iris.

The search for Miss Foy is Hitchcock's metaphor for Iris's quest for identity. By contrast, Reed's Anna is first and foremost a daughter, seen in the company not of any female friends but of her father, whose importance as a scientist caught in a tug-of-war between Britain and the Nazis overshadows her own pursuits. The pattern of Reed's female-centred 1930s films is reversed here as Anna's story is relegated in importance beneath Dickie Randall/Gus Bennett's (Rex Harrison) fulfilment of his heroic role in the secret service. With Britain now at war, the focus on male, not female, heroics might have seemed in the circumstances more appropriate. Unlike her roles in *Bank Holiday, A Girl Must Live, Girl in the News* and even *The Stars Look Down*, Lockwood's Anna is an altogether more conventional character, where even her costume marks her out as a stereotype heroine of feminine romance. Her femininity is defined by daughterliness and by love. Her heart – or emblazoned hearts – are not here worn on the sleeve, but, surrounded by patterns of leaves and flowers, on her chest. After initial anxieties over playing the bad girl in *The Stars Look Down*, Margaret Lockwood seemed relieved to revert to an earlier type, defining Anna as a 'nice girl' (Lockwood 1955: 79), but Iris's initiative is replaced by Anna's incompetence, leading to mistakes from which she must be rescued by others, chiefly Gus/Dickie Randall. Her daughterliness is compounded, after imprisonment with her father at the Nazi concentration camp, by her role as nurse, tending to male prisoners. There she makes the first of her errors, failing to see the villainy beneath the charm of Karl Mauser, the disguised Nazi (Paul Henreid). 'I am a desperate character' Karl confides to her, but Anna reads his confession only as that of a patriot being persecuted by the Nazis, insensitive to its ambiguity. Paul Henreid's charm is usually flaked with a certain tension or unease, here probably attributable to what Val Guest recalls as his nervousness about being picked up for security reasons, as an Austrian, by the Home Office (2001). Karl is indeed desperate, but only to track down Anna's father. Gus/Dickie Randall, though, is no stranger to duplicity. When informed about Karl's part in the staged escape from the concentration camp, he wonders whether the escape has been organised by the Nazis. Anna's flaws of perception and blunders multiply from this point on, culminating in her failure to take proper precautions when followed by Karl's Nazi henchmen *en route* to her *rendez-vous* with her father.

The film's discreet use of symbolism indicates the shortcomings of innocence in a woman available for rescue by a man of experience. Accompanied by Karl, Anna, reaches England's shores in a rowing boat christened 'Skylark', to be greeted by a fisherman with a Cockney accent. The beautiful Anna's detachment from the reality of her situation recalls Shelley's description in a famous poem of another skylark. Like a 'blithe spirit' Anna's innocence has removed her 'higher still and higher' from awareness of danger. The fisherman's banter as she and Karl climb out of the boat onto the pier suggests that, like the fisherman's catch, she too has been hooked by Karl. Anna's girlish innocence is further highlighted through images of sight. Karl's contact in London is Dr Fredericks (Felix Aylmer), an optician. When Karl begins to read the eye-test letters on the clinic board, he sees the usual letters but reads out others, substituting for those on the board the letters of a secret code. After repeating the process, as a way of confirming his identity to his contact, he utters the words 'Heil Hitler', a salute also given by Dr Fredericks. Like Anna, these men have a skewed vision of reality: Anna's innocence is matched by the blindness of Nazi ideology. Her myopia is given its clearest visual representation in the scene following the disclosure of Karl's true identity when, in the foreground of the frame, and looking towards the viewer, she listens on the phone to an unseen interlocutor with news of her father's whereabouts, while in the background, behind her, Karl's shadow falls on the staircase wall. Anna's positioning, designed to ensure her failure to see the shadow and to realise that her conversation is being overheard, is the measure of her naiveté.

That naiveté is what initially attracts Gus/Dickie Randall. Rex Harrison's light comedian persona, exuding self-confidence bordering on arrogance and even ill-temper finds an easy target in Anna. His irascibility is linked to the aristocratic air and brisk, impatient response to duller wits, qualities that serve him well in the darker roles in his repertoire of tetchy lovers such as the jealous husband in *Unfaithfully Yours* (Sturges, 1948) and, towards the end of his career, Professor Higgins in *My Fair Lady* (Cukor, 1964). Through Rex Harrison's Gus/Dickie Randall the film examines Englishness, above all heroic Englishness. In that respect his rivalry with Karl invites speculation on questions of sexuality as well as of ideology. Gus/Dickie seems at one level a cross between Bulldog Drummond and Raffles. Of the two, Bulldog Drummond represents the straight action-man, unquestioningly doing what he regards as his duty on behalf of comrades, class and nation. Raffles – later impersonated on screen first by Ronald Colman and then by David Niven – is the gentleman-cricketer thief. Bulldog Drummond, the creation of 'Sapper' (pseudonym of Herman Cyril McNeil) (2001, first published 1920), is the heir to the Scarlet Pimpernel and the progenitor of James Bond, fighting international criminals, rescuing damsels in distress, defending the superior, more virtuous culture of England. He is the upper-class sophisticate, as much at ease in smart gentlemen's clubs or aristocratic soirées as on sports fields or duels against evil foreigners, especially Communists and Germans. Many of Drummond's attributes apply to Gus/Dickie, and when he remarks to Anna, who thinks he is giving up the struggle against the Nazis, 'What do you take me for? Bulldog Drummond?', a direct connection is made between the two, though the comparison also invites reflection on their differences. The missing element in the Drummond persona is supplied by Raffles, E. W. Hornung's creation of the gentleman thief, the relation of Lubitsch's Gaston Monescu in *Trouble in Paradise* (1932) and the forerunner of Cary Grant's John Robie in *To Catch a Thief* (1955). The comparison with Raffles is not made by Gus/Dickie himself but by Charters when he suggests that Gus/Dickie might be an international crook. Raffles's description by Bunny, his faithful companion, in the short story 'Gentlemen and Players', could serve as a pen portrait of Rex Harrison's Dickie Randall:

'I looked at Raffles. I had done so often during the evening, envying his high spirits, his iron nerve, his buoyant wit, his perfect ease and self possession' (Hornung 2003: 46). When Caldicott remarks that crooks don't generally play for the Gentlemen, Charters replies that Raffles did. This exchange develops from the earlier moment when Caldicott recognises the Nazi officer 'Ulrich Herzoff' as the Dickie Randall who was up at Balliol with him, who used to bowl slow leg-breaks, and played for the Gentlemen. When Charters wonders whether Dickie Randall has become a traitor, Caldicott replies: 'Traitor? Hardly old man. Played for the Gentlemen.' The more innocent of the pair, Caldicott, lives in a private inner world where codes of gentlemanliness are sacrosanct. Equally blind to realities, but with a slightly more suspicious nature, Charters counters amusingly: 'But only once.' Charters and Caldicott are both right. Dickie/Gus is no crook, but his heroics align him with Raffles, and draw attention to an underside of cunning and devilry that extend beyond the rescue of the scientist and his daughter. Caldicott had already inadvertently referred to Dickie's underside in a casual remark: 'Well, I can't help it if Dickie Randall has a double'. The doubles motif, so common in Reed's films (as in *Odd Man Out, The Third Man, The Agony and the Ecstasy*) not only highlights in *Night Train* Harrison's dual roles as Dickie Randall, the Oxford graduate, and Gus Bennett, the spy and seaside entertainer, but also, more darkly, invites comparison with Karl Mauser, the Gestapo officer, an alliance that however shocking for a wartime audience nevertheless draws on narrative traditions that narrow the distance between sinners and saints.

Gus/Dickie's devilry, though, has a lightness of touch denied the Teutonic villain Karl with whom he is inevitably compared as a sexual rival for Anna. Dickie's fondness for role-playing partly reveals an ingrained tendency towards characteristically English self-mockery. Karl's play-acting – he starts off, after all, by pretending to Anna he is an enemy of the Nazis – is deadly serious, a necessary disguise in the service of a political philosophy. 'Ulrich Herzoff' seems as much a comic turn as his song-and-dance man on Brightbourne pier. His song, 'For only love can lead the way', conveys less through its banal lyrics than through the singer's assumed role and the proletarian seaside setting the attitudes of the English. The constant lightness of touch, and the resort to humour for even the gravest subjects characterise even the most peripheral English characters. So, for instance, when the top brass at the Foreign Office meet to discuss the weighty matters of state, especially those concerning the refugee Czech scientist, the atmosphere is lightened by Roberts's remark to one of his colleagues, urged on instruction from Mrs Roberts, to remind his wife not to forget to bring her recipe for pickled walnuts to their next meeting.

The undermining of gravity by lower-order items or references is a characteristic form of British humour. It belongs more generally to a fondness for understatement, an aesthetic of litotes recognisable as much in the literary art of George Eliot and Jane Austen as in films scripted by Launder and Gilliat. This is not a claim for English culture's exclusive rights over this type of humour. Freud discusses it in *Jokes and Their Relation to the Unconscious*, under what he terms 'unmasking' or 'degradation': 'Under the heading of "unmasking" we may also include a procedure for making things comic with which we are already acquainted – the method of degrading the dignity of individuals by directing attention to the frailties which they share with all humanity, but in particular the dependence of their mental functions on bodily needs' (1983: 263). Such humour is exemplified in the deflation of the dignity of the Foreign Office mandarins and their talk of matters of state through commentary on the body's needs for those nourishing walnuts. Another, slightly more Rabelaisian, example is the punning juxtaposition of copies of *Mein Kampf* at the railway station beside *Gone with the Wind*. More elaborate equivalents of this subversion of loftiness appear visually through Dickie/Gus's attitude to his German uniform, and through the imagery of games, especially cricket, associated with Charters and Caldicott. When Gus/Dickie first appears dressed as a Gestapo officer he is seen fiddling with a monocle. He tries it on, then, with the amused air of someone unimpressed by its connotations of pretentiousness, puts it away. The contempt for the monocle extends by implication to the entire uniform and, beyond, to Germans as a whole, here stereotypically defined as members of a race who are strangers to humour, incapable of self-mockery, a truth borne out by Karl's more respectful, but perhaps understandable, relationship with his uniform. When he stands proudly on the prow of the submarine on which he awaits the delivery of Professor Bomasch and his daughter Anna, tricked by his henchmen into heading towards what they believe is a safe haven, his dark uniform, worn without irony, makes him seem like a cross between a Wagnerian hero and Nosferatu on board the vessel bound for Whitby.

But Karl's conversion from fake political prisoner to Gestapo officer, the living exemplar of what Susan Sontag has defined as 'fascinating fascism' (1980: 73–105), raises interesting and contradictory questions concerning his effect on Anna. Before the disclosure of his true identity Anna finds herself drawn to Karl. The companionship he offers her, the denunciation of Nazism, his beating at the hands of his so-called jailers, although all ruses, make him a plausible lover. Anna's lesson is of course that appearances are deceptive. But the part of anti-Nazi patriot, played so convincingly, signifies not only expertise in theatricals but also perhaps the revelation of a hidden and contradictory truth about himself. In his false-patriot role Karl has all the warmth and approach-ability – lent to him by the continental Paul Henreid who was to become, after all, a romantic leading man in countless Hollywood films such as *Casablanca* (Curtiz, 1942) and *Now Voyager* (Rapper, 1942) – that are markedly absent in Rex Harrison's upper-class, cool and sex-shy Englishman.

Allen Eyles's description of Karl's look of frustration when at the end of the film Dickie/Gus succeeds in getting Anna and her father by Teleferic safely across the border and into Switzerland, refers to Paul Henreid's look of a sulking, wounded small boy 'who had his ice-cream taken away from him' (Eyles 1985: 40–1). But is the ice-cream the scientist or his daughter? Judging from Karl's expression aimed at 'Ulrich Herzoff' in the train compartment during the latter's fake love scenes with Anna – designed to convince the Nazis that 'Ulrich''s pretend earlier romance with Anna gives him access to her father and his secrets – jealousy for a loathed rival suitor cannot be discounted.

The combination of gentler instincts with the imperious attributes of the Nazi man of power is a potent sexual force, taboo, of course, to a heroine in a film made in wartime, but whose effect is nevertheless manifestly uncontrollable, especially when set beside the almost adolescent projection of sexuality associated with Dickie/Gus.

The first scene of feigned sexual intimacy takes place for the benefit of the hotel waiter, who must be convinced, like all the other Germans, of a former romantic attachment between Anna and 'Ulrich Herzoff'. Anna's remark, 'You're treating all this as some sort of joke' plainly registers outrage at his impudent behaviour in the hotel room, but its latent meaning points to Dickie/Gus's culturally inbred difficulty in treating love seriously. Dickie is too much the Public School man's man, of probably restricted sexual experience, his fear of real intimacy with a woman sublimated through other pursuits, his self-esteem measured by derring-do, practical jokes, and standing among his male peers. When, for instance, he almost betrays himself by whistling a tune recognised by the waiter from a BBC broadcast, his elegant method of turning the remark to his own advantage by threatening to report the waiter for listening to enemy radio leads to his self-congratulation and an exchange of remarks with Anna that highlights the Englishman's priorities. Failing to seize the advantage of an opportunity to be alone with Anna, he contents himself with self-love: 'Handled it rather neatly,

I thought.' Anna replies: 'You know if a woman ever loved you like you love yourself it would be one of the romances of history.' Determined to have the last word, he adds: 'I'm certainly unlikely to think of a reply to that. I think we should drink a toast: "England expects that every secret serviceman this night should do his duty!".' He uncorks the champagne and exclaims: 'Flat!' The state of their relationship parallels that of the champagne, a flatness conditioned by the very qualities, lightness of touch, breezy detachment, wit and self-confidence, that in other spheres bring their own rewards.

The national characteristics that identify Gus/Dickie with heroes form the pages of Buchan, Conan Doyle, Sapper, Hornung and the rest appeal above all to certain types of male, their alter ego represented here, in comic form, by Charters and Caldicott. Reed's deconstruction of the couple's appearance in *The Lady Vanishes* leads him into some of the more dubious areas of masculinity. Taken to extremes, and applied more widely to the culture in general, these virtues perpetuate the stereotype of the Englishman's suspicion of foreigners. For every gesture or remark, for every action taken by Caldicott and Charters that earns approval for its merited criticism of foreign – in this case Nazi – barbarity there is another that exposes the insularity of the English, a tendency already noted in Reed's films, above all, in the satirical remarks made by the Swiss hotelier in *Climbing High*. Charters and Caldicott are a comic double act, the Public School Morecambe and Wise of their day, the subjects as well as the objects of the film's humour. As allies of the hero and heroine in their struggle with the Germans, their status is not in doubt. Here, as in *The Lady Vanishes*, they subordinate their personal interests and safety to the cause of England. But they are also, for all Charters's interest in *Mein Kampf*, which he takes the trouble to read, little Englanders. Charters is surprised *Punch* is not sold at the German bookstall: '*Punch*. English magazine. Very humorous', he exclaims to the bookstall vendor, painstakingly describing its features, ever the Englishman abroad who speaks his own language very slowly in the expectation that the foreigner will understand him. In 'England Your England', Orwell comments: 'Even when they are obliged to live abroad for years they [the British] refuse either to accustom themselves to foreign food or to learn foreign languages. Nearly every Englishman of working class origin considers it effeminate to pronounce a foreign word correctly' (1988: 49). Charters and Caldicott are not working class, but the rule still applies: first, when at another station, attempting to make a long-distance call to England, Caldicott expresses irritated surprise that the operator speaks 'all in German'; and second, when the pair join Dickie/Gus, Anna and her father in the getaway car awaiting them in Munich, Charters begins to drive on the left. The benign satire of English insularism is paralleled by comic reformulation of English attitudes to sex, indirectly scrutinised in the triangular relations involving Dickie, Karl and Anna.

The joke about the Englishman's awkwardness in the company of women, and associated speculation about the repression or denial of homosexual tendencies, is first developed by Charters and Caldicott in *The Lady Vanishes*. There, forced to spend the night in the chambermaid's room in a hotel overcrowded with stranded passengers, the inseparable pair are uncomfortable in her presence, even horrified at the prospect of sharing a room with their buxom hostess. Even more suggestively, they share the same bed and a single pair of pyjamas, Charters awarded the top, and Caldicott the bottoms. The most telling gesture is made when, as the maid unexpectedly enters the room, now occupied by the odd couple, Charters hastily covers Caldicott's chest to protect his modesty. The joke is replayed in *Night Train to Munich*, only here the *mise-en-scène* of desire is not a woman's bedroom but the train lavatory. Dickie/Gus bursts in on Charters and Caldicott in a sort of prelude to the more elaborate scene between Noel Coward and Alec Guinness in *Our Man in Havana*, setting plans in motion to frustrate Karl's to arrange the scientist's return to Nazi headquarters. Whether this tendency to show men unfazed by communal beds or lavatories simply acknowledges the Public School ethos of collectivity, or whether the homosocial bonding contains elements of homosexuality – a pattern repeated throughout the history of British popular culture and extended beyond Public School types to lower-class heroes like Morecambe and Wise – it emphasises at the very least the unthreatening (because, to men, known) nature of male friendships and identity. The threat (because, to men, unknown) is the female, even if, as in *Night Train to Munich*, the woman is of the 'nice', daughterly kind portrayed by Margaret Lockwood's Anna.

Kipps (1941)

Like *Night Train*, and Reed's next film, *Girl in the News*, *Kipps* was scripted by Gilliat, although the film did not meet with his ultimate approval: 'My script was written faithfully to fit Wells's account of Folkestone society, which was transformed by Carol Reed and Cecil Beaton into quasi-Mayfair society and played far too much that way ... It was said by some that Carol was not very happy outside the square mile or so of the West End' (in Brown 1977: 100). Impressed by the box office returns of *The Stars Look Down* and *Night Train to Munich* (its title trimmed to *Night Train* in America), Fox offered Reed the opportunity to direct a sound version of H. G. Wells's *Kipps*. *The Story of a Simple Soul* (1899) (a silent film version had appeared in 1921), a novel about class and identity that gave him greater scope than *Night Train to Munich* for dividing attention equally between female and male characters. It reunited Reed and Redgrave for the third and last time. Here, Redgrave plays the lower-middle-class draper's assistant whose unexpected legacy of £26,000 enables him, lured by the artificial trappings of a higher world, to abandon temporarily his own class. The casting of Redgrave as Kipps drew a mixed response. Some (e.g. Agate 1941) would have preferred to see John Mills or John Carol as Kipps, arguing that Redgrave was too tall, and too alert for the role. Dilys Powell thought (1941) that well though he played the part, Redgrave 'neither conveys, nor is intended to convey the awkward misery of Wells's hero', a view more or less echoed by C. A. Lejeune (1941), who found Redgrave 'an odd choice for Wells's badgered little draper's assistant', adding that 'Mr Redgrave may have a simple soul, for all I know, but with that presence and that headpiece he is hard put to it to convince us that he is one of life's natural orphans, and a victim of capitalism and an inferiority complex'. But a more sympathetic view is not hard to find in other reviews, such as in the *News Chronicle* (Anon 1941a), where Redgrave's diction and comportment, and the film's wardrobe of high collars and stiff tailoring – in Cecil Beaton's first film – do justice to the characters.

Work on *Kipps* began on 16 September 1940, at the start of the Battle of Britain, shot – with interruptions from German bombs – over thirteen weeks. The *Sunday Despatch* reviewer, Moore Raymond, in a piece entitled 'There's a New Spirit in Britain's Film Studios', even composed some doggerel verse in honour of films, like *Kipps*, being made in dangerous times: 'Though the Blitz / May give some people fitz / It'll take more than this bit of row and ruction / To stop British film production' (Raymond 1940). At a moment of great uncertainty, there was room for a film that looked back nostalgically to more tranquil Edwardian times, celebrating the nation's heritage, with *The Scotsman* going so far as to comment that the film would bring the 'British people a deeper appreciation of their own land' (Anon 1941b). As nostalgic as Mamoulian's *Summer Holiday* (1948), *Kipps* transfers its audience to the somnolent world of a bygone era, of bandstands, boas, silver teapots, boaters and blazers, to offset the lived realities of bombs, air raid sirens and uncertainty.

Underneath the nostalgia, *Kipps*, in those parts that dwell on the draper's assistant is, as Marcia Landy observes, a 'male melodrama' (1991: 256). Where in a conventional romantic comedy the narrative is arranged – as in *Climbing High* – to facilitate the eventual union of true lovers, melodrama, more sceptical about the course of true love, concentrates on the vicissitudes of desire in ways that damage more than superficially the viability of the ideal couple. In *Kipps* the lovers destined for each other are wounded by deeper scars in their long day's journey towards union, learning to find fulfilment not by escaping but by embracing their true nature. Melodrama, with its emphasis on feeling, often stresses the forming influences of childhood, a tradition that Kipps respects. In common with films as varied as *Written on the Wind* (Sirk, 1956), or *Wuthering Heights* (Wyler, 1939), the destinies of Kipps and Ann (Phyllis Calvert) in *Kipps* are settled in childhood. The circularity of the narrative, as Ann and Kipps finally tie the knot, makes of the lovers, characteristically for melodrama, the playthings of external forces. When, after the news of his legacy Kipps returns home, he heads for the beach, the setting for the games he played with Ann in infancy. Like Marylee, Kyle and Mitch Wayne, who yearn in *Written on the Wind* to go back to the river of their lost Edenic innocence, Kipps is driven back to a fantasised time and place of irretrievable security. Like Ann, he has kept the half-sixpence that, in a modern version of Plato's account of the origins of love, has symbolised their ultimately inseparable union, the definition in cash terms of these divided halves of a single spirit nevertheless pointing to their troubled destiny. The magnetic force of their urge for union competes with a more conscious determination, in Kipps's case, with an ambition prepared to sacrifice roots for the illusory material and social rewards offered by a higher world, here represented by the Walshinghams and their apologist, Chester Coote, a feeling described by Wells as a 'vague dissatisfaction with life [that] drifted about him, and every now and again enveloped him like a sea-fog' (1999: 42). The Walshinghams are the less comic middle-class equivalents of the impoverished aristocratic mercenaries with whom the Redgrave character becomes entangled in *Climbing High*. As soon as Kipps receives word of his legacy the film develops into a tussle between loyalty to, or betrayal of, class.

The stifling lower-middle-class world into which Kipps is born is given its most vivid expression at Shelford's, the department store where he begins his suffocating life of apprenticeship drowned in a sea of chintz. Here, the hierarchical world of the retail trade allows owners to act dictatorially over a cowed and exaggeratedly respectful workforce. An early montage sees the harassed Kipps facing a barrage of orders from his superiors. The stuffy environment and poor salary that allows for only free forms of entertainment, such as attending bandstand music concerts, eventually hasten Kipps's growing impatience for self-improvement, a feeling that leads to enrolment at the Folkestone Institute. But the hierarchies of Shelford's are only replaced by the equally moribund shabby gentility of the Walshinghams and Chester Coote, who fall on Kipps like leeches as soon as they become aware of his new found prosperity. The views of Edgar Anstey (1941) and Dilys Powell (1941) concerning the film's failure to be true to Wells's theme of class snobbery seem unjust. Through the Walshinghams's mercenary exploitation of Kipps, Reed stresses Wells's theme of English aversion to class mobility. For all the money Kipps has inherited he is never allowed to forget, despite his new genteel friends' attempts to educate him, his place. The film faithfully represents the novel's sentiment that all Kipps's efforts at social advancement, at becoming a gentleman, are doomed to failure, since in 1940s as much as in turn of the century Britain, a man finds himself trapped by his low birth, his low connections tied like a dead weight about his feet. Reed's *Kipps* addressed the class prejudices and hierarchies of 1940s Britain in the forlorn hope perhaps that the war might finally expose the triviality of social division when more serious issues were at stake.

The most extreme caricature of English class prejudice relates to the portrayal of Max Adrian's Chester Coote, who exemplifies the notion that all classes acquire their own identity through comparison – and usually disparagement – of others. Now quoting Carlyle, now teaching Kipps table etiquette, he drips with oleaginous charm, administered in the cause of Helen Walshingham's mercenary ambitions. Wells's description of Coote could hardly be improved on in Max Adrian's impersonation: 'prominent nose, pale blue eyes, and a quivering quality in his voice' (1999: 43); 'a curious rectitude of bearing' (1999: 109), and of whom 'from amateur theatricals of a nice refined sort to science classes, few things were able to get along without him' (1999: 109). Initially, before news reaches him of the legacy, Kipps is attracted to Helen (Diana Wynyard), the teacher of wood-carving at the Institute, and finds the courage to declare, but only in a dream, his feelings for her. As soon as she becomes aware of the legacy, Helen takes the initiative in preparing Kipps for marriage. His name is altered to its more distinguished, foreign, even aristocratic form as 'Cuyps', his pronunciation – especially his unaspirated 'h' – syntax, dress, gaucheness, innocence of poetry and chamber music, all come under scrutiny through the combined efforts of Helen and Chester Coote. Meeting Ann again after his engagement to Helen, Kipps answers, when asked whether he is happy, 'I ought to be happy. I've been lucky enough haven't I?' The reply carries little conviction, and indicates his growing awareness that if luck has brought him wealth and social standing it has also meant losing control of his own life.

Fortune, as the medieval poets knew, is a wheel, bringing moments of material success followed by failure. Trusting to fortune, rather than to morality or conviction, is to place oneself at the mercy of external forces. Kipps's attempt to regain control of his life occurs at the anagram party where he comes across Ann, now in service at the Walshingham household. There he breaks his engagement to Helen and asks Ann to marry him.

The exchange of Ann for Helen, the re-unification of the two halves of the sixpence, would have been a perfect ending for romantic comedy, where experiments with unsuitable partners are typically the prelude for marriage to the ideal. In melodrama the ending is usually, even when seemingly happy, at best arbitrary, and at worst a mark of resignation or even surrender. As *Kipps* is a melodrama, the contradictions of choice resonate beyond closure, and in Kipps's case relate to his conflicting desires for two women from different worlds.

Diana Wynyard – Reed's first wife – as Helen, and Phyllis Calvert as Ann, bring to their roles opposed connotations. More a stage actress, Diana Wynyard projects through firm, emphatic features, and a statuesque, remote beauty, a more forceful personality, ideal for Helen Walshingham. Phyllis Calvert, on the other hand, the sweet English rose, the foil to Margaret Lockwood's Gainsborough *femmes fatales* and precursor to Deborah Kerr, exudes a soft, warm, even submissive femininity posing little threat to male authority. While Kipps's engagement to Helen was an escape from self and background, marriage to his childhood sweetheart is not only a return to the familiarity of the past, the embrace of his own nature, but also an admission of a preference for a complaisant woman, whose respect and admiration offer no challenge to his constantly judged and wounded self-respect.

Kipps's choice of Ann for a wife is, furthermore, a statement of identity and recognition of his station in life. In returning to Ann, he seemingly repudiates the world of social pretence but, as represented by Helen, it is also a rejection of the unknown. Kipps seeks in Ann his mirror image, a woman who confirms his own values and ideals, whose behaviour is not marked by the aggression that characterises the more predatory Helen, over whom there was never any possibility of exercising control and authority. Marriage to Ann declares his longed-for restoration to childhood innocence, a regression that also clearly registers fear of development. Kipps ends as he began.

Yet even though the film's conclusion shows Kipps as a contented bookshop owner, married to Ann, their income supplemented by the return on an investment in 'The Pestered Butterfly', a play written by their friend Chitterlow (who first drew Kipps's attention to the notice in a newspaper calling for Kipps to claim his inheritance), the shock to his system of involvement with Helen is enough to leave doubts in the minds of protagonist and audience. Kipps may have had to scale down his delusions of grandeur, for instance, over the size of the marital home he is planning with Ann, but the decision to be satisfied with a smaller building comes only after news that Helen's brother (Michael Wilding) has lost all the money with which he was entrusted by Kipps. And as for Ann, Kipps has never had a dream of her. Only Helen, the different, glamorous object of desire has had that honour. Ann will make Kipps 'some buttered toast, just the way you like it', but the memory of the gourmet fare served by Helen may not easily fade from his memory.

The Way Ahead (1944)

After *Kipps*, Reed turned his hand to more directly patriotic projects. *A Letter from Home* (1941), a seventeen minute documentary, starring Celia Johnson, on the heroic endurance of Londoners in wartime, followed by *The Young Mr Pitt*, a wildly inaccurate film using the Napoleonic Wars as ill-concealed allegory for Britain's current war with Germany, were followed by another documentary, *The New Lot* (1942), the basis for what is still regarded by many as one of the finest British war films, *The Way Ahead*. Nicholas Wapshott claims it provided 'the blueprint for a number of post-war projects which fondly looked back at the war and the camaraderie enjoyed by those who fought' (1990: 1643). In 1942 Reed enlisted in the Royal Army Ordnance Corps, was awarded the rank of Captain, and commissioned to make films for the army. The first of these was to be a training film, in which he was joined by Eric Ambler and Peter Ustinov, as screenplay writers, and Thorold Dickinson as producer (Wapshott 1990: 158–9). Nothing came of this initial project, but Reed, Ustinov and Ambler were then assigned to the Directorate of Army Psychiatry, their brief a film to boost the morale of new recruits. That film was *The New Lot*, and although shelved because considered too negative, it eventually formed the basis for *The Way Ahead*, once David Niven, who had left Hollywood to join up, used his influence for official backing from the army, as well as to help arrange Reed's release from his commission, in order to advance the project for Two Cities Productions.

At many levels *The Way Ahead* retains the documentary format of its precursor. In this it recalls the pseudo-documentary structure of another war-time narrative, C. S. Forrester's *The Ship* (1949), a novel that prioritised accurate description over formal experiment. *The Way Ahead* does for the army what *One of Our Aircraft Is Missing* did for the RAF, or *In Which We Serve*, for the Navy. Noel Coward had been approached in vain by David Niven to write the screenplay for *The Way Ahead*, put together in the end mainly by Ambler and Ustinov, with some contributions from Reed himself, who up to now had relied on the work of specialists, particularly of course Launder and Gilliat. In its portrayal of the heroism of infantrymen from varied social backgrounds, and the support of their families and friends, the film is a response to the more satirical portrayal of the Army in *The Life and Death of Colonel Blimp* (Powell and Pressburger, 1943), and paints a portrait of a society of men and women pulling together, unified by war and, despite the impediments of class, to affirm the common values of a nation under threat. Like *In Which We Serve*, *The Way Ahead* is a double-focused narrative, concentrating simultaneously on the group and the group leader. *In Which We Serve* follows in flashback the lives of a group of seamen – chiefly those played by John Mills and Bernard Miles – whose leader Kinross, the captain of HMS Torrin (Noel Coward), a character based on Lord Mountbatten, is given narrative prominence in often being positioned in set pieces standing above the men to deliver his latest harangue or morale-booster. Coward, the producer and co-director of the film, was also its major star. Even though there were misgivings in official circles concerning the appropriateness of his light comedy background for the role of a ship's captain in wartime, his fame clearly set him apart from the other actors, some of whom, like John Mills and Richard Attenborough, would eventually become big stars in their own right.

The Noel Coward equivalent in *The Way Ahead*, a less class-bound film (Drazin 1998: 64) was David Niven, whose Captain Perry, not a regular like Kinross, discovers through call-up natural qualities of leadership that inspire his troops to rise to the occasion and to overcome their initial resentments in deference to a common cause. Like *In Which We Serve*, *The Way Ahead* follows patterns, noted by Marcia Landy (1991), repeated in a cross-section of British war films made after 1939: the use of documentary footage, the stress on pulling together in a 'people's war', the solidarity of the group, cross-sections of society, appeals to patriotic unity over class or ethnic difference, and the conversion of callow or resentful recruits to the embrace of the good of the community.

As Benedict Anderson argues, communities are largely imagined, since the members of even 'the smallest nation will never know most of their fellow-members, meet them, or even hear of them, yet in the minds of each lives the image of their "communion"' (1991: 6). *The Way Ahead* illustrates this argument. Through its portrayal of British society it may intend to instil into the viewer that knowledge, but in reality the film merely dramatises the viewer's imagining. And, in hoping its upbeat tone will stir the patriotism of the British viewer, it further examplifies a point made, via Freud, by Anderson, that nationalism should not be understood exclusively as a pathological state governed by fear and hatred of the Other, but as a concept that inspires love and even self-sacrifice (1991: 141). The characters in *The Way Ahead*, the imagined representatives of the community, are willing to die – like the viewer – for such imaginings.

The Way Ahead produces its rhetorical effects through a blend of formulae and realism. Unlike the more romanticised, and what James Chapman (1998) has termed the 'Boys' Own' fantasies of films like Reed's *Night Train to Munich* and Leslie Howard's *Pimpernel Smith* (1941), it belongs to the more realistic crop of war films, characteristically made at Ealing (e.g. *Went the Day Well?* (Cavalcanti, 1942) or *San Demetrio London* (Frend, 1943)), that were clearly indebted to the documentary tradition. Unlike the glamorous fantasy of British or Hollywood war films, such as *Objective Burma* (Walsh, 1945), or the Audie Murphy films of heroic young warriors sacrificing all for their country in modern versions of the romances of chivalry, *The Way Ahead* prepares the ground carefully by anticipating the real horrors that await the soldier – in this case at the end of the film on the battlefields of North Africa – by dwelling for long stretches on the gruelling experience of training. The brutal realities of war are not entirely eclipsed by the celebration of manly resolve and eventually willing service in the call of duty. Though not in this sense in the class of *La grande illusion* (Renoir, 1937), or *Paths of Glory* (Kubrick, 1957), *The Way Ahead* is a thoughtful contribution to the war film genre, its silencing of the real drama of the battlefield an indication of the rejection as much as the denial of military glory.

As Christine Geraghty notes (1984: 63–7), male genres like the Western or the Gangster film, are characterised by groups in which, nevertheless, a hero shines. She further argues that in the war film the male group 'is a crucial base both ideologically and formally' (1984: 63). Films often 'centre on a group of men, some of whom may be more important than others, but all of whom represent some attitude or response to war. The concept of the male group allows the films to work in certain ways and to explore certain areas which would not otherwise be open to them' (1984: 63). As in *In Which We Serve*, where upper-middle (Coward), lower-middle (Walter), and lower-class (Mills) individuals and families come under scrutiny, or in *One of Our Aircraft Is Missing*, where the stranded crew includes an actor, a diplomat, a Yorkshireman and an older man, the group – the recruits – in *The Way Ahead* is a microcosm of British male society: the men come from varied backgrounds, walks of life, class and regions. Other films follow this pattern: in *San Demetrio London*, for instance, after the ship is rescued and makes its way back to Britain, the men take turns to define home in nationalistic terms. 'First stop England!' cries one crew member; 'first stop Wales!' shouts another; and 'first stop Scotland!' yet another, the unity of the kingdom unambiguously asserted in wartime. A curious variation occurs in *The Halfway House* (Dearden, 1944), where an Irishman initially defends his country's neutrality, but eventually, like *Casablanca*'s Rick, accepts the need for engagement after experiencing first hand the effects of Nazi aggression. 'Swine! Filthy swine!' the Irishman declares on abandoning neutrality.

The group dynamics of *The Way Ahead*, appealing to common interests and unity in regional or national diversity, but also highlighting the role of the leader, is given a slightly different emphasis in *One of Our Aircraft Is Missing*. Here all the members of the crew, stranded in Holland after a crash, are given equal prominence as they attempt to return to England. Because of their team-spirit they struggle to nominate a leader. Part of the point here is surely to stress the democratic tendencies of the British over the fascist, leader-obsessed ideology of the Germans. Audiences both for *One of Our Aircraft Is Missing* and for *The Way Ahead* are expected to identify themselves not only with the characters but with the film's imbued democratic ideology. Even though in a memo prior to shooting David Niven stressed the need to avoid giving the impression of propaganda (Morley 1985: 124–5), the effect is little short of the propaganda that James Chapman identifies as the motivating force behind the making of these and similar films in the war years (1998). *The Way Ahead*, after all, started life as a morale-booster for recruits in its rougher, abbreviated version as *The New Lot*.

In 'The Disillusionment of the War', the first section of Freud's 1915 essay on the First World War, 'Thoughts for the Times. On War and Death', Freud writes, on states at war: 'The state exacts the utmost degree of obedience and sacrifice from its citizens, but at the same time it treats them like children by an excess of secrecy and a censorship upon news and expression of opinion which leaves the spirits of those whose intellects it thus suppresses defenceless against every unfavourable turn of events and every sinister rumour' (1985c: 66). The state, in fact, treats the recruits like children, reserving the status of parenthood to the officers and the drill sergeants who will ultimately achieve through love rather than discipline the aims of their mission. In *The Way Ahead* Lieutenant Perry, very much in the style of Kinross in *In Which We Serve* informing them of the 'good news' about imminent active service, treats his men like an affectionate father. Perry's sympathetic advice to the recaptured deserter Parsons, as well as his efforts to put on a regimental revue, suggest parallels with fathers devising games and pastimes as well as developing paternal anxiety over the welfare of children. As Anthony Storr argues, shifting Freud's focus to a more political level, the need for cohesion makes of democracy – even in democratic countries like Britain – the first casualty of war: 'military organization is based upon a strict rank order and absolute obedience. The dress of soldiers is misnamed 'uniform'; for, although an officer may garb himself in the same colour as a private, his rank will be emphasised by tabs or badges which indicate that he is far from uniform in status. The whole of military training is designed to inculcate the notion that men are by no means equal' (1982: 46–7).

The emphasis on obedience and regression to states bordering on infancy is typified by the fate of the recruits in *The Way Ahead*. First, all traces of resistance are systematically erased; second, even when the order finally comes to send them on their way to battle, the troops are treated like children, kept in the dark about their destination, the secret only known to the officers and Sergeant (William Hartnell), who is gently warned by Lieutenant Perry (Niven) not to disclose to the troops what he knows he is thinking, namely that they are about to go into battle.

The assembly of the group, well before the scene of their deployment by sea to North Africa, celebrates, like the films already mentioned, variety of background: Perry, Fletcher, Brewer (Stanley Holloway), Lloyd (James Donald), Luke (John Laurie), Beck (Leslie Dwyer), Stainer (Jimmy Hanley) and Parsons (Hugh Burden), represent British society. Their assembly is intercut with shots of the Chelsea Pensioners, on parade at the Royal Hospital and, subsequently, by two of their number who act as a sort of chorus for the action. The editing maintains continuity and tradition, emphasising debts owed by the present to the sacrifices of the past. The commentary of the old soldiers, though, offers a mixed message of reassurance and regret. One, in particular, while praising his Boer War comrades benignly derides the efforts of the modern soldier. His carping is inspired by what he believes is the degeneracy of the modern age, a view that seems lifted directly from

J. B. Priestley's 1934 essay 'English Journey', a sort of elegy on the demise of an earlier, nobler age and its values. The Chelsea Pensioner gestures to Priestley's lament for 'old England' and the triumph of a modern industrial culture in thrall to American popular music, dance halls, Woolworths and cinema: 'it's all this education and machinery and goin' to the pictures ... it's all right to 'ave a good regiment, but where's the men to fight in it? That's the point. Where are they?'. Even though the Pensioner's devotion to the past and suspicion of the present is gently but unmistakably satirised by the film, as he laments the falling standards and the dearth of real men, despite the ordeals endured by the modern recruits, the rhetoric of nostalgia does not fail to leave its mark.

In an original draft, the screenplay began slightly differently from the completed film. The initial idea for the credits was as follows: 'Credit titles: superimposed over sky of swiftly moving clouds. As the last of these titles fades out, a specially [sic] dark cloud can be seen approaching. As it approaches it begins to take the shape of the map of Europe. S. T. (soundtrack). Overture building up to the appearance of the dark clouds which introduces a new theme suggestive of crisis and approaching danger. Overlaid sound to marching feet getting louder and rising to a crescendo with title in next scene' (Ambler and Ustinov n/d: 1). The ideas for both sound and vision, as outlined here, were scrapped. It might have seemed that the effect would have been too gloomy at a time when the outcome of the war was still uncertain. The screen-writers were in some respects responding to up to the minute events taking place on the battlefields. As Reed himself scribbled on the screenplay typescript, he, Ambler and Ustinov were adjusting their story to changing circumstances: 'The action described here and the circumstances surrounding the last part of the picture were based on the information about the course of the war available at the time of writing the original story. It was understood, however, that should a second front be opened in the near future, the story would be adjusted accordingly. 'Village x' would be in, say Sicily instead of Tunisia' (Ambler and Ustinov n/d: 109). In fact, although the film's interiors were shot at Denham, the exteriors were indeed filmed in North Africa. As to the original, discarded opening, the ominous beginning of dark clouds, marching feet and sombre music gave way to the much more upbeat beginning of credits rolling against a regimental insignia accompanied by William Alwyn's martial music, which starts as a march before developing into a less formally militaristic but still rousing melody, at first in a minor and subsequently, as the credits end, leading into the scene at the Royal Hospital, in a triumphant major key. The regimental insignia points to the standards by which the conduct and attitudes of the recruits must be judged. It is the badge of excellence and tradition, a reminder to the recruits of the sacrifices made by previous generations of soldiers, whose history begins in Napoleonic times.

At first the recruits fail to live up to these standards: early on, still resentful of their treatment by hard task-masters, they deliberately subvert a field exercise in order to return sooner to their barracks. Lieutenant Perry's response is to shame the men, informing them that since the regiment's creation the 'badge ... hasn't been disgraced yet'. The dressing down goes even further when he adds, looking ahead to the day they will be expected to take to the battlefield themselves: 'If you're lucky you'll have soldiers like Captain Edwards and Sergeant Fletcher to look to. If they're lucky they'll be with another company.'

Perry's words perform at least three important functions. First, they bear out what Peter Hennessy argues was Churchill's sense of the importance of language to the leader in times of war: 'In 1940 he commandeered the English language for war. His words stood up and fought' (1992: 26), Second, they affirm the importance of cultural memory: Perry's speech conjures up not only the valour of past generations of nameless soldiers, but also significant moments dating back to the early eighteenth century of British history; memory and identity are indissolubly linked in Perry's description of a nation that has defined itself ever since the eighteenth century as Jerusalem. The England that, for the moment, Perry evokes here is not the 'green and pleasant land' of croquet, tea-drinking, eccentricity and good humour, but of bravery, fair play and comradeship, all epitomised by regimental codes of honour. But, thirdly, the rebuke has the required effect of converting the sheepish men from skivers to soldiers, thus conforming to the conversion-pattern narratives noted by Marcia Landy (1991). In *The 49th Parallel* (Powell and Pressburger, 1941), Johnny's (Laurence Olivier) light-hearted approach soon yields to the same suspicions of the Nazis felt by fellow Canadians when he too falls victim to their barbarity; in *San Demetrio London*, another Canadian (Robert Beatty) is transformed from an irresponsible, boozing free-loader into a much valued member of the ship; in *The Demi-Paradise*, the Russian (Laurence Olivier), at first bemused and even irritated by the British way of life, with its endless interruptions for tea breaks, its seduction by tradition and seemingly arbitrary customs and rituals, is eventually charmed by even its most trivial idiosyncrasies. These films all stress the importance of the Western alliance, to the point where, as in *The Demi-Paradise* (Asquith, 1943), even the Russians are praised. In *The True Glory*, Reed's later documentary collaboration with Garson Kanin, General Eisenhower's prelude to the film includes this remark: 'Teamwork wins wars. I mean teamwork among nations.'

In *The Way Ahead* the transformation affects an entire group, but perhaps above all, Lloyd (James Donald), the malcontent who initially complains to Perry that Fletcher's strict regime of discipline is provoked by revenge following overheard unflattering comments about the army and its sergeants. His leading role in subverting the field exercise, in the eyes of his commanding officer an act that dishonours the name of the regiment, at least shows initiative and enterprise, qualities that earn him recognition and promotion as a corporal, once his irresponsibility has bowed to discretion. Before this Pauline conversion the film strives to emphasise the ordinariness of the group. These are not, essentially, self-serving individuals. On the contrary, their decency and eventual willingness to serve their country mark them out as civilians who may be strangers to army discipline but not to the imperatives of the national cause. When England expects, no Englishman disappoints. The people, here represented by a cross-section of the population, are in a sense allowed to speak for themselves in a 'people's war'. The controlling voice-over informs the audience: 'This is our people's story. In their words.'

While *The True Glory* (the title a quote from a prayer by Sir Francis Drake) was intended to give the impression of ordinary people expressing their thoughts and observations in voice-overs played against carefully edited documentary footage of the war, *The Way Ahead* adds performance, character and narrative to discrete and disembodied voices. These men from different backgrounds come burdened with their own problems, some self-inflicted, some created by circumstances. The men are introduced in the following sequence: (1) Brewer in the House of Common boiler room; (2) Beck at the Travel Agency; (3) Lloyd collecting rent at a Cardiff terrace slum; (4) Perry at a country garage; (5) Fletcher at a drill hall; (6) Parsons at home; (7) Davenport at work in a Department Store, interrupted by Parsons who also works there; (8) Davenport, Parsons and Beck on a train heading for the recruitment centre; (9) Stainer, Lloyd and Luke in the railway bar at Crewe station, soon joined by the others. Each of these introductory vignettes, interrupted by the nostalgic reminiscences and proud claims of the Chelsea Pensioners, gives a thumb-nail sketch of what the film regards as some of the characteristic features of British life and customs.

Played by Stanley Holloway, in films since 1921, Brewer is a blend of irreverent humour and an agnostic attitude to authority. Holloway's major roles as a slightly bombastic Ealing Comedy loser in films like *Passport to Pimlico* (Cornelius, 1949), *The Lavender Hill Mob* (Crichton,

1951) and *The Titfield Thunderbolt* (Crichton, 1953), all lay ahead. Here his comic persona is given a southern Andy Capp inflection, complete with fag drooping out of the corner of his mouth, as he rails against self-indulgent politicians, and approves of resolve in a leader, delivering his broadsides in the witty demotic of the British working class, here represented by its Cockney variant. Following the chimes of Big Ben, we move from the sound of political authority to *vox populi*, Brewer's complaint to a colleague that 'Things are getting serious. You know what time I got home last night? Half past ten.' Likewise, the 'serious' situation for Brewer is not Hitler, but the effect on his domestic arrangements. His approval of Churchill, also expressed in the scene, is consistent with Anthony Storr's argument that, in times of war, politicians considered in peace time unsuitable on the grounds of excessive resolve seem highly appropriate for a different set of demands: 'When confronted by the threat of an external enemy there is a strong tendency for even the most democratic country to abandon some of its liberal principles and to revert to a group structure in which dominance is the most essential feature' (1982: 47).

The introduction of Beck, the chirpy Cockney, in the following scene raises different issues. While Brewer is a humorist, Beck is partly a target of humour. His cheerful, travel agent's eager-to-please manner allows his innate British pragmatism to cloud his judgement of political realities ('War? Not a chance of it Madam. Not this year. Not in anybody's interest, is it really?'). Ever the practical race, the British pride themselves on taking advantage of a commercial opportunity, and in that spirit Beck continues, when his female customer enquires about sandstorms in Benghazi, that the Italians have missed an opportunity – as colonisers of the country – to turn Libya, 'the only unspoilt playground in the Mediterranean', into a tourist haven. The jibe against the Italians is more fully developed at the end of the film when the recruits finally reach North Africa. Meanwhile, through the customer's enquiries about holidays in California and Libya the film introduces less flattering images of the British, as some citizens appear not to be taking developments on the continent seriously enough. A further blemish is revealed in the scene of Lloyd's collection of rent in a Welsh slum. Overwhelmingly patriotic and propagandistic, the film nevertheless allows itself brief moments of self-scrutiny, bearing out Stuart Hylton's unassailable argument in *Their Darkest Hour* (2003) that, on the home front, London (which could stand for the rest of the country) hardly lived up to its projected image of Utopian collectivity, a nation of classless philanthropists, singing Vera Lynn songs and endlessly drinking cups of tea. Much of the population was indeed governed by finer feelings, but many others saw the war as an opportunity to profiteer, to take advantage of circumstances, in a country that only superficially, and temporarily at that, overcame class and other forms of prejudice. The slightly discordant Welsh rent collection scene rapidly dissolves through the introduction of Jim Perry, a Territorial Army officer who works in a country garage. We are immediately returned to a prouder version of Britain. Perry is played, after all, by one of the major British stars of the day, someone who had begun to make a name for himself in Hollywood. His work at the garage, seen here not in what was to become a film cliché profession of chicanery and untrustworthiness (as in Dennis Price's second-hand car salesman in *The Naked truth* (Mario Zampi, 1957)), but as a manly occupation, the power and beauty of automobiles affirming the virile masculinity of Perry's officer-class personality, additionally marked by his voluntary involvement in the TA. His reliability is further enhanced through marriage to an attractive wife (Penelope Dudley Ward). The casting of Niven ensures that although, as a garage foreman, Perry's democratic credentials are impeccable, his aura as an already established Sandhurst-educated star lift him above the ordinary level of the recruits. Niven's real-life officer status at that time in the British Army gave him what Peter Haining (1984: 25) calls his archetypal gentlemanliness.

It is instructive to compare Niven, the star of *The Way Ahead*, with Robert Donat, the star of *The Young Mr Pitt*, made only two years previously, another of Reed's films that focused on leadership, and as remote from historical accuracy as George Arliss's version of Wellington in *The Iron Duke* (Saville, 1934) of a decade earlier. Donat's mellifluous voice, gentle manner and overall impression of tenderness, even in heroic roles, and put to such good effect in films like *The Count of Monte Cristo* (Lee, 1934), *The Thirty Nine Steps* (Hitchcock, 1935), and *Goodbye Mr Chips* (Wood, 1939), makes of his Pitt the Younger a strikingly thoughtful and measured prime minister. Contrasted with the boisterous Charles James Fox (Robert Morley), Donat as Pitt cuts an elegant, introspective figure, a man of resolve, but also of sensitivity and grace, the film's embodiment of ideal leadership, even though the films' writers – again Launder and Gilliat – were unhappy, as James Chapman notes (1998: 237) at what they regarded as Reed's simplistic, Manichean identification of Pitt and Fox with heroism and villainy respectively. Reed's Pitt serves the film's partly allegorical propaganda in his clear invocation of the Churchillian standards demanded by the nation in times of crisis. Pitt the Elder remarks: "'William Pitt, the great commoner". I would not wish you a better title. My son, evil days are coming to us. There may come a time when only a single-minded man can save us.' Pitt the Younger becomes that single-minded man, standing up to Napoleon as Churchill defied Hitler. He risks his health, foregoes marriage to Eleanor Eden (Phyllis Calvert), and neglects his own finances, building up ruinous debts amounting to £30,000, all in the service of his country. And yet, although he comments 'until victory is won there must be no softness in my heart', Donat's softness is undisguised. The remark is delivered tenderly, spoken by a man whose gentle voice and expressive eyes, slack facial contours tending slightly towards puffiness in the jowls, whose slightly sad and weary expression, and whose eagerness to play pillow-fighting games with children, offer a variant of masculinity at odds with both the superman Germanic models and the British stiff upper lip ideals then in vogue.

But heroism is a coat of many colours, as proved by Niven in *The Way Ahead*. Where Donat is softness bordering on femininity, Niven, beyond what in common with Jack Hawkins is his 'quiet English integrity' (Mackillop and Sinyard 2003a: 7), conveys a certain levity, his crisp manner informed by identification with debonair roles in light swashbucklers (such as *Bonnie Prince Charlie* (Kimmins, 1948)) or romantic comedies (such as *Bluebeard's Eighth Wife* (Lubitsch, 1938)). Lightness, though, does not invalidate authority, and in *The Way Ahead*, Niven's training in the Rifle Brigade lends weight to his performance. The military bearing served him well throughout his film carer, most poignantly in his role as the lonely middle-aged sex pest pretending to be a decorated retired officer in *Separate Tables* (Delbert Mann, 1958). In *The Way Ahead* the clipped speech and unflappable manner of the phlegmatic gentleman officer is matched with William Hartnell's more robust proletarian drill sergeant, a couple who form the army equivalent of the good cop / bad cop relationships of many thrillers. Both Sergeant Fletcher and Lieutenant Perry are patriarchal figures, their class dictating the division between the former's abruptness and the latter's civility as outward expression of a shared belief in discipline. Sergeant Fletcher barks at his recruits, but in preparing them for the worst, has their best interests at heart. Lieutenant Perry's approach is lighter and even though, as befits a gentleman, more civilized, no less governed by discipline.

Perry is at ease among his men, but even though in wartime some divisions vanish, the barriers of class remain in place. On this point Storr argues: 'the barriers which divide men in time of peace tend to disappear ... When the danger is past, the barriers descend once more, and the aggressive component in human nature resumes its normal functions of seeking where it may divide. This increase in fraternal feeling may at first sight seem to contradict the principle that in face of external danger men revert to an authoritarian group structure, but the two phenomena are not wholly incompatible' (1982: 48). Storr's point is exemplified in the attitudes of Davenport and Parsons, employees at the same department store, thrown together in the same regiment, their hierarchical relationship at work placed under stress in the army. Now equals, the smug superior and the timorous junior have no other option than to set aside differences for the duration of the war. On the train, Davenport – whose self-importance anticipates that of Grace Brothers' Captain Peacock – further emphasises the film's unwillingness to paint a wholly idealistic portrait of Britons at war, when he is made to suggest that the men's civilian status should be of no consequence in the regiment: 'By the way Parsons, I think it might be less, shall I say, embarrassing for both of us if we forget, disregard, any differences in status which may have existed at the store'. Unable to adjust immediately to this temporary reprieve from form, Parsons replies: 'Yes, sir'. Significantly, too, when Davenport, on leave, returns for a visit to the store, he fails to curb his salesman's instinct when rushing to help a customer, even though, of course, no longer employed to do so.

The film's point is that when the recruits eventually return to civilian life, once the war is over, old habits, attitudes and routines will resume, including adherence to the prejudices of class. As Peter Hennessy argues: 'A case could be made for mid-century Britain as the most settled, deferential, smug, un-dynamic society in the advanced world. The fundamentals of its constitution – Crown, Parliament and the Civil Service at the centre, strong municipal tradition at the periphery – were unquestioned apart from a tiny band of Welsh or Scottish Nationalists' (1992: 435). What was true of the institutional structure applied equally to social ones.

As well as allowing a glimpse of Davenport on leave in his normal habitat, the film shows the other recruits at home. Of special interest is the way it places the women. There is no woman here as commanding and active as the Dutch resistance heroines played by Katherine Byron ('you know, young lady, you've got your head screwed on all right', observes Eric Portman) and Googie Withers in *One of Our Aircraft Is Missing*. 'You don't seem to think much of women', Withers complains to the British crew she helps in their attempts to return home. But when she asks Godfrey Tearle 'Are you in command?', he replies, on behalf of the crew, by now clearly impressed by her, 'No, you are.' Googie Withers was one of the most forceful actresses of her generation, as ready to flout gender roles as to conform to them, such as when deploying her self-conscious sexuality to seduce a German officer into a trap. These are not the harridans from whom husbands hide when guiltily indulging in bouts of outlawed behaviour, such as when Stanley Holloway and

Robert Newton continue their alcoholic binge under the hallway stairs in *This Happy Breed* (Lean, 1944), in fear of Celia Johnson's deprecations. As a rule, *The Way Ahead* shows women in support roles for the men, keeping the home fires burning, not entirely driven to do so by propaganda, but in response to the demands of social realism: Mrs Parsons's struggle with creditors is matched in much lighter mood by Brewer's daughter's insubordination. Even so, the overall impression is of backstage involvement, the most interesting example of which is Mrs Gillingham (Mary Jerrold). While her daughter (Renée Asherson) conforms to stereotype, running a canteen, and while Mrs Perry serves as decoration and to cue more significant lines from her husband, such as when he recognises the change in attitude of his recruits ('Were those the awful men you wrote to me about?' 'No, that's another lot; quite different'), Mrs Gillingham provides the men with the comforts of home but in subtle, comic ways that gently mock the self-importance of the male. Her house is a civilised space, a refuge from the Spartan ambience of the barracks, where fresh towels, hot baths, tea and scones, comfortable armchairs and the homely air of an English living room are reminders of values worth defending. Even her Kentish name emphasises her symbolic provincial Englishness. A benign witch in a modern version of Hansel and Gretel, welcoming the troops to her house of delights, this Good Mother is blessed with healing and other powers. Firstly, she succeeds in reconciling Lieutenant Perry and his discontented troops; second, her refusal to be tricked by Brewer's pretence that her boiler has suddenly stopped working now that Lieutenant Perry has requested a bath demonstrates that women see through the petty rivalries of men. Mrs Gillingham mothers the men, and in so doing provides a necessary complement to their otherwise exclusively patriarchal environment. Jeffrey Richards rightly notes that 'when the soldiers gather round a wireless in North Africa it is talk about the countryside at harvest that plunges them into nostalgia for their homeland' (1997: 99). But equally important is the memory of Mrs Gillingham. The image of Mother and home that she creates lives in the minds of these homesick boys as they do their duty in North Africa, an 'Orientalist' space from which they long to return and by which they measure their own values and culture:

> BREWER: What a dump! Not even a flick house with an army picture! I'd hate to be an Arab in peace time.
> LUKE: How about them harems?
> BREWER: I haven't seen any yet. Nothing but flies. Talk about the mysterious East. I reckon Lyons Corner House, Coventry Street's got more mystery than what this has.

DAVENPORT: Well this isn't strictly speaking the East.
BREWER: What is it then?
DAVENPORT: Well, I suppose you'd call it the Middle East or Near East at a pinch.
BREWER: Well heaven preserve us from the Far East, that's what I say.

The familiar – Coventry Street, Lyons Corner Houses – is celebrated not just in contrast to but also at the expense of the unfamiliar – the East, near, middle or far – though there is nothing 'uncanny' about this unfamiliarity. The contemptuous treatment of North Africa is made all the more apparent by comparison with the less disparaging portrayal of a European 'other', Italy. Italians often serve as targets of abuse even as they simultaneously arouse the admiration and envy of the British. Here, though, because the Italian bar-owner is played by Ustinov – an actor/writer who had already begun to establish himself in films as a sympathetic comedian – the jibe is not as contemptuous as in *In Which We Serve*: 'never get the maccaronies to tackle a dangerous job like that, not for love or money'; 'Ities would do anything for money'; 'Ah! Anything but fight. That's why they were so lousy in the last war. That's on account of their warm, languorous, southern temperament.' Of Russian extraction, a speaker of many languages, and friend of many cultures, Ustinov could have neither written nor tolerated those sentiments, spoken by a group of men that included actors as distinguished as Bernard Miles. *The Way Ahead* contents itself with less demeaning observations and, as far as the Italian bar-owner is concerned, restricts its barbs to a patronising account of a nation with no stomach for war, eager for the cessation of hostilities and a return to the service of customers in a run down bar in the middle of nowhere. The 'way ahead' for the British soldiers is home, but only after engagement not with Italy but with a serious enemy, Germany, on the beaches of North Africa.

Although the film did poorly in the USA, it was a huge success in the UK and, as Niven comments, was used as a training film at Sandhurst for years afterwards (1971: 225). Perhaps its most enduring success was, as Robert Murphy remarks, in 'propagating a democratic "everyone pulling together" ethos which became one of the key myths of the war' (2000: 225). With the outcome still uncertain, the film ends with the recruits going into battle in earnest in the midday sun, defending what many in the audience would have regarded, in the words of William Ernest Henley (1849–1903), as 'England, My England'.

Odd Man Out (1947)

After *The True Glory* (1945), Reed came across F. L. Green's recently published (1945) novel about the Troubles in Belfast, that appealed to his taste for thrillers. He visited Green in Belfast, bought the rights to the novel, hired R. C. Sheriff – whose credits as scenarist included *Goodbye Mr Chips* – and Robert Krasker for the first of his four films with Reed (the others were *The Third Man*, *Trapeze* and *The Running Man*), cast James Mason in the lead role, and raided the Abbey Theatre Dublin for actors to fill many of the minor parts. Made for J. Arthur Rank's Two Cities Productions, and earning the deep suspicion of Stormont (Loughlin 1995: 148), *Odd Man Out* was shot on location in Belfast and at Denham. In its concentration on the dying IRA gunman Johnny McQueen (James Mason), it delves, like almost no other Reed film, into the unconscious as well as the consciousness of a character, as Johnny's mind begins to disintegrate after his fatal gunshot wound. Reed brings his hero into line with the protagonists of modernist English novels of the early twentieth century. As in the narratives of, say, Virginia Woolf, the confusion of memories, sense impressions and urgent desires, as Johnny finds it increasingly impossible to comprehend his life in time present, seems conditioned by the widespread influence of, above all, Freud, Bergson and Einstein, all of whom, in their various ways, highlighted, through their analyses of character, time and space, the fragmentation of identity.

Reed's concentration in *Odd Man Out* on identity focuses mainly on male heroism, on a man of action who sacrifices himself for others and a noble cause. In a Jungian discussion of ancient myths of heroism and their modern relevance, Joseph L. Henderson (1978: 95–156) argues that the structure of hero myths is reducible to six key elements: the hero's miraculous but humble birth, early proof of superhuman strength, rapid rise to prominence or power, triumphant struggle with the forces of evil, vulnerability to the sin of pride, and fall through betrayal, or heroic sacrifice that ends in death. He further argues that in many cases the hero's weakness is offset by the pairings with stronger companions or guardians who ensure the accomplishment of his task. Examples are given of the roles played by Poseidon, Athena and Cherion in the lives, respectively, of Theseus, Perseus and Achilles. A list of similar couplings could be added from heroic film narratives: Dunson and Matt in *Red River* (Hawks, 1948), Christ and Judas in *King of Kings* (Ray, 1961), or even Johnny and Dennis (Robert Beatty) in *Odd Man Out*, although here the relationship is further complicated by the 'shadowy' meanings attached to the latter's involvement in the hero's fortunes in a narrative that destabilises the very foundations of heroism. The disintegration of Johnny's mind is paralleled by the degeneration of his body, as the blood flows out of his heroic frame, the stiffness of the male hero (Theweleit 1987) softened through the reluctantly tolerated contact with femininity, in the person of his aspiring girl friend, Kathleen (Kathleen Ryan).

As Henderson acknowledges, not all of these elements are found on every occasion. In *Odd Man Out* very little is known of Johnny McQueen's background. He makes his first appearance as an adult, a fugitive from prison, plotting a raid with his comrades to finance his political cause. Released in 1946, the film seems to refer not only directly to the Troubles in Ireland but also, indirectly, to the recently concluded wider conflict of the Second World War. The heroism of *The Way Ahead*, made in the heat of war to rouse the morale of the nation, gives way to scepticism. Johnny McQueen has magnetism and charm, but his conviction and sense of mission are gradually eroded, and the flag-waving euphoria of the nation's triumph is seen from the perspective of breakdown and failure. Nevertheless, clear indications are given from the outset of the special qualities of this modern hero: first, the role stars James Mason, among the most romantic of the day (who claimed incidentally that Reed was his favourite director [1982: 213]); second, the photography and editing of the first sequence involving Johnny immediately emphasises through isolation his superiority, the singular attributes of the hero, famously defined by C. M. Bowra: 'Whatever a hero's birth may be, and of course it is often natural enough, he is recognised from the start as an extraordinary being whose physical development and characteristics are not those of other men' (1952: 95).

Although Mason had often antagonised British audiences with carping remarks about British cinema, he was clearly also one of its most revered idols. The popular press veered between condemnation and eulogy. While Reg Whiteley (1946) in *The Daily Mirror* relished the Mason character's nemesis in *Odd Man Out*, *The Evening Standard's* Patrick Kirwan (1947), still mindful of his periodic outbursts, praised the film and Mason's contribution under the headline 'James Mason Vindicates Himself.' The Mason of the Gainsborough melodramas, battering and bruising his heroines, is through poetic justice himself in pain in *Odd Man Out*. The pain, though, is of an almost messianic variety, for here, as Johnny McQueen, Mason is an odd man out in the sense not only of being cast adrift from the hold-up men at the mill, but also of being a man alone, the solitary hero, or voluntary scapegoat, who takes upon himself the suffering of the community, in whose cause he dies. Blending into the background of sombre Belfast streets, made even more unwelcoming by Robert Krasker's wide-angle photography, he is the victim of the world's disorder. His fellow citizens, sometimes shunning him, sometimes coming to his aid, are all, in a sense, represented by him, their collective personification, a sacrificial lamb and surrogate for a nation's suffering.

Although the film reveals nothing of Johnny's early biography, form alerts the viewer to his qualities of leadership. After the rolling graphic commentary informs the viewer that the story is told against a background of political unrest in a city of Northern Ireland, an aerial shot eventually brings the action down to street level, at first through concentration on a clock tower, and then fixing on a man standing, reading a book. Next, the camera follows this man into a house, where he is admitted by an old woman (Kitty Kirwan) and, as the camera tracks these two, a voice is heard, Mason's as Johnny, remarking in an accent intended to pass for Irish: 'Anyway, I know you're quite clear up to that point.' But the quality of voice, not the infelicities of pronunciation, are what matter. Other than his Byronic looks, Mason's voice, that combination of whistle and whisper, is his most characteristic feature (Evans 2001: 108–19). The remarks are a prelude to his unveiling in a packed room. For the greater part of this sequence, putting the final touches to a raid on the mill, Johnny is isolated. The exceptional, even eccentric quality of the voice, dispensing its characteristic blend of honeyed venom of the masterful Gainsborough anti-hero converted here into what Joseph Campbell (1988) might have defined as the redeemer hero, finds its visual complement in the respect accorded him through photography and editing. In keeping with all heroes, Johnny has something of the unearthly about him, and is often shot in this sequence alone. In a series of ten shots that follow an alternating pattern, Mason appears in four, only on one occasion framed with another character. Sometimes, even when not in shot, his presence is felt through the voice that speaks across the visual compositions of other characters, confident, but also relaxed, at one point deployed to settle the nerves of his companions with the words 'There's no need to hurry; time for a cup of tea.' Even when Johnny's isolation is interrupted through the arrival of another woman the pattern holds. As she enters, the camera, now behind Johnny, allows the group to be viewed, as it were, across him, from over his shoulder, adopting his perspective.

Although a man apart, Johnny is a hero whose strength has little in common with the Nietzschean ideal of the superior man's aspiration to be set free from the crowd. His superiority, on the contrary, is on behalf of the many, here struggling to be liberated from what are considered occupying forces representing an alien culture. Nietzsche's idea of nobility depended on rank, where difference 'of worth between man and man needs slavery in some sense or other' (1984: 173). Where life is conceived by Nietzsche as 'essentially appropriation, injury, overpowering of the strange and weaker, suppression, severity, imposition of one's own forms, incorporation and, at the last and mildest, exploitation' (1984: 175), Johnny's will to power is ultimately driven by devotion to the service of others, even by the messianic self-sacrifice rooted in his un-Nietzschean Catholicism.

The film's Catholicism, the rallying flag for nationalism in Northern Ireland, is often signalled. Early on, the iconography of Madonna and Child contributes to the dissident *mise-en-scène* of the old woman's house where, in this scene, preparation for the raid takes place. Much later, the speech Johnny makes towards the end of the film, where he quotes St Paul's remarks in the *Epistle to the Corinthians* about the man of charity, emphasises even more the film's ideological allegiance. The speech, a tribute to F. L. Green's Catholicism, is really the climax to Johnny's journey of self-discovery, the moment that signals the hero's awareness of the limitations of his cause, and specifically, its dependence on violence. The contradiction between the politicised hero's violence and the redeemer hero's growing rejection of it is delivered in a moment of hallucination that bears all the hallmarks of religious conversion, the defining moment of a tendency that began in his own agony in the garden, a Belfast prison, and that climaxes on the Golgotha of the Belfast docks. Reed's indifference to religious nuance, however, borne out by the use of the Protestant Authorised Version instead of the Catholic Douai Version, provoked ridicule in some Irish quarters (Wapshott 1990: 187). This insensitivity to cultural specificity belongs with other examples of hybridity. As in *The Stars Look Down*, where no respect was shown for Geordie pronunciation of English, the Irish accents in *Odd Man Out* ignore the idiosyncrasies of region with, for instance, the Southern Irish accents of the Abbey players like Cyril Cusack (Pat) or Maureen Delaney (Teresa), the English accents of Robert Newton (Luke) and Elwyn Brook Jones (Tober), and the unclassifiable patchwork-quilt attempt at Irish brogue by James Mason as Johnny, sitting uncomfortably beside the authentic accents of, say, the chorus of picaresque Belfast street urchins. But then again, as Wapshott argues, with his eye fixed on the American market, the accuracies of regional pronunciation might not have been a top priority for Reed. And yet, as Reed's aim is less to comment documentary-style on the up to date political realities of Northern Ireland, and avoids, as Wapshott argues (1990: 185), controversially arousing sympathy for a killer unashamedly identified as a member of the IRA by drawing instead on the Troubles to develop a story with more timeless relevance, this apparent indifference to detail deserves a more generous interpretation.

Reed's art, meticulous, carefully planned, leaving as little as possible to chance, even here in a film that, after all, seems coy about identifying its urban setting as Belfast, that maintains the novel's preference for the more universal term 'the Organisation' to the more specific IRA, explores the internal turmoil of characters in various forms of crisis, struggling with the imperatives of their conscience, or attempting to reconcile split allegiances. A film made at the end of the Second World War, *Odd Man Out* is also a statement about a nation's surfeit of killing, not only in Ireland, but also in continental Europe, and the other theatres of war.

Reed, though, is no Godard. He avoids the directness of political discourse. The film's focus is more personal than political, Johnny's struggle less ideological than psychological. Although no account is given of his rise to prominence there is no doubt about his status in the Organisation where his comrades refer to him as the 'Chief'. And yet, even though Johnny's childhood and early years are ignored, the theme of childhood, as ever in a Reed film, forces itself into view, and is related to Johnny's metamorphosis from man of action to the man of charity.

In contrast to the more innocent eye of the child in, say, *A Kid for Two Farthings* (1955) or *The Fallen Idol* (1948), the feral children who inhabit the grubby streets of 1940s Belfast are characterised by wilder, more *id*-driven impulses, their presence defined by Dai Vaughan as 'an anarchic, inchoate, corrosive substratum of the city's consciousness' (1995: 22). So, when in the film's third moment of dream-like hallucination (the earlier two occur first in the shelter and then in the pub), Johnny begins to quote from St Paul's *Epistle to the Corinthians*, Chapter 13, the references to children are as significant as those to charity. He actually inverts the order so that the references to children, originally Verse 11, appear now before the reference to charity, Verse 2: 'When I was a child I spoke as a child. I thought as a child. I thought as a child; but when I became a man, I put away childish things.' St Paul's meaning here, later clarified in Chapter 14, Verse 20, emphasises the importance of maturity as a basis for understanding: 'Brethren, be not children in understanding; how be it in malice be ye children, but in understanding be men.' Mason, who noted the film's prioritisation of morality over politics highlights the importance of Johnny's allusion to St Paul: 'He has done his duty but he has forgotten the one important thing: he is without love' (1982: 218). As Johnny comes to recognise the incompatibility of charity and worldly power, the audience steadily realises that the film's main theme, through its focus on the heroic, concerns different forms of justice, one worldly, intent on fulfilling the demands of a secular law, another, inspired by the Gospels, characterised by mercy, an antithesis crystallised in the conversation between Father Tom (W. G. Fay) and the Inspector (Denis O'Dea):

> FATHER TOM: Tell me this. From your experience of men and women, would you say they are all bad?
>
> INSPECTOR: In my profession, Father, there is neither good nor bad; there is just innocence and guilt, that's all.
>
> FATHER TOM: I have seen the bad in them. We condemn that rightly so, but what do we do when we find something that is good in them? Shouldn't we recognise that?
>
> INSPECTOR: I am sorry, Father, but it is our duty to bring this man to justice.
>
> FATHER TOM: That's the duty of all of us.

Crime, guilt and punishment are set against mercy. The sterner qualities are represented by a man of the law, the forgiving ones, by a priest, an almost comical, certainly unworldly figure, who asks the fugitive's pursuer to accept evil as willingly as virtue. The folly of mercy and charity, the lesson Johnny learns, returns from the repressed of his unconscious in the hallucinatory scene at Lukey's.

The certainties of the man of action have been under threat from early on. Even as the gang prepare for the raid on the mill they sense a wavering in Johnny's convictions, using the excuse of his time in prison *hors de combat* to persuade him to leave himself out of the robbery. Clearly, Johnny has by now become a reluctant killer. Emerging from the mill, with the rest of the gang, after the robbery, his vision is blurred on the steps of the building, forcing him to hold back before joining the others in the getaway car, a fatal moment's delay allowing another man to accost him. A struggle ensues, and both Johnny and his assailant are shot, the latter fatally. At periodic moments from then on Johnny asks whether he has killed the man. Two points are especially interesting here: (1) Johnny's failing vision; (2) his concern for the assailant's fate. His reservations about violence mark the transition between immaturity and maturity, leading to a change of attitude expressed most sharply in his dream-like hallucinations.

In the sequel to the robbery scene Johnny's impaired sight registers, following St Paul, growing disenchantment with the child's eye. In this process of maturation the hero must triumph over the regressive or childish drives of his personality, in Jungian terms the 'shadow', carried 'with us, to wit, the primitive and inferior man with his desires and emotions, and it is only with an enormous effort that we can detach ourselves from this burden ... Mere suppression of the shadow is as little of a remedy as beheading would be for a headache' (Jung 1983: 88–9). As Henderson points out: 'For most people the dark or negative side of the personality remains unconscious. The hero, on the contrary, must realise that the shadow exists and that he can draw strength from it. He must come to terms with its destructive powers if he is to become sufficiently terrible to overcome the dragon' (1978: 112). Johnny, the hero archetype, has the negative or dark side of his personality made explicit to him in these dreamlike states. He confronts his shadow, given shape by more than one character. His comrades (Dennis above all), the prison warder, the inspector, and Lukey the painter, are all variants of the displaced shadow from which he struggles for release. All of these characters, along with many others, like the priest, Shell, and the nameless street urchins, want something from Johnny: love, a soul, thirty pieces of silver, a role model. But in addition to their function as characters in their own right, they also serve as split projections of his shadow. Dennis, the comrades, the prison warder and the inspector are all to some extent projections of his inner violence, serving the film's interests in social and national themes. Dennis's identification with Johnny becomes explicit when he wears Johnny's bandage to mislead the police. He is the committed party member whose inflexible adhesion to the cause allows no compromise. The novel permits him saving graces: 'His whole nature was submitted to his ideals, submerged beneath the purpose of the Organization; looking at his hard features, and touching his hard flesh, she felt only the coldness of him. Yet below that coldness there was heat. The immeasurable heat of courage, resource, patience and unyielding resolve' (Green and Sherriff 1948: 29). There is also, though, the unstated envy, perhaps even resentment, of the inferior man, to whom the call of martyrdom has not been made, making of him another of the film's odd men out. When Kathleen asks for permission to go to the wounded Johnny, Dennis replies: 'As long as he lives he belongs to the Organisation.' He is visibly Johnny's shadow, in dark hat and clothes scouring the night streets in pursuit of Johnny to keep him safe for the Organisation before discovery by the police. His role parallels the Inspector's, also on Johnny's trail, but for an obviously different reason. Like Dennis, the Inspector is wedded to an ideal, and although regarded charitably by Granny as not a 'bad fella, as them fellas go', the imagery of power, even of cruelty, associated with this servant of an occupying force remains in the memory long after her defence of him. Seated in her parlour, Kathy replies to the Inspector's questions about Johnny's whereabouts. At one point, standing beside Kathy, he places his baton under her chin to raise her face towards him, a gesture that expresses even more vividly than his stony countenance or steely remarks the true measure of a man accustomed to achieving results through violence. In addition to the exercise of power, the gesture perhaps also expresses the repressed sexual desires of the policeman, the substitution of a truncheon for the revolver originally referred to in the sceenplay emphasising the point even more graphically.

If Dennis and the Inspector are the projections of Johnny's violence, Lukey, the painter, mirrors disaffection with his own notoriety. Lukey is no betrayer. Appalled by Shell's intention to sell Johnny to his pursuers, he informs Shell: 'I'm going to hit you hard for trying to sell a man on the run.' The irony of Lukey's use of a sinner as a model for a portrait of Saint Francis talking to the birds is not lost, but beyond commentary on loyalty and betrayal his role highlights another of Reed's abiding themes, observable in *The Third Man, The Agony and the Ecstasy* or *Follow Me* (1972): the scope and limits of art. Lukey's recognition of his own limits as an artist comes when he tosses away his painting of the fugitive Johnny, whom he has himself transported from his last place of refuge, the pub. The failure of the artist to capture the essence of his subject may be viewed in part as the dislocation between the reality of Johnny and his public image, so admired by the boys, of the notorious gunman, 'Johnny McQueen'. In Johnny's unconscious the struggle between the transcendent truths of Christianity and the imperatives of politics or art ends in this scene with the triumph of the former. In the religious sense, though, Reed is no Bresson, nor even a Hitchcock. Catholicism, like the Troubles in Ireland, provided an opportunity for a story about a man's response to conflicts of interest, and although the viewer's sympathy clearly lies with Johnny, the force of the film, for viewers as well as for Reed, stems from the hero's growing aversion to one set of values and developing attachment to another.

In his surreal hallucination at Lukey's flat, paintings on the wall come to life, in a way reminiscent of Cocteau's *La Belle et la bête* (1946), where the objects in the Beast's castle take on a Daliesque life of their own, but here their serried ranks are defeated by the solitary human figure of Father Tom, whose message of love triumphs over the immortality promised by the painter's art. Even as some of the boys on the street, like their precursors in *Angels with Dirty Faces* (Curtiz, 1938), hero-worship the notorious gunman, others are already proclaiming his demise. Johnny's conscious life has hitherto been a dream, his dream-world, or unconscious, the world of a truer reality. The film's dream imagery is inspired by the novel's insistence on Johnny's dream-like state as emphasised in the first two chapters, where the word 'dream' is reiterated by the narrator and by Johnny himself at regular intervals, to create not so much a blur as a distinction between different realms of being.

This inversion is most sharply focused in the first hallucinatory sequence, where, wounded, hiding in an air-raid shelter, Johnny imagines he is back in his prison cell, chatting to a warder, in actual fact a little girl – another of the film's street children, so poor she only has one roller skate – who has ventured into the shelter to retrieve her ball. He tells the warder: 'What a dream I had ... I dreamt I'd escaped from prison.' The dream is Johnny's reality, lived as though it were a dream, where actions – as in a dream – are beyond control, and every move as if governed by external forces, the will subjected to alien desires. Johnny's conscious life has been determined by the Organisation, but his unconscious, his dream-life, is where his real interests lie. His allegiance to the Organisation eventually seems to him no more substantial than the bubbles of the spilt pub beer from whose centres stare back at him the faces of his own inner demons. A life ruled by the Organisation is, as even Kathy knows, an illusion. 'Touch me if you're real' she says at the end, a remark ambiguous enough to refer not only to the joy of reunification with him, but also to the doubts about which of the two Johnnys, the dreamer or the wakeful, stands beside her.

Although it is the fatal decision that finally allows him to come to terms with his growing disenchantment with violence as a means of achieving political ends, Johnny's refusal to back out of the raid on the mill points to a psychological flaw. The hero's commitment to his mission often results in tragedy, and Johnny is no exception to the rule. Despite the misgivings of Dennis, who is exclusively concerned with the success of the raid, and of Kathy, more preoccupied with Johnny's welfare, Johnny, as befits all heroes, does not waver: 'Dennis, I'm the leader of the Organisation in this city ... I've got orders and I'll see them through.' Like the disastrous choices made by the heroes in, for instance, *The Song of Roland* (c. 1100), or *The Cid* (c. 1140), Johnny's mistake in *Odd Man Out* epitomises what, in a discussion of heroic poetry, C. M. Bowra describes as the genre's sense of doom. In the novel, Kathy (there named Agnes) comments: 'He is doomed ... and you know it' (1952: 33). We know that Johnny has no option, that his fate is sealed: the Belfast setting with its attendant history of the Troubles, compounded by William Alwyn's bleak music that recalls the sacred film scores of classic Christ or Roman Christian epics (such as *King of Kings* (Ray, 1961) or *The Sign of the Cross* (De Mille 1934) respectively), and the black and white urban *mise-en-scène* of a scourged metropolis, set up his inevitable downfall.

Pride, of course, is partly what makes Johnny a hero. Initially, at least before the gunshot wound that also damages his mind, he is the self-assured leader who takes action, however ill-judged, on behalf of the persecuted community. His energy and drive are pressed into collective service, and the arrogant brio of the leader is a tonic for comrades and viewers alike. The speed of thought, coolness under pressure, efficiency of manoeuvre and unquestioned authority, once the raid is under way, are all underscored by editing of sound and image. At first the camera concentrates on breakneck speed, its lens glued to the road as the raiders' car heads for the mill; once inside the accounts office of the mill, where the men make their demands, only natural sounds are heard as the non-diegetic music halts, returning only when, wounded and unable to climb aboard properly, Johnny falls off the moving car. Karel Reisz's brilliant analysis of the mill raid sequence has highlighted the ways in which Reed intensifies the realism of the scene through various formal devices: for instance, through the sound of the 'dull, pulsating beat of the mill machinery', or the 'track of footsteps ... from men walking over wooden boards, emphasising these sounds to add to the atmosphere of suspense' (Reisz and Millar 1999: 265). But these effects serve not only the interests of realism. The scene's dramatization of a plausible occurrence – daylight robbery – also becomes a defining moment in the career of a hero in full flow, the modern-day Prometheus answering the call for the overthrow of tyranny, searching, as Joseph Campbell puts it *à propos* the heroic quest in general, 'for the principle of regeneration ... within the very walls of the tyrant's empire itself' (1988: 17), the empire here indirectly identified as British rule in Northern Ireland. As he accomplishes his mission, blind to his own weakness – defined literally as the result of months of inactivity in a British jail – the hero has no inkling of the catastrophe awaiting him, even though perhaps unconsciously, in those fatal few seconds, as he hesitates before joining his comrades in the car, he is beset suddenly by self-doubt and uncertainty over the justice of his cause, which he seems almost on the point of betraying.

There are many around Johnny poised to fulfil the role of betrayer that is often an indispensable feature of heroic narrative. In Reed's work the role of the betrayer is most memorably played by Holly Martins (Joseph Cotten) in *The Third Man*. In *Odd Man Out*, Shell (F. J. McCormick) is ready to sell Johnny to the highest bidder, but as he is an incompetent traitor the deed is never done. The film's true betrayer is Teresa, the blowsy Irish matriarch, full of surface charm and concealed menace. Maureen Delaney's Teresa is a sinister Mae West, the personification of what the screenplay describes as a 'massive figure, but she moves with an energy and an air of confidence suggestive of a quick mind which has a deadly ability to formulate rapid plans to her own advantage. She is dressed gaudily, with a necklace about her neck and a crucifix on her breast. Her hair is fashioned in an elaborate style, which she constantly touches with her hands that are heavily ringed' (Green and Sherriff 1948). Teresa's victims, though, are not Johnny but Johnny's accomplices, whom she hands over to the police, though we suspect he would have fared no better had he fallen into her clutches. Johnny's delivery to the police, though not by betrayal, falls to Kathy.

The film's last moments express the ultimate frustration of her attempts to help Johnny evade capture. In the unrelenting cold and darkness of the wintry night, the couple reach the docks where, positioned right in front of the gates' iron bars, their imprisonment is complete. Belfast is a place of false hope and liberation. The ships anchored in the docks are a promise of freedom and access to foreign places and influence, but the steel gates barring the flight of the lovers define the city's true identity. Johnny eventually falls in a *mise-en-scène* of captivity, his destiny fused with the history of sectarian violence associated with the city.

The film cuts to a long shot of an approaching phalanx of lit torchlights as the police slowly converge on their victim. Kathy reaches for Johnny's gun and fires in the certain knowledge that her fire will be returned. This duly happens, and both are fatally wounded. In a rhyming shot the camera turns to the clock tower that had marked the beginning of this tragedy that, following almost classical rules, has unravelled over twelve hours. As if to register the ebbing life of the wounded hero, the clock strikes the hour, prompting reflection, like the opening lines of a famous Metaphysical poem by Vaughan, 'I saw eternity the other night,' on the contrasts between clock-time and hourless eternity. The clock marks the conclusion of a life brought to an abrupt and untimely end through devotion to a political cause; Johnny's death fulfils the requirements of a ritual drama that prioritises the eternal truths of morality over the time-locked beliefs of a political cause.

The doubts expressed by Granny about the Organisation, and her advice to Kathy to consider abandoning it for the rewards of love, marriage and family, had already begun to make an impression on her young compatriot. And although her ashen, dark-eyed Celtic beauty fails in life to prise Johnny away from the hold over him of the Organisation, her suicidal gunshot aimed at the police is her means not only of sparing Johnny a fate at their hands perhaps worse than death but also of completing a vendetta on the Organisation that claims in death a hero for love not politics.

Johnny's initial reluctance to treat Kathy as much more than a friend had been in line with the hero's resistance to sexuality, the consequence of submission to a cause. The response to what he regards as a higher calling distorts his view of Kathleen – until his political convictions begin to waver. The advertisement that appeared in the *New York Times* (21 April 1947) for the New York release of the film refused to accept that Johnny's feelings for Kathy amounted to friendship rather than love. A vertical, poster-style advertisement has Johnny at the left of the frame, occupying almost the full length of the box, gun in hand. On the right, and beneath the capitalised credit, 'JAMES MASON', and dignified by a quotation ('packed with suspense'), from one of the most prominent commentators of the day, Walter Winchell, the following summary appears: 'A killer on the loose ... hiding in shadows ... seeking desperately to claw his way to the arms of the woman he loves ... the woman who sticks by him while an angry city screams for his blood.' At the bottom of the frame there is a photo of Johnny's bust, this time with Kathy's head resting on his chest. The Hollywood publicity machine has turned a complex relationship characterised by the competing demands of love and friendship, sexual denial and longing, into a straightforward love affair.

The generic, formulaic explanation for Johnny's indifference to sex may also encapsulate self-conscious, and even psychological motivation. Johnny is, after all, played by sexuality's tormented enforcer, whose sadistic treatment of women enslaved as much as liberated the caddish lovers of all his Gainsborough films, the James Mason who is here rescued from sexual obsession, gripped instead by other desires. The self-conscious play with the Mason persona – with Reed subverting it in much the same way that Hitchcock played up the sinister as opposed to the Screwball elements of Cary Grant – is complicated even further in an early scene when a courting couple seek the privacy of the shelter in which Johnny is hiding to pursue their furtive love. Before the sound of his uncontrollable movements alerts the couple to his presence in the shelter, Johnny is transformed from protagonist into spectator, watching a scene of mortifying squalor and infinite pathos as love threatens – on the part of the younger man at least – to degenerate from self-transcendence into what Shakespeare called 'the expense of spirit in a waste of shame'. Here in miniature is the film's riposte to Granny's idealised vision of love, marriage and family life. As it follows the one in which, before the raid, Johnny relies on the word 'friend' to define his affection for Kathy, the scene cannot be read as a projection of Johnny's attitude to sex. Nevertheless, by its very inclusion, it seems intended to encourage the comparison with Granny's comments on the subject and, in hindsight, to relate them to Johnny. In a film that, through its dream or hallucinatory sequences, especially, exposes Johnny's inner life, this connection, for all its chronological disorder, may bear such a reading. Sexuality in a post-Freudian age is the key to the self, its absence in Johnny's life legitimately opening up his psychology to speculation about the libidinal as well as the ideological premises of his heroic mission.

Hearts of the matter: the Graham Greene films

4

Well before their collaboration on three of Reed's most memorable films, Graham Greene (1980) wrote highly favourable reviews of Reed's work. *Midshipman Easy, Laburnum Grove* and the *Stars Look Down* earn lavish praise for different reasons. In *Midshipman Easy* Greene admires the pace of the boys' adventure yarn, surprisingly finding it possible even to enthuse over the young Hughie Greene in the title role. Admittedly, some of the mannerisms of his TV *Double Your Money* and *Opportunity Knocks* later years mercifully appear only sparingly. But, more plausibly, Greene finds here, as in *Laburnum Grove* and *The Stars Look Down*, much to admire in the form of these films: the cutting and pace of *Easy*, the eye for visual detail in *Laburnum Grove*, and the documentary effects of *The Stars Look Down*. Greene looks for the distinctiveness of cinematic form, and finds it in *Laburnum Grove*: 'Mr Reed's camera has gone behind the dialogue, has picked out far more of the suburban background than Mr Priestley could convey in dialogue or the stage illustrate between its three walls: the hideous variegated Grove itself, the bottled beer and the cold suppers, the crowded ferny glasshouse, the little stuffy bedrooms with thin walls, and the stale cigarette smoke and Bertie's [*sic*] half-consumed bananas ... the picture of suburbia seems to be drawn simultaneously from two angles – which is as near as the screen can come as yet to stereoscopy' (Greene 1980: 90–1)

In discussing *The Stars Look Down*, form again holds Greene's attention, allowing him to compare the film favourably with *Kameradschaft* (Pabst, 1931) (Greene 1980: 265). The admiration was mutual. Greene's characteristic interest in betrayal, the overlaps of guilt and innocence, the glamour of evil and the dullness of virtue, the hypocrisy of governments and just causes, are all themes that also appealed to Reed. In *The Quiet American*, the cynical English journalist Fowler's constant rebukes to the blundering but implacable conviction-politician Pyle recall not only the moral and psychological ambiguities of *The Third*

Man, but many of the films Reed made without Greene: 'I hope to God you know what you are doing there. Oh, I know your motives are good, they always are ... I wish sometimes you had a few bad motives. You might understand a little more about human beings. And that applies to your country too Pyle' (Greene 2001: 3). These could be the unspoken sentiments of Harry Lime to his friend Holly Martins. But they could also be Rex Black's in *The Running Man*, George Redfern's in *Laburnum Grove* or Chris Ford's in *The Key*. 'God save us from the innocent and the good' Fowler says elsewhere, as Leslie James in *A Girl Must Live*, Helen Walshingham in *Kipps* and Willems in *Outcast of the Islands*, might have put it. A dominant pattern of Reed's films combines irredeemable outcasts (Willems, Lime, Black) with blundering heroes (Kipps, Martins, Philippe, McQueen and Wormold) who, usually too late, learn the lessons of experience.

The Fallen Idol (1948)

Followed by *The Third Man*, *Outcast of the Islands*, *The Man Between* and *A Kid for Two Farthings*, *The Fallen Idol* was the first of five films made for Alexander Korda's London Films. Reed's reputation, on the back especially of his war films and *The Stars Look Down*, obviously attracted Korda. Partly financed by David Selznick, *The Fallen Idol*, of all Carol Reed's child-centred films, dedicates, along with *A Kid for Two Farthings*, greatest amount of screen time to a child actor – Bobby Henrey – and provides an opportunity for more leisurely treatment of a child's response to a crisis in which he, his friend, the butler Baines (Ralph Richardson), Mrs Baines (Sonia Dresdel) and Julie (Michèle Morgan), Baines's mistress, are all embroiled. When Philippe's ambassador father and mother entrust him to the care of the house-keeper and butler, Mr and Mrs Baines, he stumbles on the clandestine affair between Baines and Julie, described by the latter as his niece. Mrs Baines discovers the affair and, pretending to leave the embassy, in the basement of which she and Baines also reside, she returns to catch the pair together. After an argument with her husband, Mrs Baines falls to her death from a window sill on to which she had climbed to spy on the couple. Philippe imagines Baines has murdered her and makes matters worse through comments to the police that he hopes will clear Baines. Police suspicions of Baines vanish once Mrs Baines's footprints are discovered by the window. The departure of the police coincides with the return at the end of the film of the boy's parents.

Neil Sinyard (2003: 54–5) argues plausibly that there are echoes here of *These Three* (1936), the version by William Wyler – a favourite director of Reed's – of a play by Lillian Hellman about the destruction of the lives of two schoolteachers by a malicious child. Developed from Graham Greene's *The Basement Room* (1935), a short story that had appealed to Korda as a possible subject for a film, *The Fallen Idol* ranges over familiar Greene territory: the blurred boundaries of guilt and innocence, the rotting of the will, the lure of the exotic. Like many of Reed's films, it is shot through characteristically unsettling tilted angles, and addresses parent/child relationships. Previously an admirer of Reed's other work, Greene now extolled the virtues of the director who had worked on his own material: 'Of one thing about these films I have complete certainty, that their success is due to Carol Reed, the only director I know with that particular warmth of human sympathy, the extraordinary feeling for the right face for the right part, the exactitude of cutting, and not least important the power of sympathising with an author's worries and an ability to guide him' (Greene 1980: 124). One change for which Reed cannot be credited, one of the few by which Greene remained unconvinced, was the distributors' decision to replace the title 'The Basement Room' with 'The Fallen Idol'. Even so, the emphasis now given to the relationship between Baines and Philippe, bringing Philippe's disillusioned idolisation of Baines more into focus is appropriate. Other more substantial changes to the story earned Greene's approval: 'in the conference that ensued the story was quietly changed, so that the subject no longer concerned a small boy who unwittingly betrayed his best friend to the police but dealt instead with a small boy who believed that his best friend was a murderer and nearly procured his arrest by telling lies in his defence' (Greene 1980: 123). In the short story Mrs Baines falls to her death as a result of the struggle with Baines; in the film she slips unaided by Baines from the widow sill but, as Baines himself concedes, his legal innocence is not untouched by moral or psychological guilt, an awareness that, for all her portrayal as a witch-like, Bad Mother figure, alerts the spectator even more poignantly to the film's inquest into the complexity of human relationships. The ambiguity of the film's happy ending was perhaps predictably highlighted by the Catholic paper *The Tablet* whose reviewer saw in Baines's exoneration the seeds of perpetual agony: 'The unthinking may, if they must, accept the proffered hint of a happy ending in the new moral Greene has added, subtler in a way and characteristically compassionate ... Only the unthinking will miss the point that Baines is going to suffer an agony of conscience more painful than legal punishment; and that the child, watching his parents arrive at the embassy door below, has learnt his first bitter lesson of "omnis homo mendax"' (Anon 1948).

On its release, the film – universally praised, with only rare dissenting voices – attracted attention for the remarkable performance by Bobby Henrey, the small boy whose long, usually unkempt flaxen hair, expressions of rapt idolisation alternating with terror and, finally, when no one will hear his explanations once Baines has been absolved of all blame, vexed exasperation, make Philippe a convincing study in child psychology. Representative views include *The Sunday Chronicle*'s reference to Henrey as 'the Greatest Kid since Coogan' (Dehn 1948), putting the film, in this respect, on the same pedestal as Duvivier's *Poil de carotte* (1932), a film concerned with mother–child relationships, and Chaplin's *The Kid* (1921), about surrogate father–child relations. In Reed's treatment of childhood there is nothing insipid or mawkish, after the Hollywood fashion of, say, the Bobby Driscoll or Shirley Temple films. In *A Kid for Two Farthings* and *Oliver!* his small boys, for all their vulnerability, belong to narratives that address without condescension adult audiences. Elsewhere, Almayer's plump little daughter Nina in *Outcast of the Islands*, for instance, unsentimentally mirrors through her over-indulgence the egotistic excesses of her obese father. In *The Fallen Idol* Reed's mature gaze falls on the immature eye of the small boy whose alternating fits of activity, childish imaginings, uncomprehending, sometimes fear-driven withdrawals from the adult world are stamped with an authenticity that has earned him praise for his famed powers of observation, and led to these generous comments by David Lean: 'Well, I think I know as much as Carol about the technical process of making pictures – but he knows so much about human beings, and about acting' (Watts 1950: 7–8).

Although released three years after the end of the war, *The Fallen Idol* is readable in the context of Reed's own interest in child's eye narratives as well as within the wider tendency in the 1940s by other film-makers such as Lean (e.g. in *Great Expectations*, 1946), Crichton (e.g. in *Hue and Cry*, 1946) or Asquith (e.g. in *The Winslow Boy*, 1948), as well as by writers like Rosamund Lehman, L. P. Hartley and others, to use childhood as a convenient focus for reflection on the loss of pre-1939 innocence in the crucible of war, and the promise of renewal symbolised by child-centred narratives. The post-war years were a time of rebuilding, the repair to family life a clear priority, as fathers returned from war to resume their roles as breadwinners, women as mothers and wives in structures where children could once more feel safe. *The Fallen Idol* dramatises through metaphor its own realistic commentary on the claims of ideology. The fractured structure of family life at the embassy indicates deeper causes of dysfunctional relations, not easily remedied by appeals to reparation and renewal. Unlike the Utopian family films of the period, such as *The Happy Family* (Muriel Box, 1952), *The Fallen Idol* offers no reassurances to the new society: Jack Warner's reassuring, avuncular persona in *The Happy Family* contrasts with Ralph Richardson's more anguished presence. The restoration of order to family life – represented by the return of the ambassador – is no more than an arbitrary ending providing no solution to the problems of a deprived child, whose frustrations born of parental neglect are transferred on to his relations with Baines the butler.

The adult world of marital strife, adultery, obsession and hysteria is the eventual destination of the child whose innocence, far from being an idyllic phase, is already compromised in *The Fallen Idol* through contact with unstable adults. While the film often dwells on the child's view, as he struggles to make sense of events taking place around him, the adult's perspective, especially through the twinning of Baines and Philippe, is not neglected. All the characters play their part in Reed's variant of the Gothic film, only here the male, not the female, is at risk from a partner's malevolent designs. In that respect *The Fallen Idol* seems to gesture to Hitchcock's *Rebecca* (1940). Like *Rebecca,* it traces the attempts of an immature character – young female in *Rebecca,* male child in *The Fallen Idol* – to sever itself from the mother, and to attach itself to the father, although in both cases the child displaces on to surrogates parent-related feelings of love and hate.

The literal child in *The Fallen Idol* is Philippe, but Baines, with whom he is so closely identified, is also childish. Through friendship, games, secrets and other mutual interests, Baines replays his own childhood, sharing not only the realities of Philippe in time present but also, his own recollected childhood. In his own way Baines, like Philippe, is still attempting to detach himself from the Bad Mother (Mrs Baines), identifying himself with the father – the fantasy figure the butler creates of himself as an African big-game hunter – and searching for the Good Mother, Julie (Michèle Morgan), or, in her more *grand guignol* version, Rose (Dora Bryan), the local tart.

The links between Philippe and Baines are thus related to childish idolisation of a heroic ideal and adult regression to childhood. Philippe's awe-struck love for Baines finds tender expression on many occasions, especially early on. For instance, on their trip to London Zoo, a close-up shows Philippe, face cupped in his hands, listening to Baines with an expression bordering on rapture. Their fondness of animals, also stressed through Philippe's devotion to McGregor, his pet snake, reveals a shared curiosity about life. Mrs Baines, who is anti-life, eventually assassinates McGregor. Baines's tomfoolery, played for the benefit of a single spectator, Philippe, is also a form of relapse to his own childhood, a ludic rebellion against the Bad Mother. The bond between Baines and Philippe recalls Greene's reflections on love and identity in *The Quiet American:* 'To be in love is to see yourself as someone else sees you, it is to be in love with the falsified and exalted image of yourself. In love we are incapable of honour – the courageous act is no more than playing a part to an audience of two' (Greene 2001: 112). The spectator's first sighting of Baines comes when he is glimpsed helping the ambassador prepare for his departure knowing, in another sign of empathy with the child, that 'Phil', as he calls him, is at the top of the stairs watching him. Occasionally Baines looks up at him conspiratorially, raising his eyebrows, winking, making amusing hand and foot gestures, slightly at odds with the solemn office of stewardship, a profession he seems elsewhere – superficially, at least – to respect through measured, controlled movements, more in keeping with the role. As we look down with Philippe at the hectic activity below, the chequered tiles of the embassy hall resemble a chessboard, the embassy staff and others who cross it, now and throughout the film when high angled shots repeatedly bring it into view, seeming like pieces in a game where the moves are determined by the laws of desire.

In the short story Baines's regression arouses Phil's mild contempt. There, the child prefers to idolise an adult whose tales of heroic exploits and adventure in exotic lands are untainted by infantilism. In the film, on the other hand, Philippe bears no such resentment towards an adult's reversion to childish ways; quite the reverse. During the night of Mrs Baines's feigned absence from the embassy, Philippe thoroughly enjoys the game of hide and seek played in the dark with Baines and Julie. Suffering from parental negligence and denial of friendship with other children, he finds child substitutes in Baines and Julie.

Both through the lens of childhood and in more general terms, the film, unlike the short story, approves of the survival of the child in the adult, while simultaneously arousing audience compassion for a character infantilised by his domineering, ill-humoured wife, someone whose melancholy remark in the short story, 'I was a man once', continues in the film version to apply.

The game of hide and seek is a pivotal moment in the film. Its simple, dual structure of concealment and exposure crystallises in childish terms the double-edged realities of the lives led by the embassy residents. The ambassador, for instance, a pillar of the establishment, the married family man, is later discovered to be acquainted with the prostitute Rose. The whole episode involving Rose at the police station caused Reed enormous difficulties with the American Production Code authorities. The police station scene, where Rose remarks with unmistakable *double entendre* 'Oh, I know your daddy', drew the following comment from Gordon S. White, of the Motion Picture Association, in correspondence with Morris Helprin of London Films: 'In the police station sequence the purpose is of course to eliminate anything in either pictorial action or dialogue which tends to brand the woman a prostitute' (White 1948).

The moralistic tone extends to comments about another scene, at the embassy, involving Julie and Baines: 'The bedroom sequence can hardly be connected satisfactorily without the recording of a new dialogue track. In re-writing this dialogue and cutting this sequence you must, of course, eliminate the footage which shows Julie looking shyly at the bed and pointing to it and also must eliminate anything and everything in the questions and answers which has to do with the idea that Julie was on the bed, that she was undressed, that she had to dress before she could leave the room and that she had been sexually intimate with Baines ... You will, of course, as mentioned above, cut out the piece which shows Julie looking at and pointing to the bed, so that there will not at any time be any reference to or attention to the body ... I shall report to Mr Breen your sympathetic understanding of the Production Code, Administration's report on your picture and your sincere desire to do everything possible to make the necessary revisions to meet the Code Requirements' (White 1948).

Reed had no option other than to implement these recommendations for the American release, leaving his British audiences to the mercy of the uncensored original. What by today's standards seem like the ludicrous strictures of the Production Code nevertheless point to the divided nature of the embassy residents. Like Julie and the prostitute-consorting ambassador, Mrs Baines, Baines and Philippe are all split characters: Mrs Baines's mask of domestic efficiency conceals hysteria on the verge of a nervous breakdown; Mr Baines's persona of the unruffled, self-controlled butler cloaks passion (for Julia) and fantasies about his fictitious exotic past that belie his chosen profession; Philippe, the playful child, is also dragged into the world of the adults, with whose secrets (Mr as well as Mrs Baines's), he is at different times entrusted. The *mise-en-scène* of this world of hide and seek, of secrets and lies, of affirmation and denial, is above all the embassy, but also the outlying Belgravia streets of police station, pubs and tea rooms, as well as, most especially, London Zoo, all of which play their part in clarifying the desires by which these characters are either vitalised or tormented. Twice in the film the embassy is defined as a foreign place: initially by the First Secretary, who objects to police enquiries into the death of Mrs Baines, by exclaiming 'This is officially foreign territory;' next by the Scotland Yard detective who makes a similar remark in a later scene.

The embassy's foreignness is definable in two ways: literally, since the building belongs to another country, its sacrosanct environment not subject to the laws of the host nation; but also, and perhaps more significantly, in view of the film's themes of identity and desire, figuratively, in the sense that its laws and values are at odds with the aspirations and drives of its residents.

The embassy's interior *mise-en-scène* is overpopulated with period furniture, ornaments, oriental screens, marble statues, paintings, all affirming the material status of a wealthy Western nation. But interiors and exteriors are also sometimes shot in ways that transcend political commentary to give a disturbing, even uncanny, perspective to the space's many dramas. In what has come to be recognised as the characteristic visual style of many Reed films, the camera is again often tilted to create the sensation of disturbance, of a familiar space made uncanny through repression (Freud 1990: 372). Especially during the nocturnal game of hide and seek, the embassy takes on the appearance of a Gothic mansion, a place of entrapment, ghosts and shadows. At the conclusion of one carefully edited sequence, Philippe actually thinks he sees a ghost. First Julie and Baines in long shot are caught kissing in a doorway, framed by its structure on either side, with shadows falling on their bodies; next a choker close-up of, alternately, Baines and Julie, followed by a glimpse seen through the window by Phil, of someone in long shot, prompting Philippe to scream (not recognising Mrs Baines) 'I thought I saw a ghost!', suggest that the love affair between Baines and Julie will be haunted, even after her death, by Mrs Baines and, through her, the inner torments of her guilt-racked widower.

Frame composition often traps characters between the bars of burglar-proof windows or stair banisters; they are sometimes positioned in door frames, reflected in mirrors, or marked on their faces by the shadows of window panes or bars. Philippe, one of the film's most persistent watchers, as he spies on the secret or public dramas of the adults in his midst, is often placed at the top of the stairs, witnessing scenes through the bar-like appearance of the spindles or railings of the main staircase banister.

The definition of the embassy as a kind of prison loses all ambiguity in the cut from a scene in which Philippe overhears Baines engaged in a telephone conversation with Julie to a shot of a caged lion at the zoo, roaring and making hostile gestures. The notion that all human beings are trapped by circumstances is treated humorously at the zoo when Philippe attempts to feed what he imagines are animals through the bars of what turn out to be the turnstiles of the men's lavatory. Bemused by the gesture, an emerging patron declines Philippe's offer of food, inadvertently playing his part in Reed's ironic commentary on the human condition. As Calderón puts it in *Life's a Dream* (c. 1638) man is born free but is everywhere in captivity.

Sometimes the characters in *The Fallen Idol* are allowed temporary parole from the different forms of imprisonment represented visually and metaphorically by the embassy. At crucial moments, for instance, Philippe – sometimes accompanied by Baines, sometimes alone – steps out of his garret to look at the world outside from his rooftop eerie, momentarily freed from the sombre realities of the interior life, the domain of troubled secret desires symbolised by the indoors world of the embassy. So, for instance, after the first altercation between Philippe and Mrs Baines, in which she accuses him of lying, and he retorts by exclaiming, 'I hate you!', Philippe, ordered to his room by Mrs Baines, rushes immediately out onto his rooftop balcony, and sees Baines leave the house. He cries out after him 'Baines!' and, having failed to make himself heard, climbs down the outside back staircase, in pursuit of his idol.

Both Philippe and Baines seek release from the prison of the embassy and from Mrs Baines, who is both its captive and warden, a woman whose obsession and hysteria are rooted in a mixture of natural and socially motivated pressures. She fits the compulsive-obsessive pattern of enslavement to tidiness and order, of a life led according to a rigid plan that brooks no challenge. Hysteria is an illness that from its earliest definition in the work of Freud and Breuer (1991) has often been linked, controversially, with women. As Julia Borossa argues, 'hysteria picks up on a problematic, paranoical relationship to conformity, played out primarily in the arena of the body: gendered, out of control and refusing an easy categorisation ... hysteria is a reaction to certain aspects of human subjectivity ... The fact that it is women who have most often been designated as the ones who bear and embody that reaction is itself a significant part of the issue highlighted by hysteria' (2001: 7). Mrs Baines, paired with the ambassador's wife through illness, mental in the case of the former, and an unspecified malady in the latter (from which she only recovers on her return at the end of the film), are both further associated through motherhood: real in the case of the former, surrogate and frustrated in the case of the latter. Mrs Baines, the hysterical obsessive, is thus also the personification of the uncanniness of the embassy, a patriarchal space, in which women become ill (the ambassador's wife) or lead unhappy lives (Julie, the love-lorn secretary, and Mrs Baines). At first, Mrs Baines seems content to play out her complaisant role as housekeeper, attending to the superficial order and hygiene of the house, her covering of the furniture readable as denial, a sign of repression and perhaps ultimately of frustrated motherhood, a condition the film defines through awareness of the processes of victimisation and her troubled sense of identity.

Clues to Mrs Baines's inner turmoil surface almost immediately. She first appears as a shadow projected against the main staircase wall, announcing her verbal presence through almost hypnotic control over Baines, tolerating no challenge to her commands from husband, child or subordinates. In Reed's most disturbing image of an adult relationship that has evolved from mutual attraction to ownership, Mrs Baines appears as a monster whose twisted features have been formed, too, it must also be acknowledged, by the neglect of a faithless husband. We read in her expression bitter resignation to a life no longer held together by love. Once she comes into full view we see a woman dressed in smart, practical clothing, sensible shoes, with a hairstyle that in its tied-back, braided style does justice to prison-warder fashions. The disciplined hair becomes dishevelled only at the end. In one of the most chilling sequences, with Philippe lying at night in bed, his face in close-up, a hairpin suddenly drops on to his pillow, loosened from Mrs Baines's hair, who now appears in extreme close-up, her haggish face hanging over Philippe's look of terrified innocence. A limp lock of hair, formerly held in place by the fallen hairpin, dangles across her forehead revealing a sweaty and manic face wearing the expression of a modern Medusa who will stop at nothing, not even violence, against this surrogate son, to discover the truth about her husband – his surrogate father – and his lover.

Mrs Baines's pitiless eyes and hollow cheeks belie the significant emphasis in both film and short story on her association with food. In appearance, Mrs Baines (like Hitchcock's embittered harridan, Mrs Danvers) is both apologist and scourge of the ideology she serves, a woman who refuses the femininity embraced by Julie. Her restrained dark hair contrasts with Julie's Joan Fontaine look from *Rebecca*, of shoulder-length blondeness, her practical clothes inviting comparison with the frillier ones worn under her more sober work uniform by Julie. As scholars of fashion have increasingly been arguing (e.g. Bruzzi 1997, Street 2001), clothes are key markers of identity in film. Shoes, for instance, are used in *Strangers on a Train* (Hitchcock, 1951) to register the wilder character of Bruno through his two-toned footwear, while the straighter character Guy's nature is to some extent marked by his more conservative Oxfords. In *The Fallen Idol* Mrs Baines's sensible thick-heeled shoes are shamed by Julie's elegant, more finely heeled ones, in another example of visual short-hand for contrasts of character. When Philippe hides under a table and sees, alternately, the shoes of Julie and

Mrs Baines, the audience is expected to note the differences in the predicaments of their wearers.

The varied way the two women speak to others (especially Baines and Philippe), their facial expression, their every gesture, could not be more striking. Mrs Baines's hard as nails personality is counteracted by Julie's softness, her hysteria by calm. Unlike Mrs Baines – 'on the warpath again' Baines warns Philippe – Julie is characterised not by belligerence but by docility. Tenderness, so lacking in relations between Mr and Mrs Baines, is a feature of all contact between Baines and Julie. An especially poignant instance, one which, in a further example of playful allusion to Lean, recalls the touching scenes of another illicit romance in *Brief Encounter* (1945), occurs in the tea room where Julie and Baines have met to make their farewells. Reed manages to compress, in a prelude to the spectator's view of the encounter, a host of interrelated themes that have a bearing on this and other scenes. In pursuit of Baines, Philippe at first tries looking for him in a nearby pub. Told, in another of the film's references to barriers and thresholds, that 'you mustn't come in here, sonny,' Philippe eventually tracks Baines and Julie down to a tea room, a shabby trysting place not unlike the station bar in *Brief Encounter*. Reed cuts from the publican's refusal of entry to Philippe to a shot of cakes on which wasps are feasting in the tea shop window. Philippe's eyes lift from the cakes to the shop interior where he sees the furtive couple. The boy's immature gaze once more draws attention to the film's preoccupation with impressions of reality drawn from innocence or experience, momentarily baffled but later satisfied – as only a child could be – by Baines's explanation that Julie is his niece.

The film's interest in sense perception is reformulated humorously in the scene involving Rose at the police station. On observing the natural affinity between prostitute and child, the duty sergeant asks Rose to accompany Philippe home. Rose can only phrase and inflect her remarks in the hallowed manner of a lady of the night: 'Hello, dearie, where do you live?' 'Shall I take you home?' 'Now you'd like to come home with me, wouldn't you?' The tone and idiom earn the disapproval of the duty sergeant but, in passing, they highlight Reed's fascination with discourse and reception. In the tea shop scene the food imagery recalls Mrs Baines's obsession with food – sublimation of a sexual desire no longer felt for her husband – and the way it is used by her as a means not only of imposing discipline on Philippe, but also of trans-ferring on to the latter the hostility she feels towards Baines. Seeing him, Philippe exclaims 'Baines!'. The name is called out in a way that crosses a child's natural joy at the discovery of a friend with a half-jocular angry tone borrowed from Mrs Baines's earlier imperious hailing of her husband at the embassy.

Here, the attitude of the watcher seems to approximate to Freud's observation in 'Instincts and their Vicissitudes' on the scopophilic, autoerotic drives of the voyeur (1984a). The element of aggression further noted by Freud in this drive is also apparent in the boy's form of address to Baines. Quite apart from serving to highlight the position of the spectator of the film as a voyeur, thereby identifying the spectator with Philippe and other watchers in the narrative, the scene pinpoints the hostility in the attitude of the little boy towards his father – here represented by his proxy, Baines – who threatens once more, like his real absent father, to destroy the exclusivity of the relationship with the son, now through the developing relationship with his 'niece'.

The scene that follows sees Philippe scoffing cakes to his heart's content as the intimate conversation between uncle and niece resumes awkwardly. Although inhibited by the boy's presence, the restrained dialogue maintains the lovers' characteristically mutual tenderness, only the occasionally fidgety body language of the pair indicating anxieties caused by the prospect of the seemingly unavoidable termination of their relationship.

From the point where Philippe begins to eat his bun the camera focuses, at first in medium shot, on the profiles of the lovers. As they agonise, softly, tenderly – in keeping with the slow, mainly stringed-instrument background music – over their separation and possible ways out of their predicament, the varied movements of their heads (now bowed, now raised, drawing near or withdrawing), of their eyes (now lowered, now meeting the other's gaze), of their hands (clenched and unclenched), and arms (placed on and off the table), draw attention to what they themselves refer to as 'torture'. The closing moments of the scene show Julie in a close-shot that celebrates her beauty, while also highlighting her soft femininity, and her submission to the laws of love rather than efficiency and routine by which Mrs Baines, in order to overcome her deep unhappiness, is ruled. As Julie leaves the tea room, the camera follows her out, adopting Baines's viewpoint, and takes in the word 'closed' on the back of the shop door, a word that alerts customers who will see its reverse side as a sign that the shop is open for business, while also indicating Baines's domestic and emotional captivity from which there appears to be no rescue.

Julie is the idealised partner, the fantasised Good Mother for the boy with an absent mother, the alternative to the hysterical monster who tyrannises and infantilises both man and boy, Philippe and Baines, the former an abandoned waif, the latter an adult transported emotionally and psychologically back in time, to a childhood at once remembered, desired and also resented. As no clear explanation is given for Mrs Baines's hysterical infantilisation of Baines the viewer is left to speculate over the deep unhappiness that leads to monstrosity.

The remark made by Baines about his contribution to his wife's unhappiness confirms the way her individuality is eliminated through marriage, her identity defined exclusively through attachment to Baines. When the inspector asks whether he pushed his wife to her death, Baines tellingly remarks in a way that recalls another Greene hero's awareness of his contribution to his wife's misery in *The Heart of the Matter*: 'I'd done enough to her without that.' The confession reveals his touching self-awareness, a recognition that besides humiliating her through the affair with Julie, he has also contributed towards the construction of the resentful woman his wife had eventually become. In his exposure of the origins of the female monstrous Reed is very close to Hitchcock, Mrs Baines little different in that respect from what Barbara Creed has called the monstrous-feminine (1993), the mothers of Marnie, Frances Stevens (*To Catch a Thief*), Roger Thornhill (*North by North West*) or Norman Bates (*Psycho*). Mrs Baines's reaction to Baines's gentle suggestion that they should consider ending a marriage that brings only misery is met by her reply that she will commit suicide, a scandal that would make him the sensational victim of the Sunday papers. The reaction is hysterical, its emotional blackmail an indication not only of Baines's difficulties in being a husband to her, but also of Mrs Baines's unstable personality.

Baines's honest appraisal of his part in the formation of his wife's personality is in line with post-Freudian psychoanalytical accounts of human personality measured not exclusively by archaeological models searching for defining moments in an individual's childhood but also by attention to object relations, to the attachments and identifications of the individual during the course of a lifetime. Mrs Baines's role as a watcher belongs to this pattern, leaving the viewer to wonder whether her voyeurism is to some extent conditioned by her frustrated motherhood, by an introjection of a sense of failure, through barrenness, as a woman. The monstrosity of Mrs Baines is thus both self-directed and a form of revenge against a victimising ideology. She is in some senses the equivalent of Mrs Danvers who, as Tania Modleski has argued (1988), is allied with Rebecca, visible and invisible presences asserting their womanhood through an appropriation of the male gaze (Mulvey 1989) to assert and impose themselves on their environments.

On this reading, Mrs Baines, like Mrs Danvers, is an image of displaced motherhood whose power must be destroyed through specularisation or fetishisation. Removed at first (admittedly, of her own free will) from the embassy, the domain of patriarchal power, Mrs Baines returns in monstrous form to assert her femininity, taking control of the gaze, in her secret involvement during the nocturnal family romance game of hide and seek, where Baines and Julie become Philippe's idealised parents, simultaneously inviting the viewer's horror and compassion. Although the film sees not only the patriarchal order restored through the death of the Bad Mother, but also the return of Philippe's real parents, and the union of their fantasised versions, Baines and Julie, the resistance to this order, the trouble caused by Mrs Baines, will survive in the memory of her husband and his beautiful young lover as well as in those of the boy and audiences disturbed by the film's excavations of identity and desire.

The Third Man (1949)

In *The Third Man*, as Reed and Greene shift attention from female to male monsters, concern with the overlapping boundaries of innocence and guilt transfers from the stifling environment of Diplomatic Belgravia to the ruins of post-war Vienna. Korda had always wanted to make a film about the four-way post-war occupation of Vienna by the Americans, British, French and Russians, who also took it in turns to control its central international sector. Greene's successful collaboration with Reed on *The Fallen Idol*, his known involvement in MI6, and his fondness for thrillers (e.g. *Brighton Rock* (John Boulting, 1947)), seemed to him ideal qualifications for making a film about penicillin racketeering in a city at the mercy of individuals whose moral instincts were as inviolable as the bombed architecture of a once proud city. The inspiration for Harry Lime (Orson Welles), the chief racketeer, may well have been, as some argue (e.g. Connolly 1999: 5; Drazin 1999: 144–59) Kim Philby, whose middle name was 'Harry', the eventually exposed traitor labelled the 'third man' in the Burgess/Maclean spying scandal. Robert Murphy, though, claims that, closer to home, Greene would have been aware of the notorious 1940s gangster Max Intrator (1986: 292), on whose exploits he might also have drawn. But as well as being possibly inspired by real individuals, Greene would also surely have been aware of a short story written by *The Times* Eastern Europe correspondent and double agent about black market penicillin racketeering in Vienna. These were clearly some of the tributaries that led to the creation of Harry Lime, a character bearing the indisputable Greene trademark, a grown up version of *Brighton Rock*'s Pinkie, less overtly sadistic, more charming, but rotten to the core, his narcissism leading to another drama hewn from contradictory drives leading towards redemption or damnation in an eternal battle between good and evil.

Greene himself explains that a sentence composed a year previously and carried around in his head was the real starting point for the story: 'I had paid my last farewell to Harry a week ago when his coffin was lowered into the frozen February ground, so that it was with incredulity that I saw him pass by, without a sign of recognition, among the host of strangers in the Strand' (Greene 1982: 4). This sentence was then written up as a novella, which eventually became the screenplay of the film. From that starting point, the search for a dead man, Greene launches into a narrative about identity, a quest that will reveal as much about the subject as the object of enquiry, the racketeer who betrays all – including his girl friend – to safeguard his own survival, pursued by another of Greene's well-intentioned but blundering innocents, the school friend, another 'quiet American' whose refusal to believe in Lime's wickedness eventually ends up like the rubble of a city whose ruins attest to the vanity of human aspiration and achievement.

The Third Man, unlike its near neighbour, the Hollywood film noir, grounds its narrative not in a domestic city but in the chaotic, shattered continental theatre of war, often viewed through Robert Krasker's tilted lens, chiaroscuro effects, and low angles that exaggerate the size of monuments and buildings towering over dwarfed citizens. These effects of form – which Rob White (2003) attributes to inspiration by Julien Duvivier's *Un carnet de bal* (1937) – link the analysis of personal devastation with commentary on the failures of European culture itself. Neil Sinyard argues that *The Third Man* is to the Second World War what *The Wasteland* was to the First World War: 'a definitive evocation of ... decadence, demoralization and dismay' (2003: 27). The 'mad, bad, and dangerous to know city' of American film noir, over which, according to Reid and Walker (1993), the gloom of the Depression has never lifted, is here replaced by a demonised continental European metropolis, a dystopia already presaged in Lang's 1926 classic.

The war, symbol of a bankrupt civilisation, has been over for four years, but its terrible impact remains. Amid the debris of a scarred city, viewed by Marcia Landy as an 'extension of the characters' personal and interpersonal divisions' (1991: 183), the film's authors examine the circumstances that turn human beings into sinners or saints. While the film clearly comments through Vienna on European waste and failure, the foreign setting is also a hyperbolised metaphor for Britain in the late 1940s.

After the dampening of initial euphoria created as a result of Labour legislation – the nationalisation in 1946 of coal, the railways, health, gas and electricity – as strikes appeared in 1947, for the first time since the end of the War, and with crime on the increase, a more cynical attitude towards the new society had started to take hold, changes reflected in the British cinema in the revival of crime films with urban settings, such as *It Always Rains on Sunday* (Hamer, 1947), *Brighton Rock*, or *Good Time Girl* (Macdonald, 1948). Social conditions, though, in Greene's universalist, atemporal Catholic world view do not exempt individuals from responsibility. Circumstances may influence but not seal an individual's fate, determined only by freely made acts of will. While Holly Martins eventually decides to bring his friend to justice, Lime's will has become so rotten it is used solely to gratify egoistic needs, viewing his fellow mortals from the Olympian heights of the ferris-wheel, treating them like insignificant dots reducible to the statistics of his own five-year plans.

Like Macbeth who, once Duncan is stabbed in his sleep, fails to free himself from the downward spiral of murder, Lime knows no way out of the mire of his own creation. And yet, the split between Holly and Harry – linked by their Christian name initials – is in some senses arbitrary, since as well as being about friendship and identification, the film also ranges over the overlaps of good and evil.

The relationship between Holly and Harry is sketched out by Greene in the screenplay, and even though the film versions are not faithful to their original pen portraits, the rudimentary descriptions clearly inform their eventual construction:

> Rollo (Holly) Martins: a Canadian, aged about 35. He has been invited to Vienna by his old friend, Harry Lime, to write propaganda for a volunteer medical unit Lime runs. A simple man who likes his drink and his girl, with more courage than discretion. He has a great sense of loyalty to Lime, whom he first met at school, and even his blunderings are conditioned by his loyalty. His love for Anna arises from the fact that she shares his devotion to Lime. He is an unsuccessful writer of Westerns, who has never seen a cowboy, and he has no illusions about his own writing; Harry Lime: Harry Lime has always found it possible to use his devoted friend. A light, amusing, ruthless character, he has always been able to find superficial excuses for his own behaviour. With wit and courage and immense geniality, he has inspired devotion both in Rollo Martins and the girl Anna, but he has never felt affection for anybody but himself. (Greene n/d b)

The film retains the brio of the character, whose energy and dash are admirable even though the ends they serve are not. Harry Lime's bravado recalls the brilliance of the Renaissance man of distinction – to whom he indirectly compares himself in his 'cuckoo clock' speech – his original demonic allure eventually giving way to insipid bowdlerised versions in the radio and TV series, the latter starring the improbable Michael Rennie.

The changes from Greene's original sketches include, in Martins's case, the substitution of the first name 'Holly' for 'Rollo'. In the preface to the novella Greene writes that Joseph Cotten objected to the name 'Rollo', and although an unusual name was still thought necessary for the part, he settled on 'Holly', an allusion to 'that figure of fun, the American poet Thomas Holley Chivers'. This reference is consistent with the film's pattern of literary self-consciousness. There is an element of autobiography in Holly Martins, whose Western pulp fiction – the equivalent of Greene's 'Entertainments' – admired by the proletariat, here represented by Sergeant Paine, who has read many of Martins's works, is dismissed by the intelligentsia and the middle classes, symbolised by Major Calloway and Crabbin, the British consulate cultural events officer, who have never heard of him.

These nuances of literary taste belong to a more sustained satire of the class system in Britain, which Orwell famously described as the most snobbery and privilege-ridden country under the sun (1988: 52). While celebrating British understatement in the inveterately English characters played by Trevor Howard (Major Calloway), Wilfrid Hyde-White (Crabbin) and Bernard Lee (Sgt Paine), all of whom enjoy moments of understated humour, the film is also, not unusually for a Reed film, sharply satirical of British attitudes to class. So, after Lime's first 'funeral' (in which Joseph Harbin is made to impersonate Lime in the coffin), in a scene found neither in the novel nor in the screenplay, Sgt Paine is seen sitting alone at a table in the bar where Calloway and Martins, at another, are discussing Lime. The novel omits Paine's presence altogether; the original screenplay has him enter the bar just in time to prevent Martins taking a swing at Calloway. But in the film Paine is already there in the bar, his NCO rank barring him, Reed seems eager to emphasise, from the table reserved for the officer class.

Martins's literariness – both through association with the poet after whom he is christened, and as a writer of Zane Grey-style novels – belongs more seriously to the film's interest in the fictionalisation of experience. With characteristic insight, Anna at one point urges Martins, once referred to in another cultural in-joke – in keeping with Reed's playful rivalry with Hitchcock – as the 'master of suspense', to stop making Harry in his image: 'Harry was real. He wasn't just your friend and my lover. He was Harry.' Literary and cultural self-consciousness – highlighted by the film title's reference not only to the known character

Harry Lime – the 'third man' present at the road accident that apparently claimed his life – but also to the novel's being supposedly written by Martins (so he menacingly informs Popescu at the British Council), is integrally related to questions of identity. 'The Third Man', the novel being written by Martins, narrativises his own drama of friendship with Lime. More specifically, Martins's pursuit of the 'third man', both the fictional character intended for one of his own novels, and the mysterious stranger who witnessed the 'death' in suspicious circumstances of his boyhood friend, becomes at once a quest for Harry Lime, a scrutiny of his own self and, by extension, of the very rudiments of identity. Popescu's response to Martins's remark about writing a novel entitled 'The Third Man' is a warning not to mix fact and fiction. But his Manichean approach to literature and, by extension, to film, seems designed both as regards the overlaps of fact and fiction and in relation to Martins's perception of Lime – confusing reality and desire – to provoke controversy. In that sense Martins's identification with his fictionalised hero, the 'third man', stands for everyone. As Koch the porter remarks when asked by Martins about the identity of the third man, he 'could have been anybody'.

The links between Harry Lime and Holly Martins, as friends and projections of each other, grow steadily clearer. At first glance, though, a world of difference apparently divides them. One exudes public-spirited self-denial, the other self-centred opportunism, a taste for risk, for living on the edge between darkness and light, an egocentricity that even neglects to inform Anna about his best friend Holly ('He never told me about any of his friends'). The former is played by Joseph Cotten, many of whose films see him cast in worthy roles marked by solid values and the natural courtesy of a Southern gentleman. In *Citizen Kane* (Welles, 1941), for instance, he is the drama critic whose refusal to compromise his principles forfeits the friendship of a powerful employer, also played by Orson Welles, whose own declaration of principles turn out to be less substantial than the paper on which they are written. In *The Magnificent Ambersons* (Welles, 1942), too, his loyalty to the woman he loves remains unruffled by even his most persistent detractors. Much of the Cotten persona was fashioned in these Welles films. His elegance, height, softly spoken, mildly Southern drawl, and his thick crinkly hair, suggest class and dependability, while his consistently furrowed brow and heavily lidded eyes point to a man of a meditative, philosophical turn of mind.

The thoughtful, equitable character he plays in early films is repeated in *Duel in the Sun* (Vidor, 1946), where again as in *The Third Man*, his man of reason is set against a demonic rival, there played, against type, by Gregory Peck, in some ways that film's less polished, more libidinal Harry Lime. And yet, the link between Holly and Harry is visually emphasised very early on, as Holly bounds up the staircase to Harry's Vienna flat, the spring in his step undermined by the shadow cast by his body on the staircase wall, lighting here drawing attention to the unshakeable presence of the sinner in the life of the saint. Cotten's shadow, the darker side to his Everyman persona, was teased out by Hitchcock, above all, in *Shadow of a Doubt* (1943) and, to a lesser extent, in *Under Capricorn* (1949). In *The Third Man* the inner darkness is projected on to Harry Lime, his friend and ego ideal.

Harry Lime is another of Reed's outsiders, 'outcasts' or 'men between'. Sometimes the emotional damage is given physical expression, as in *Trapeze*, where the Burt Lancaster character's limp is symptomatic, like L. B. Jefferies's broken leg in Hitchcock's *Rear Window* (1954), of inner torment. At other times, immoral choices are prompted by psychological trauma. No physical deformity betrays Lime's twisted psyche. In appearance he recalls the most terrible of all outsider figures, Satan himself. His shadowy allure, emphasised by his invariable outfit of black cashmere coat, scarf and matching hat, gives him a devilish appeal. This is a stylish, secular and dandified Satan, a sharply dressed upper-class spiv, heir to British (Murphy 1986: 292–3) as well as American gangster traditions of dandyism, a rebel of the kind associated in Hollywood with Cagney and, in the British cinema (Spicer 2003), with lesser luminaries like John McCallum and Sidney Tafler, his elegance made all the more striking through contrast with Martins's shabbier, less narcissistic, drearily reliable look.

Significantly, in an extension of the film's patterns of shared complicity and betrayals, Major Calloway is also given a dandified moment on his first appearance. Whereas, indoors, he is usually later seen in battle dress or, outdoors, in a duffel-coat that makes him look like Monty's double, at Lime's first, 'false' funeral he wears a black patent leather full length overcoat that in some senses aligns him with the villain he pursues and thinks he has just buried. Calloway's accoutrement comments ironically on futile attempts to bury evil: Lime is still on the run, his darkness mirrored in the lawman who pursues him, his resuscitation prefigured here, displaced onto Calloway in a process where the raising of the dead, Harry's return halfway through the film, becomes a vivid metaphor for the restoration not of life but of death. Harry's reappearance is a regeneration of evil, the return in monstrous form not just of perverse desires but of a culture's imperfectly interred collective wickedness. A mainly nocturnal demon, he emerges from the shadows to stalk his victims, the great betrayer who has sacrificed even his devoted mistress Anna for the price of his own infernal salvation, his wickedness easily accommodated by Orson Welles's persona. Welles, though, was not Reed's first choice for Lime. David Niven, Robert Taylor, Kirk Douglas, Trevor Howard, James Stewart, Robert Mitchum and even Noel Coward were all in the frame. Reed had initially favoured Cary Grant, and although Hitchcock managed to draw out the more sinister tendencies in what was, at that time, his overwhelmingly romantic comedy leading man persona, Harry Lime is now unthinkable without Orson Welles. Of all those considered for the part, Welles is closer to Calloway's description of Lime in the novella, a man with stocky legs, 'big shoulders a little hunched, a belly that has known too much good food for too long, on his face a look of cheerful rascality, a geniality, a recognition that his happiness will make the world's day' (Greene 1982: 103). The taste for good living extends in the film to all his decadent associates, such as Dr Winkel who, when visited on the first occasion by Martins, is caught slicing a plump roast turkey in a city where others starve.

In *Citizen Kane* Welles is, if not actually satanic, predominantly monstrous, an over-reacher, a Tamburlaine, lost to his own limitless egocentricity. *Macbeth* (Welles, 1948), *The Prince of Foxes* (King, 1949), *Genghis Khan* (Levin, 1964), and other films take to extremes, in some cases risking the hyperbole of *grand guignol*, the persona's capacity for evil. The overfed cheeks and heavy frame become signs more of predatoriness than of bonhomie. And yet, Welles is no Boris Karloff or Bela Lugosi, lugubrious, unnerving monsters, usually unredeemed by humour. In contrast, Welles's menace is often either offset by irony, or marked by understandable, even if unpardonable, human failings. In Lime, more attractive qualities are allowed expression, inspiring devotion in friend, lover and even animals, who are either blind or prepared to overlook the cruel egoism of the racketeer.

Animals often appear in Reed's films to indicate the merits, failings or saving graces of a character. For instance, birds in *Oliver!*, elephants, lions, horses and snakes in *Trapeze*, a snake in *The Fallen Idol*, a kitten in *Girl in the News*, perform the role of chorus, commentators on the behaviour of their human entourage, warning against an exclusively anthropocentric view of the world. In *The Man Between*, Kestner, a Western agent, and therefore on the side of the angels in a film about East–West relations during the Cold War, is bitten by a dog. The incident, like the cockatoo's nipping of Martins's finger in *The Third Man* points to the precariousness of moral absolutes.

The detail of the cat's devotion to Harry Lime is revealing. Whereas the cockatoo's assault marks out Holly as a flawed character, the cat's loyalty to Harry identifies saving graces. When he first appears, caught at night in a doorway, his unexpected presence exposed by the suddenly switched on light shining from un upper window, the film aligns him with the cat, an animal notoriously independent, graceful and mysterious, often used in art to incarnate libidinal drives, as in the work of Decadents like Rops or Moreau, or in films like *Cat People* (Tourneur, 1942) or *The Leopard Man* (Tourneur, 1943). As the cat nestles in Harry's handmade Church's shoes, playing with his laces, the moment recalls an earlier exchange between Anna and Holly: 'Not very sociable, is he?' 'No, he only liked Harry.' A kitten performs a similar role in *Girl in the News*, comforting a self-indulgent hypochondriac (Irene Handl) who behaves like a spoilt child.

In addition to the monstrous, feral qualities, there is also something in Lime, not untypically for a Reed character, of the hidden child, whose innocent, playful mischief has not been entirely stifled, whose malevolence is partly rescued by wit and playfulness. Anna remarks pertinently, 'He never grew up. The world grew up around him.' The prankishness and humour are conveyed through Welles's characteristic chuckles and laughing eyes. When he realises he has been seen by Holly in the doorway his face creases into the smirk of an unruly fifth-former, caught out in one of his daring after-lights-out escapades. Welles's outsize girth, not yet at the Gargantuan limits of his Detective Hank Quinlan in *Touch of Evil* (Welles, 1958), give him an almost cherubic look. The rounded, softened contours of the jaw suggest over-indulgence, an affront to the gaunt, ascetic, slightly self-righteous appearance of Cotten as Martins.

The links between Lime and childhood are further strengthened in two ways: (1) the street statue of the cherub, (2) the little Austrian boy, Hans. Neither in the novel nor in the screenplay is there any reference to the statue of the cherub beside which first Holly and then Sergeant Paine are positioned, as the trail for Harry goes cold, before they and Calloway suddenly realise their quarry eludes them through entry into the sewers via the tubular kiosks found all over the city.

The cherub belongs to a pattern of associations linking statues and characters. For instance, at Dr Winkel's home, Martins comments on his host's abundant collection of religious ornaments, statuettes of saints, holy relics, crucifixes and so on, drawing attention to the schism in this household between their owner's official calling as a healer, and his death-dealing involvement in penicillin racketeering, crimes given silent, ironic commentary through the sacred symbols with which he is surrounded.

The cherub, towards whom Paine makes a gesture of frustration, seems to represent Harry's spirit, superficially an angel of childish innocence, but inwardly a harbinger of wickedness, mocking the efforts of his pursuers or, as Holly had earlier put it, 'laughing at fools like us all the time', the cunning ruthlessness of the anti-hero expressed as the indomitable wilfulness of the selfish child.

The identification of the cherub with Lime is compounded by his projection as the little boy Hans. Attempting to recover his ball, Hans has earlier seen Holly in conversation with Koch, the porter in Harry's flat. When Holly returns to find a crowd around the flat, driven into the street by news of the porter's murder, Hans accuses Holly, in German, of the murder. For a moment, through this childish surrogate, Lime is the accuser, Martins, at one point framed in close-up to encourage the suggestion, the accused, as if in falsely identifying Martins as the murderer of the porter, the child becomes the agent through whom Greene and Reed indicate the complicity of Martins in murder, a prefiguring of the killing of a friend that will later be his fate.

The Holly/Harry relationship opens up questions about the nature of friendship and identity. The film is partly about male friendship: the comradeship, shared interests, reciprocity of feeling, loyalty and empathetic willingness to understand 'what is inherently foreign to our ego in other people' (Freud 1985b: 137). It is also a film about role models and hero worship for another 'fallen idol' for, as Greene puts it in the novella, Martins had hero-worshipped Lime for twenty years (1982: 190), the kind of hero worship of which the stronger, more charismatic man could take advantage, easily persuading him to come over to Vienna to help provide cover for his deadly schemes.

Additionally, though, the film opens up questions about the wellsprings of identity and desire. In 'Group Psychology and the Analysis of the Ego' (1985b), Freud makes a distinction of degree between friendship and other forms of love, all of which ultimately belong, he argues, to the same spectrum of feelings:

> The nucleus of what we mean by love naturally consists (and this is what is commonly called love, and what the poets sing of) in sexual love with sexual union as its aim. But we do not separate from this ... on the one hand self love, and on the other, love for parents and children, friendship and love for humanity in general, and also devotion to concrete objects and to abstract ideas. Our justification lies in the fact that psychoanalytical research has taught us that all these tendencies are an expression of the same instinctual impulses, in relations between the sexes these impulses force their way towards sexual union, but in other circumstances they are diverted from this aim or are prevented from reaching it, though always preserving enough of their original nature to

keep their identity recognisable (as in such features as the longing for proximity, and self sacrifice). (Freud 1985b: 119)

He goes on to argue in the same essay that the intensity of such relationships is accompanied by a 'sediment of feeling of aversion and hostility, which only escapes perception as a result of repression' (130). Returning to the topic of friendship in the later 'Civilization and Its Discontents' (1985a), he adds the further nuance that while 'genital love leads to the formation of new families' (1985a: 292), what he defines as aim-inhibited love leads to friendships, one of the advantages of which is its refusal, in contrast to what he refers to as genital love, of exclusivity. For all the various differences noted by Freud between friendship and genital love, his stress on their common roots and on the residual feeling of aversion or hostility, and the implicit acknowledgement of the homoerotic basis of friendship have been acknowledged and developed in the work, above all, of Eve Kosovsky Sedgwick (1985).

A cause of much anxiety for Selznick (White 2003: 18–19), the homosocial or homoerotic and displaced desires of Holly and Harry belong to a clear pattern. Holly's relationship with Harry is characterised by friendship as well as by the melancholia resulting from abandoned homoerotic attachments and, perhaps even more, by drives towards identification, where Harry becomes to some extent a model to whom Holly looks up. Freud's comments on identification also serve as a useful theoretical framework for discussion of the links between the pair. For Freud, identification is ambivalent, characterised as much by aversion as by tenderness: 'It behaves like a derivative of the first, oral phase of the organization of the libido, in which the object that we long for and prize is assimilated by eating and is in that way annihilated as such. The cannibal, as we know, has remained at this standpoint, he has a devouring affection for his enemies and only devours people of whom he is fond' (1985b: 134–5). He summarises his thoughts on identification by describing it as the original form of emotional tie with an object, a substitute through introjecting the object into the ego for a libidinal object-tie, and arises through perception of shared qualities with another person who is not the object of sexual instinct (1985b: 137). The friendship and processes of identification that bind Harry and Holly together are acknowledged unconsciously, if not consciously, by Anna (Valli), the woman loved by Holly partly because she is Harry's girl, whose refusal to accept Harry's betrayal as the price of freedom from the Russians is repaid by Harry's betrayal of her in exchange for his own life. Her attitude marks her out further, as if loving the rebel Harry were not enough, as someone determined to take control of her own destiny, a 1950s Antigone (Rob White's suggestive analogy (2003: 66–7)), making decisions for herself, refusing the offer of a part in a conventional happy ending by rejecting union with Holly, and walking straight out of the frame and romantic closure at the end of the film. Her unwillingness to acknowledge Holly at the end, to respond to his silent overture of passion, registers all the more poignantly the emptiness of her loveless life without Harry.

This ending, as Greene admitted, was Reed's idea: 'One of the very few major disputes between Carol Reed and myself concerned the ending, and he has been proved triumphantly right. I held the view that an entertainment of this kind was too light an affair to carry the weight of an unhappy ending. Reed ... felt that my ending ... would strike the audience who had just seen Harry die as unpleasantly cynical ... I was afraid few people would wait in their seats during the girl's long walk from the graveside and that the ending was as conventional as mine and more drawn-out. I had not given enough consideration to the mastery of Reed's direction' (Greene 1982: 11).

Anna's blind spot is Harry. She is one of the most vivid examples of a Reed character drawn to a lover in a way that seems to bear out Bataille's notion of eroticism as the affirmation of life to the point of death. Stella in *The Key*, Catherine in *Bank Holiday* and Kathleen in *Odd Man Out*, are others who embody a constant theme of Reed's, that love leads not to life but death. Her sad eyes still perhaps recalling the witnessed horrors of war on the continent, Anna is the personification of anguish produced by awareness of death through erotic affirmation of life. In identifying herself with Lime, the harbinger of death as well as the deliverer of life, Anna embraces transgression, asserting, as Bataille would put it, her sovereignty, declaring her own truth regardless of social responsibility (in Richardson 1994: 39). When she deflates Martins's declaration of love with the words 'if you'd rung me up and asked me if you were dark or fair or had a moustache, I wouldn't have known', the hypnotic effect of Lime on Anna to the point where symbiosis even leads to wearing his monogrammed pyjamas, combines with her tendency to call Holly 'Harry' on a number of occasions, not only to express the force of her idealisation of Harry, but also to draw attention to the links between the two men. The detail of the pyjamas is one of many that confirms Reed's refusal to be bullied by Joseph Breen and the demands of the Production Code. In a letter to Selznick, Breen had written: 'There will be no dialogue definitely pointing up an illicit sex relationship between Anna and Harry. The sequence in the bedroom will be played without any emphasis on the bed, or other sex suggestive flavour to the scene. In the scene where Anna is arrested and has to dress, she will at no time be shown in anything less than a slip, and there will be no suggestive reactions from the soldiers present' (in Falk 1990: 81–2).

Anna's slips of the tongue echo those made by Martins when he addresses Major Calloway as 'Callaghan'. Martins's linguistic confusions may simply be a conscious lack of respect for protocol, a way of irritating a man seemingly ruled by military routine. Or they may indicate American indifference to British sensibilities over the troubles in Ireland (Calloway complains to Holly, 'I'm not Irish'), an issue still fresh no doubt in Reed's mind, from his recently completed *Odd Man Out*. Even more intriguingly, these muddles of identity created by linguistic slips, like 'Callaghan' for 'Calloway', and 'Harry' for 'Holly', underline beyond questions of perception, in which characters see objective reality through the distorted lenses of prejudice or fantasy, the aleatory laws governing nationality, gender or class.

So, when Holly complains to Anna, after again being called 'Harry', 'For heaven's sake stop calling me "Harry"', his plea invites a mixed response. From one point of view, Martins and Anna are variants of the pattern, given most extreme form in Lime, of the film's denunciation of refusals to respect the individuality of others. From another, Anna's error means she sees not the friend before her but the mourned lover, language here, prompted by the agony of yearning, recording the power of memory and loss to shape reality. From yet another, it stresses the film's interest in the complications of friendship and identification. Accordingly, Holly and Harry are mirror images of each other. While Harry has sought the Limelight ('It's a far far better thing that I do. The old limelight. The fall of the curtain', he muses beside Holly at the top of the ferris-wheel) among the ruins and sewers of Vienna, looking for a self severed from his roots in a foreign place, Holly remains, like many Noir heroes, traumatised by the laws of the superego. Obedient to the Law of the Father, he destroys in the pursuit of his idolised friend his own shadow, personified by that friend, surrendering to Major Calloway, a policeman, the upholder of more than the criminal law.

The theatrical references in Lime's speech, of a piece with the various other elements of theatricality, such as Anna's career as an actress, make Holly as well as Harry a post-war Sidney Carton. Through their indissolubility the film examines the overlays of egocentricity and self-denial, of awe-struck friendship and absence of mutuality, a *mise-en-scène* of upper world rubble and an underworld of rat-infested sewers.

The famous sequence in the sewers is the final place of definition for Harry's blackened soul, where in defiance of Breen's warning to

Selznick not to make it look like mercy killing, he is shot by his other self, Holly, who is given the go-ahead in Harry's muted gesture of approval. The scene recalls the closing sequence of *He Walked By Night* (Werker, 1948), where the criminal anti-hero (Richard Basehart) is finally chased by policemen in the storm drain system, providing him, as one of the cops puts it, with 'seven hundred miles of hidden highway' under the Los Angeles streets through which to make his getaway. The chase through these drains is almost identical to the pursuit of Harry in the Vienna sewers. For all its many virtues, though, *He Walked by Night* cannot be compared with *The Third Man*. For one thing, it lacks a zither score, that lilting Karas melody that in its sometimes jaunty, sometimes slower, more plangent harmonies, serves as a musical cloak of Viennese gaiety for the concealed horrors of a fallen world.

Our Man in Havana (1959)

Our Man in Havana was Carol Reed's third collaboration with Graham Greene. Hitchcock had attempted unsuccessfully to buy the film rights, which Reed, much to Greene's pleasure, secured shortly after the novel was published in 1958. Losing no opportunity to run down his films, he would not have approved of Hitchcock as the director for *Our Man in Havana*. In *The Pleasure Dome* Greene comments: 'Hitchcock's inadequate sense of reality irritated me and still does – how inexcusably he spoilt *The Thirty-Nine Steps*. I still believe I was right (whatever Monsieur Truffaut may say) when I wrote: 'His films consist of small "amusing" melodramatic situations ... they mean nothing. They lead to nothing' (1980: 1–2).

Having by this time set up his own production company (Kingsmead Productions), Reed offered the film to Columbia Pictures, who took on the project in October 1958, offering him the choice, according to John Box, of either making it in Spain in colour, or in Havana in black and white. Reed took the latter option.

All three Reed–Greene collaborations are part thriller and part quest narratives. Greene's novels and 'entertainments', like Reed's films, typically concentrate on individuals searching for authenticity or redemption – often in foreign settings – measuring and testing their identities against the norms and ideals of class and nationality. These exotic spaces are perfect for narratives about the destabilisation of the self, especially when in the service of thrillers where identity is endangered by the uncontrollable laws of desire or crime. *The Third Man* evaluates the sincerity and conception of themselves as men of its two central characters, Holly Martins and Harry Lime, in the devastated surroundings of post-war Vienna; in *The Fallen Idol* the foreign ambassador's son is trapped between the prerogatives of his own nationality and the appeal of the heroic ideals associated with the English butler, Baines; *Our Man in Havana* dispatches its two major characters, the Englishmen Wormold, the vacuum-cleaner salesman, and Hawthorne, the master spy, to the Caribbean, where the clash between Englishness and otherness (chiefly Hispanic, but also Germanic) leads to readjustments of the Englishman's attitudes towards self and other. *Our Man in Havana* takes advantage of a turning point in its history to pursue its explorations of identity in the changing conditions of Cuban society. Made only three years after the Suez fiasco, the film is also a comic statement about Britain's decline as a world power, and satirises the wish-fulfilment fantasies of spy narratives, like Ian Fleming's *Casino Royale* (1953), whose hero, James Bond, was yet to be given screen life by Sean Connery in films where British power and expertise still commanded respect. All the British characters in *Our Man in Havana*, in one way or another involved in Foreign Office affairs, are ludicrous, caricatures of the real boffins and mandarins in a country humiliated by the Suez crisis. The film was released only three years after Osborne's *Look Back in Anger* (1956) and three years before Wesker's *Chips with Everything* (1962), plays by the 'Angry Young Men' generation disenchanted with the unresolved problems of post-war Britain. No 'kitchen sink' drama, *Our Man in Havana* responds to shrinking British influence abroad not with anger but ridicule, no longer confident after the loss of Empire and overseas political influence about what Jeffrey Richards and others have highlighted as one of the main characteristics of the pre-war national character, an unshakable sense of superiority (Richards 1997: 31)

The action of *Our Man in Havana* takes place in the pre-revolutionary dictatorship years of Batista's Cuba. Although the decision to proceed was taken while he was still in power, by the time the film went into production Batista had been overthrown (2 January 1959), a turn of events that in the end failed to deter Columbia from keeping faith with the project. Greene's interest in Cuba grew out of a fondness for a country he had often visited, attracted by both its natural beauty and its decadent nightlife. Nevertheless, the narrative was an adaptation of a treatment Greene had written for Alberto Cavalcanti about a spy inventing information for his gullible controllers, an idea based on Greene's own experiences in the Secret Service (1943–4), where as an agent responsible for Portugal, he was able to see, first hand, how German spies – recognising the game was up – were sending false reports back home (Wapshott 1990: 293). Greene used his material to develop a story set in Estonia about a man who satisfies through this deception his wife's mundane needs. Cavalcanti's reservations about the plot led him to ditch the project, arguing that the British Board of Censors would never have condoned mockery of the Secret Service. When in the 1950s Greene returned to the story, he offered this explanation for the switch from Estonia to Cuba: '... the reader could feel no sympathy for a man who was cheating his country in Hitler's day ... However, in fantastic Havana, among the absurdities of the Cold War ... There was a situation allowably comic' (in Moss 1987: 227–8).

Columbia's early anxieties about the attitudes of the new regime towards the film were soon allayed once it became clear that Castro, a good friend of Greene's, had taken an interest in it, and actually visited the set on one occasion. Nevertheless, government officials demanded a Spanish translation of the screenplay, and observers were sent to the set. The national dailies in Britain picked up on these intrusions. *The Daily Telegraph*, for instance, reported under its headline '*Our Man in Havana* Runs into Trouble' (Anon 1959), that Cuban ministers were insisting that 'Cuba be projected in a proper light', that Dr Rodríguez, the Minister of the Interior, ordered an observer on the set to ensure 'there was nothing disparaging to the revolutionary government', and that a Dr Junco, the Secretary of the Film Revision Commission, visited the set. *The Daily Express* published an interview with Reed:

> What they want ... is to make sure that our story, which is set in the old regime under dictator Batista, shows just what a police state it was then. We are doing that anyway with odd little scenes outside police stations and reference to torture of political prisoners. But most of the plot is comedy and we cannot make it too heavy. The authorities here don't want to make it appear that anything that happened under Batista could possibly happen again now. So when they saw Noel Coward being pressured down a street by three musicians twanging guitars in his face they thought this might give a bad impression. It does not happen now – but that sort of thing did happen in the old days. We are just going on filming and there is no question of our having to stop because of trouble.
> (Lewin 1959)

In the novel Greene allows room for detailed descriptions of a favourite city. For all its decadence and corruption, Havana for Greene, as well as for Reed, was an attractive, lively capital, its charm – owing much to its Hispanic legacy – an affront to the squalor, ugliness and inhospitableness of Jamaica. For Greene, 'to live in Havana was to live in a factory that turned out human beauty on a conveyor belt' (Greene 1971: 108), while Jamaica was defined by dirt and heat, leading Wormold to ask

'What accounted for the squalor of British possessions? The Spanish, the French and the Portuguese built cities where they settled, but the English just allowed cities to grow. The poorest street in Havana had dignity compared with the shanty-life of Kingston – huts built out of old petrol tins roofed with scrap metal purloined from some cemetery of abandoned cars' (1971: 158).

The novel gives a clear impression of the geography of Havana, with passages on the downtown areas of Old Havana, as well as on the more suburban, residential areas like Vedado and Miramar, the sea-front – the Malecón – and the provinces. A key scene, where Wormold and Beatrice set off in search of Professor Sánchez, one of the agents Wormold is supposed to have recruited, takes place in one of the luxurious homes just off the famous Quinta Avenida in Miramar. All of this is scaled down in the film leaving the emphasis firmly on Old Havana – with its Casbah-like labyrinths of bars, hotels, night-clubs, busy streets – and the country club, included partly in order to depict the privileged life-style of the old order's ruling classes. But the Havana, especially Old Havana, of the film is no museum piece. The film avoids the travelogue genre's eulogy of an island's cultural heritage. Like the novel, the film is primarily interested in the decadent, sexualised other-ness of, as Greene himself terms it, 'fantastic' Havana, an ultimately unreal, tarnished version of a Caribbean paradise lost, an island of natural beauty and cultural diversity polluted largely through foreign, especially North American, interference and local greed. Wormold himself, in line with the riven English heroes and anti-heroes of many novels and films from the period, is simultaneously drawn to and suspicious of this inflammable mixture of tropical daiquiri and sex. Like the Guinness character Holland – or 'Dutch', his own preferred moniker – in *The Lavender Hill Mob* (Crichton, 1951), whose ill-gotten gains have taken him not to Havana but to Rio, but whose conservative instincts make him probably more suited to life in the Home Counties, Wormold is a mixture of rebellion and conformity.

The tone is set in *Our Man in Havana* in the earliest sequence which serves as a kind of prologue for the main action. Before the credits roll, the camera, on a crane, swoops down on a dark female swimming backstroke, in leisurely fashion, to the adagio cadences of a mandolin-led Latin rhythmical score, on a rooftop swimming pool, which despite its lofty position, seems as if located at the base of the sunlit city, the carnal capital of the Caribbean, chosen even by Marlon Brando's Sky Masterson as the destination for the seduction of his Salvation Army victim, Jean Simmons's Sister Sarah Brown, in *Guys and Dolls* (Mankiewicz, 1955). As the swarthy girl reaches the shallow end of the pool, the words 'This film is set in Cuba before the recent revolution' appear, and the figure of a man, a policeman in uniform standing by the poolside, comes into view. In long shot, the girl remains motionless, her back to the camera, while the policeman, also in long shot, but facing the camera, seems to approach her, one hand in pocket, the other holding a cigarette, but then moves on, not having addressed her, out of the frame. The graphics fix the narrative in the recent past of Cuban history and, more significantly, define through the positioning of the policeman and the girl in the frame the authoritarianism and sexual politics of pre-Castro Cuban society. This scene, between swimmer and policeman, the former as if parading herself for his pleasure, heightens the image of a largely US-targeted economy fuelled by vice. As she swims towards him, her movements are readable as a projection of the dictatorship's unequal power relations, here focused on the state's exploitation of women. This, in miniature, is the image of Cuba as the whorehouse of sexual tourism.

As we cut to street level, our introduction to a couple – lovers? client and whore? – a dusky male of unhurried movement, and a dark, voluptuous, apple-munching female, is accompanied by the Caribbean strains of the Hermanos Deniz band. The couple give each other meaningful glances, before the man approaches the woman who responds to his advance by throwing him her half-eaten fruit, whereupon the action freezes as the credits finally begin to appear, the music now forsaking its languid pace for frenzied rhythms. Our next acquaintance with Havana is via prostitutes, pimps, street vendors, police cars – brutal treatment by the police of local citizens – a melange of urban sights and sounds.

The passionless relationship between the half naked woman and the fully dressed policeman contrasts sharply with the more natural rapport between the street level lovers. The long shot compositions of the first sequence are replaced by close and medium shots of the pair who remain mute throughout, their eye contact recording their mutual fascination. Even though not immune from stereotype – with the apple-eating maid at the balcony positioned as a Cuban Eve inhabiting a sleazy paradise – the courtship of the lovers offers a natural alternative to the imbalance of the previous scene. Less positively, and in keeping with what in *Unthinking Eurocentrism. Multiculturalism and the Media*, Ella Shohat and Robert Stam refer to as the 'reduction of the cultural to the biological, the tendency to associate the colonized with the vegetative and the instinctual rather than with the learned and the cultural' (1994: 138), the unnamed woman's association with fruit brings to mind the far more exaggerated horticultural exoticism of Carmen Miranda. To some extent the local couple reproduce what Fanon refers to as the processes of objectification, 'the determination to objectify, to imprison, to harden' (Schmitt 1996: 35), defined as they are primarily through their sexuality. But the stress on the couple's mutual attraction is also affirmative. Their libidinal *pas de deux* recalls the contrasts found in the Cuban writer Alejo Carpentier's 1953 novel *Los pasos perdidos* (The Lost Steps), where the forces of a primeval jungle threaten to undermine the structures of a civilisation imposed by outsiders. In *Our Man in Havana* the couple appear to be slaves to desire: the man, not at work, adapting a relaxed pose, idles away his hours, responding to the provocative pose of the woman who, like him, might also be whiling away her time, or else offering love for sale. Even so, the *habaneros* – the male a sort of inferior Harry Belafonte in one of Marlon Brando's cast off tee-shirts from *A Streetcar Named Desire*, the female a substandard Yvonne De Carlo – have the positive force of complicating the processes of objectification associated with the ancien regime, their rhythmic mutual attraction here seemingly in tune with the gentle, slow harmony of the music that accompanies their journey towards each other and that also places in relief the awkward otherness of the first of the Europeans to come under the film's scrutiny, Hawthorne (Noel Coward), the controller of the British agents in the Caribbean.

In contrast to the relaxed pose, unhurried movements and casual dress of the Cuban, Hawthorne's demeanour is mask-like, his pace brisk, his clothes formal, creating an overall impression entirely out of keeping with his environment. He cuts an incongruous figure, 'carrying the leathery smell of a good club' (Greene 1971: 11), dressed in a Saville Row suit, Jermyn Street tie, Homburg, trademark brolly in hand, the epitome – seen from a Cuban perspective – of the English exotic, an otherness as fantastic – to use Greene's word again – as what to him must seem like the equally alien appearance of the Edmondo Ros-style group that follows him around accosting him for money in exchange for their rendering of 'Domitila', a popular Cuban song of the day, the lyrics of which provide early clues to the film's unconventional attitudes to sex and gender. The singers identify Hawthorne with 'Domitila', a woman, and ask '¿Dónde vas con mantón de Manila?' (Where are you going in your Manila shawl?) of Domitila/Hawthorne, a question as much about sex and gender as geographical destination. C. A. Lejeune's Chandler-esque description in *The Observer* of Noel Coward in this and other scenes as 'inconspicuous as a hippopotamus in a tank of goldfish' is apt (1960). Most of the reviewers felt that Coward was the real success of the film. Robert Muller (1959) in *The Daily Mail* wrote: 'Noel Coward has done the impossible. He has walked away with an Alec Guinness picture.' In *The Evening News* J. Harman wrote: 'Sorry Alec – you're not the best man in Havana' (1959). Hawthorne is the essence of the European, specifically Anglo-Saxon, colonialist. Cuba, of course, unlike Jamaica – his base – was never a British colony (Jamaica achieved independence in 1962, a year after the film's release), and although Latin American writers and thinkers often turned to Europe for inspiration, this was often to emphasise the latinity of Latin America in order to dissociate Latin America from the economic power and utilitarianism of Anglo-Saxon America.

One of the key texts on this issue was the Uruguayan José Enrique Rodó's essay *Ariel* (1967), which contrasted the spiritual, aesthetic and imaginative qualities of Latins with the materialism of the Anglo-Saxons. While there are no North Americans in the film, their ideological and blood cousins, the British – not only the leading players Hawthorne and Wormold, but also their superiors in Whitehall, led by Ralph Richardson as 'C' – are still pursuing their colonialist designs. Hawthorne's brief is to keep an eye on anti-British (and, we must also assume, anti-American) activity, eventually succeeding in making Wormold betray his friends and innocent Cuban strangers to satisfy his venal needs.

Hawthorne's otherness, beyond his embodiment of Anglo-Saxon materialism, is relayed through the play on Noel Coward's homosexuality, and the *double entendres* that seldom fail to characterise his speech, especially in the scene where he attempts to recruit Wormold in a public lavatory.

> HAWTHORNE: A bar's not a bad place. You run into a fellow countryman, have a little get-together. What could be more natural? ... Where's the Gents?
> WORMOLD: Through there.
> HAWTHORNE: You go in there, and I'll follow.
> WORMOLD: But I don't need the Gents.
> HAWTHORNE: My dear fellow, don't be crass.
> WORMOLD: I don't need it.
> HAWTHORNE: Don't let me down. You're an Englishman, aren't you?

The links between Englishness, doing one's duty, and homosocial as well as potentially homosexual tendencies work in positive as well as in negative ways. Hawthorne's stiffness and incongruity are clearly designed to provoke amusement, marking him out comically as the rapidly vanishing ideal of the colonialist English gentleman abroad. Nevertheless, the camp and covert gayness of Coward's performance – his unstated 'shyness' of women (to use Wormold's description of the traitor Carter, another Englishman of seemingly nonconformist sexual tastes) – also works more positively to unsettle fixed categories of sex and gender. If, as Richard Dyer argues, 'gayness is, as a material category, far more fluid than class, gender or race' (1977b: 32), Hawthorne's 'fluidity' helps soften the rigidities of social categorisation, under-mining a little, through the sheer bravura of Coward's perfectly timed performance (the scene-stealing referred to in reviews of the film), the certainties of heterosexual hegemony. Furthermore, in keeping with the largely comic mode of the film, Hawthorne's otherness succeeds in ironising what might be considered the exaggerated heterosexual steaminess of Havana, initially projected through the mute couple at the beginning of the film, then through the frustrated efforts of Wormold's assistant López to find his master a serviceable woman, and especially through the predatory designs of Captain Segura, the prowling, shark-like chief of police. If, from one point of view, Hawthorne's behaviour is intended through its camp dryness to emphasise by contrast the appeal of Cuban heterosexuality, from another it reminds its audience not only of alternative forms of human relationship but also that the identi-fication of Cuba with heterosexuality ignores the traditions of homo-sexuality, celebrated above all in the work of two of its most respected writers, Lezama Lima and Reinaldo Arenas, the latter soon to be silenced by the new regime.

Nevertheless, Hawthorne, like the civil servants in Whitehall, and the traitor Carter (Paul Rogers) – whose irredeemable Englishness is confirmed by his residence, while in Havana, at the Hotel Inglaterra – is for all his ironic commentary on Cuban life, an essentially one-dimensional character. Much more complex is Wormold. Alec Guinness's complaints about the instructions given him by Reed highlight the complexity of a character that, had he been allowed to follow his own instincts, would have greatly diminished its significance:

> Carol wanted me to play the part ... quite differently from the way I envisaged it. I had seen, partly suggested by the name, an untidy, shambling middle-aged man with worn shoes, who might have bits of string in his pocket, and perhaps the New Statesman under his arm, exuding an air of innocence, defeat and general inefficiency. When I explained this Carol said, 'We don't want any of your character acting. Play it straight. Don't act'. (in Wapshott 1990: 302)

Aside from providing a necessary antidote to the more colourful acting of Coward, Ralph Richardson and Ernie Kovacs as Captain Segura, the characteristic self-effacement of the Guinness persona – masterfully analysed by Neil Sinyard (2001: 143–54) – suited Reed's aim to produce a kind of comic Everyman character in Wormold.

Guinness's enigmatic quality, that blend of knowing inscrutability and chameleon-like adaptability to roles of seemingly limitless versatility (the Oedipally fixated master criminal in *The Ladykillers* (Mackendrick, 1955)), the aristocrats in *Kind Hearts and Coronets* (Hamer, 1949), the working-class Eastender in *Oliver Twist* (Lean, 1948)), the Arab in *Lawrence of Arabia* (Lean, 1962) or the Indian in *Passage to India* (Lean, 1984)), seems ideal for a character fascinated by the exotic lure of the Hispanic Caribbean, and yet whose residual Englishness prevents him from unconditional surrender to its charm. The key to the Wormold character is a remark made in the original novel by Beatrice, the agent sent out by London to assist their man in Havana in his spying mission: 'I don't care a damn about men who are loyal to the people who pay them, to organizations ... I don't think even my country means all that much. There are many countries in our blood, aren't there, but only one person. Would the world be in the mess it is if we were loyal to love and not to countries?' (Greene 1971: 190–1). Loyalty is a recurrent theme in work by Greene and Reed; one thinks especially of the conflict between love and duty in *The Third Man, Outcast of the Islands*, or *Oliver!* In Reed's films the flawed protagonists struggle for authenticity and moral courage in parables of betrayal and guilt. Wormold, treated with a lighter touch – as befits a comedy – than the protagonists of some of these films is, even so, a divided character, full of surprise and contradiction, an Englishman who chooses to live in Hispanic America, a Protestant married to and abandoned by a Catholic, an *habanero* who plans to send his only daughter to a Swiss finishing school, a law-abiding shop-keeper/salesman who turns into a liar, betrayer and killer. Not simply, as Robert Moss maintains (1987: 232), a picture of innocence – though he is that as well – Wormold is the living conceit of Beatrice's man (or woman) of many countries, something stressed even more in the film through its gloss on the Guinness persona as, perhaps above all, an actor of comedy.

At one point Wormold begins to play the fool, impersonating a clown whose performance he and his daughter have recently attended. The scene occurs in his daughter's bedroom, so as well as serving as a moment of self-consciousness, a kind of metafictional commentary on the Guinness persona, Wormold's impersonation of a clown highlights features of the relationship between father and daughter. A contrast is made between two kinds of folly: Hawthorne's refusal to treat people as separate entities, moulding them instead into forms of subjective impression; Wormold's embrace of difference and otherness. Each, though, has traces of the other: Hawthorne's campness is a mask of otherness; Wormold's talk of finishing schools for his daughter, and his eventual seduction by Hawthorne's retainer, a sign of conformity. As the screenplay states, 'His dream is to earn enough money to leave Cuba and to send his daughter to a Swiss finishing school'. When Wormold makes his way to his daughter's bedroom, darkness has already fallen. He taps respectfully on the bedroom doorframe before entering the room. As he sits down on her bed, the tilted camera angle combines with the shadowy lighting effects to act as a sort of prelude to the slightly skewed, deficient nature of this single parent family. Wormold begins, with Hawthorne's mislaid umbrella, to untie the ribbon on a box from which he fishes out the bridle Milly has bought in the hope her father will buy her the horse to put it on. He places the bridle around his daughter's neck, a gesture that presages their eventually mutual enslavement by worldly values. Guinness's projection of 'gentleness', what Orwell considered the most marked characteristic of English civilisation (1988: 41), perfectly captures some of the ambivalence of the Wormold character. On the one hand Wormold's reserve and 'gentleness' represent a suspicion of flamboyance and militarism; on the other, this gentleness masks other forms of repression, of prejudice, violence and even barbarism. To take only the question of class, Orwell comments that the English electoral system 'is an all but open fraud, gerrymandered in the interests of the moneyed class' (1988: 45). This mixture of compromise and insularity, one suspects, has prompted Wormold to find refuge in Cuban exoticism. Significantly, in Havana, he defies stereotype by appearing to be an integrated ex-patriot, going so far as to correct Hawthorne's solecism, informing him that 'manos' in Spanish is a feminine not masculine noun, when the latter mistakes him for an interloper in his hotel room and orders him to raise his arms with the Spanish command '¡Arriba los [sic] manos!'

Wormold's reticence and self-absorption prepare the audience – both the real one, and its surrogate, his daughter Milly – for his enactment of the sad clown, a variant of what Andrew Spicer (2003) has defined as the recurrent stock type of the Fool in British cinema, a spontaneous performance that captures the essence of role and persona. Like Canio, the clown in *Pagliacci*, Wormold is a spurned husband. Nothing is known about the causes of his wife's departure, but we suspect the deficiencies, the aloofness and self-containment of role and persona may have played a part. Wormold springs up from his daughter's bedside, and approaches the wardrobe mirror, where he hunches his shoulders, stands to attention, lifts one finger, and with a slight shake of the head, admires himself uttering the words, 'Tax uh-free!' Through the pronunciation, like the pose, he mimics Noel Coward. Although at first more than ideology separates the two men, a gulf marked by Wormold's failure to understand Hawthorne's jargon ('the drill', etc.) each grows closer to the other, as the effect of Hawthorne's presence seems to tease out the dormant instincts of a personality not entirely colonised by the exotic. Significantly, as Wormold steps out of his Noel Coward impersonation and into the role of clown, he retains a key prop of the Master's, his umbrella. Formulating the words 'we should all be clowns, Milly', Wormold wears a makeshift hat – what looks like a fruit basket – holding and then opening Hawthorne's umbrella. The remark about clowning seems to refer to Guinness's own history as an actor – the clown of numerous Ealing and other comedies – as well as to comment on Wormold's attitude of mockery towards the establishment, the world of agents and feuding governments, as if suddenly disabused of conventional moral or patriotic codes to which through natural innocence he had once been inclined. The life-force of the clown is commemorated in Wormold's pirouette; but his partial reliance on a prop associated with Hawthorne, symbol not only of campness but also perhaps in this context most especially of the establishment, dramatises that tension in the Wormold character between deviance and conformity. The clown – the lower man mocking members of the higher world, the *eiron* who knows more than his privileged targets of ridicule – serves the historic purpose of subverting the laws of normality and convention. In keeping, too, with the traditions of comedy, the comedian here uses disguise as a means of both liberating and acknowledging desire, his art once more justifying the dependence on lies as pathways to truth.

The caricature version of Wormold, circus clown crossed with Noel Coward, is partly regressive – the activation of pre-Oedipal drives – and partly immanent, an endorsement of worldliness and bewitchment by the decadence all around, the domain of call girls, brothels and vice of Batista's Cuba, and its softer reflection in the world represented by Hawthorne. Once the decision is taken to make the devilish pact with Hawthorne and his paymasters, the dual nature of the Wormold character becomes increasingly pronounced. The assumption of the role of master spy unlocks Wormold's creative potential.

His relish for deceiving the establishment, as he effortlessly invents characters, situations and dangerous weapons, also unleashes darker instincts, as the film carefully steers a course between thriller and comedy. The darker elements are linked to acquisitiveness, materialism and even violence. Like the symbiotic tie between Holly Martins and Harry Lime in *The Third Man*, or Mike and Tino in *Trapeze*, the relationship between Hawthorne and Wormold if not exactly symbiotic begins to shade into uniformity, to the point where Wormold not only begins to talk like Hawthorne, he even develops an agent's killer instinct. When Wormold discovers the identity of the betrayer who is out to assassinate him, he has little hesitation in pulling the trigger himself. At times, in the later stages of the film, as the thriller mode threatens to overshadow the comic, the photography by Oswald Morris and the sets by John Box recall the camerawork and décor of *The Third Man* (photography by Robert Krasker, sets by Vincent Korda) and *Odd Man Out* (Krasker again and Ralph Brinton), with low or tilted angles, elongated shadows, momentarily transforming Havana from the sunny libidinal pearl of the Antilles into the equivalent of Troubles-torn Belfast or post-war Vienna, as Wormold, too, becomes a clone of his mentor Hawthorne. The latent violence of otherwise docile characters – like Hasselbacher, who even puts on his German military uniform in melancholy recognition of his own unconquered aggressiveness – begins to surface in worlds superficially opposed, but fundamentally similar, where Wormold, Hawthorne, and Carter temporarily mutate into the clones of the film's arch-villain and representative of Batista criminality, Captain Segura, the 'Red Vulture', who ghoulishly owns a wallet made of human skin. In the same way that the purloined umbrella indicated Wormold's affinity with its rightful owner, so too his theft of Captain Segura's pistol stresses the growing identity of two seemingly opposed individuals. But the links between Wormold and Segura are problematic. Especially in its early stages, the film is keen to represent the barbarism and brutality of the pre-Castro dictatorship, but the new government was perhaps understandably nervous about the dangers of humanising its representative (based on the real Chief of Police, Captain Ventura). Ernie Kovacs's performance positions Segura in a long line of amiable film villains, at the cost of realism and accuracy forcing him into a stereotype of Latin American villainy (e.g. Cesar Romero in countless films or, in *The Mark of Zorro* (Mamoulian, 1940), Basil Rathbone), a mixture of brutality and charm.

Wormold later returns Segura's pistol, as if ultimately rejecting his own brutal tendencies. He also returns Hawthorne's umbrella, but the more enduring effects of Hawthorne's seduction do not require the testimony of a single prop. The re-invention of himself as an agent goes beyond Reed's interest in psychology and once more into another characteristic theme, meditation on the truths of art. As in *Odd Man Out*, *The Third Man*, and *The Agony and the Ecstasy* artist and author figures allow for reflection on questions of representation and creativity. In *Our Man in Havana*, too, beyond their significance as an expression of the psychology of their author, Wormold's drawings, in keeping with his other inventions (false reports, fabrications of self and others) invite meditation on the flaws of perception in ordering reality according to prejudice and desire. The distorted view of Hawthorne and his Whitehall superiors of the vacuum-cleaner drawing as a highly sophisticated rocket or 'weapon of mass destruction' belongs to the tradition of deluded fictional characters epitomised by Don Quixote (the inspiration of course for a later Greene novel, *Monsignor Quixote* (1985)), who mistook a barber's basin for Mambrino's helmet and windmills for giants.

The end is ambiguous. On the one hand the film allows Wormold to regress to Britishness, confirming his rescue from the exotic, returning him to his native English habitat, to what Greene describes, even though he is referring to the betrayer Carter, as 'English snobbery, English vulgarity, all the sense of kinship and security the word "England" implied' (1971: 167). On the other, the absurdity of the English way is exposed through the solution of the Whitehall mandarins – led by Ralph Richardson – to decorate Wormold rather than risk their own ridicule by exposing and punishing his deception. The film seems, additionally, to veer towards romantic comedy in allowing Wormold to find redemption through love. The relationship between Wormold and Beatrice is never properly developed since, in any case, Guinness showed little talent for playing the romantic comedy gallant. Redemption, a key element of Greene's Catholic themes, makes for awkward inclusion when its strictly theological aspects are touched on (as in the clowning scene), but in its more secularised form, as the means through which Wormold's fate through suffering is ultimately sealed, it plays a vital part. The female agent's intervention in his life brings to a conclusion Wormold's conflation of father and lover, an Englishman abroad released from patriarchy – the authority of Hawthorne, the Whitehall controllers, and the fatherland – a Dante restored to the inferno of insular England but rehumanised by another, more spirited Beatrice. As the couple leave MI5 headquarters, the effect of their visual imprisonment in the *mise-en-scène* of Parliament Square, the capital's most potent symbol of Englishness – with Big Ben towering meaningfully over them – is offset by the soundtrack's recourse to Havana-coded music, indicating perhaps the couple's only partial restoration to Englishness, and their continued remembrance of things in their recent exotic past.

Outcast of the Islands (1951)

Any film directed by Carol Reed after *The Third Man* was bound to attract attention. Reviewers expecting another masterpiece found themselves almost unanimously expressing disappointment at *Outcast of the Islands*. *The Daily Mail*'s comments are representative:

> The difficulty of poor Carol Reed is that he has been the best British film-maker for so long. It is a harsh responsibility. He has himself created the dazzling standards by which he must be judged. A new Carol Reed film is automatically a special occasion. He cannot afford the luxury of being merely good ... It is necessary to go almost out of one's way to record the view that Mr Reed's new picture, Outcast of the Islands (Plaza), is a profound disappointment. (Anon 1952)

Reasons given for this widespread disappointment ranged from the failure to quarry a gripping film from the pages of a respected novel, to criticism of the film's preoccupation with the exotic spectacle of the Far East at the expense of psychological depth. Looking back at the film now it is clear that *Outcast* belongs to that group of 1950s films that, as Mackillop and Sinyard argue (2003b), challenge the conformist reputation of British films made during the decade. Madness in *Bridge on the River Kwai* (Lean, 1957), cruelty in *Orders to Kill* (Asquith, 1958), psychological crises of various kinds in *Ice Cold in Alex* (Lee Thompson, 1958) reflect the turmoil of an age caught between the conflicting impulses of deference and progress. Reed's 1950s films belong to this pattern; the behaviour of his protagonists ranges from the self-destructiveness of Willems in *Outcast* to the treachery of Ivo in *The Man Between* to the fantasy-life of Joe in *A Kid for Two Farthings*, to the complex sexuality of Ribble in *Trapeze* and the death wish of David in *The Key*, although the last two are strictly speaking American productions.

Although *Outcast* was a project of Korda's, it obviously appealed to

Reed since it enabled him to explore familiar territory: foreign settings, and a parent/child narrative. But where, say, *Midshipman Easy, The Way Ahead, The Young Mr Pitt* and *Odd Man Out* concentrate on heroism, *Outcast*, as do *Odd Man Out* and *The Third Man*, reviews its underside. The exotic archipelago setting of *Outcast* provides many of the necessary conditions for male trials of strength but, as with many Conrad narratives, it substitutes failure for heroic triumph. The elemental *mise-en-scène* – rough seas, monsoons, rotting flora – provides the appropriate background for an inquest into the very nature of the exotic itself. Set in and around Singapore, often referred to in the film as a haven of civilisation, in comparison with the outlying areas, the film locates its story of the moral abyss into which its principal character descends in the closing stages of British colonial rule in the region. Singapore had been British since 1819, becoming a colony in 1867, its strategic position, intersecting the Indian and Pacific oceans, making it a key location coveted by the Japanese, who invaded it in 1942. It was recovered by the British and held from 1945 until independence in 1959. While obviously not expected to make any direct links between the film (and its *fin de siècle* setting) and recent events in the island's history, audiences would nevertheless have probably appreciated the continuing modern commercial significance of Singapore and surrounding islands, and would perhaps have read the paternalistic attitude of the colonialists, and emerging unrest among the locals, against the background of the struggle for economic and strategic supremacy in the Far East between the Allies and the Japanese.

The clash of cultures is displaced in the film onto, on the European side, Lingard (Ralph Richardson), Willems (Trevor Howard), Almayer (Robert Morley), his wife (Wendy Hillier) and daughter (Annabel Morley), and various minor characters who appear in Sambi at the start of the film. The other, native, side is occupied by the partially blind Babalatchi (George Coulouris), the wholly blind Badawi (A. V. Bramble), father of Aissa (Kerima), and by a multitude of nameless indigenous characters, especially children, who are a sort of silenced chorus, complementing the colonised and metaphorically blinded commentary on proceedings of their elders. The opponents of the whites and, to a lesser extent, of the natives are the Arabs, led by Abdullah. The struggle by all three groups for mastery of the economic opportunities of these territories is crystallised in attempts by Willems, an involuntary exile, to satisfy his own needs, along the way compromising even those through fatal attraction to the native femme fatale, Aissa.

The film's key motif is exile, from the self, as well as from geographical and cultural roots. Both novel and film focus on the doomed attempts by their listless central character Willems to integrate himself in an alien culture. But whereas the novel partly explains his wayward-ness through hurriedly sketched childhood history, the film makes no direct connections with Willems's infancy, leaving the viewer to speculate about the causes of self-destruction. Conrad's description of Willems's origins, however hurried, is clear: 'Father outdoor clerk of some ship-broker in Rotterdam; mother dead. The boy quick in learning, but idle in school. The straitened circumstances of the house filled with small brothers and sisters, sufficiently clothed and fed but otherwise running wild' (Conrad 1992: 16). The film provides no hint, other than through his name, that Willems is Dutch. As Willems, Trevor Howard makes no attempt to speak English like a Dutchman. One wonders whether, had Orson Welles been given the role, promised him, so he claimed, by Reed, more would have been made of the Dutch nuances: 'I can only regret that he [Korda] took such a lengthy and elaborate means of dislodging me since this was not only financially very costly to myself but, as you may imagine, the most disappointing and humiliating experience of my professional life ... I am sure I don't need to tell you how many good things I wish the picture, and you may know already that my admiration and affection for you are only a little bit this side of idolitry [sic]' (Welles n/d). Welles's slightly tongue in cheek concluding flourish in his letter to Reed does not soften the force of his anger at denial of an opportunity to use a fee from *Outcast* to help finance his film version of *Othello* (1951). As the star of *The Third Man* he could justifiably feel aggrieved by Korda's broken promise over the casting of Reed's follow-up film. But Welles would have been unsuitable as Willems. The masterful over-sized sybaritic persona is inconsistent with the pinched, more famished look of Howard, whose slightly pock-marked face and sunken cheeks suggest under-nourishment, perfectly suited, as Willems, to the role of a desperate man hungry for wealth. His more gaunt features are pressed into the service here not of the understated values of the English military policeman in *The Third Man*, but of the inwardly scarred and ruthless but incompetent over-reacher, another of Reed's 'men between', caught between incompatible worlds, migrants from home and their own nobler selves.

Migration has been defined as 'man's attempts to move on in search of knowledge, wherever it may be found and also his tendency to put obstacles in the way of such an attempt, punishing it so that the migrant's experience follows a pattern of 'migration-exile-expulsion, with the resultant pain, confusion, and loss of communication' (Grinberg and Grinberg 1999: 154). The trajectory of Willems's life follows this pattern. Each step towards knowledge is followed by an act of self-destruction: rescued by Lingard from aimlessness and given financial and emotional security by the successful English trader, Willems abandons his benefactor to work for Hudink, whom he embezzles. Sacked by Hudink, and rescued once more from adversity, he is placed by Lingard at the trading-post run by Almayer, his son in law, where again, after a promising start, he reverts to type and enters into a disastrous sexual relationship with Aissa, a liaison that plunges him ever deeper into betrayal and despair, finally driving Lingard to disown his *protégé* forever.

This cycle of self-destruction, or repetition compulsion, is readable in socio-historical as well as in psychological terms, a view encouraged by Willems's incandescent answer, 'The Devil's not in me', in reply to Lingard's accusation, 'You have been possessed of a Devil!'. As regards the former, Willems stands for Europe. Like Kurtz in *Heart of Darkness*, it could be said of him that 'all Europe contributed to his making'. As such, he bears the brunt of European guilt towards its exploitation of territories to which it had no lawful claim. The chorus of natives who balefully witness the economic power games of the foreigners in their midst is not only composed of stereotypical trouble-makers but also uncomprehending elders and, above all, of bright-eyed children in whose expression may be read the anticipated joy of their country's eventual self-determination and liberation from the colonialists. On this reading, Willems's downfall is also Europe's. Lingard tells Babalatchi, with all the self-justifying arrogance of the imperialist, 'This is a peaceful place, a thriving place because I've made it so.' At what price, the colonised might well ask, and through Babalatchi's rhetorical reply, loses no time in doing so: 'Does the white man know what is best for us?,' a question as relevant to Reed's 1950s audiences as to the turn of the century readers for whom Conrad wrote. The film belongs to the tradition in literature, as well as in film, of narratives concerned with Empire. By the time of the making of *Outcast*, the focus is on loss rather than celebration, something expressed as much through the personal agonies of its protagonist, Willems, as through the post-war contraction of British colonies and dominions (e.g. India, Pakistan, Burma, Ceylon, all lost in the late 1940s or early 1950s).

The psychological implications of Willems's tragedy are as complex as the socio-political dimensions. Willems's pursuit of wealth corresponds to the migrant's 'intense sorrow for all that has been abandoned or lost, fear of the unknown, and a very profound experience of loneliness, privation and helplessness' (Grinberg and Grinberg 1999: 168–9), feelings that are consistent with the unstable psychology of many Reed protagonists. Willems, like a character from a Somerset Maugham

story, or like Firmin in Lowry's *Under the Volcano* (1947), seems
motivated by a self-destructive urgency, seeking damnation rather than
redemption in a Far Eastern paradise, his ill-defined transgression an
anticipation of the unfocused rage of the 'Angry Young Men' .

Willems's condition recalls Melanie Klein's notion of persecutory
guilt which, in contrast to the feelings of nostalgia and sense of
responsibility shown by the individual suffering from depressive guilt,
expresses itself, as Leon and Rebeca Grinberg point out, in resentment,
despair, fear and self-reproach (1999: 162). Like all migrants, at the very
least, by accident, design or necessity Willems has lost his country.
Whatever advantages seemed likely as he placed himself under Lingard's
tutelage are balanced by the inevitable loss, in the liminal spaces of a life
at sea and distant lands, of cultural roots and emotional security.
Lingard is another of Reed's father-figures looking out for a fatherless
waif, but he is also Willems' Charon, steering him to an exotic Hades,
the *mise-en-scène* of his unresolved Oedipal desires.

Since the father/son bond between Lingard and Willems is
characterised by rebellion and deceit as well as by affection and concern,
their friendship plays out a displaced and unfinished family drama.
Ralph Richardson reprises his role from *The Fallen Idol* of the surrogate
father, here also literally fulfilling the role of heroic overseas traveller
and hunter that, as Baines, he could only ever pretend to have been.
Richardson's face is almost unrecognisable beneath the layers of facial
hair that smother his characteristically clean-shaven appearance. Even
where reviewers were unconvinced by the film as a whole, Richardson
was singled out for praise. *The Daily Mail*'s reference to him as 'convincing' is representative (Anon 1952). The film capitalises on Richardson's
slightly off-centre performance style, his eccentricity fitting perfectly the
role of a skipper with the mind of a *souk* merchant, whose shrewdness
and strength of purpose manage to safeguard the secret of the seas and
the safe passage through treacherous waters known only to him.
Nevertheless, the neat and trim appearance of his Captain Lingard,
contradicting perhaps the wilder look of authentic sea dogs ploughing
the oceans around Borneo, adds an important dimension to his role as
Willems's surrogate father.

The clipped appearance is the outward sign of Lingard's self-control,
the very order by which the surrogate son is both drawn and repelled.
Lingard's patriarchal self-mastery – reflected not only in his dealings
with others but also in his smart appearance – contrasts with Willems's
gradual moral and physical dishevelment. At the height of his good
fortune, Willems cuts a dash, his well-groomed appearance, smart
colonial suit, floral tie and stylish waistcoat a dandified reflection of

Lingard's dapper Dan sense of fashion. But the seeds of his degradation have already been sown, and from the moment of his dismissal by Hudink, his gradual sartorial decline records his moral and psychological ruin. As time passes, once he is again taken under Lingard's wing, Willems's steady loss of control is conveyed through costume. As in *Carmen Jones* (Preminger, 1954) where Joe's loss of his military uniform provides the evidence of his inner collapse, so too in *Outcast* Willems's disintegration is measured by change of costume, and in both cases decline is accelerated through involvement with a fatal woman.

In *Outcast*, though, Aissa is not alone the cause of Willems's tragedy. The roots of his tragedy lie perhaps further back, in childhood, displaced in adulthood on to his father-substitute, Lingard. After his dismissal, and meeting up again with Lingard, Willem bursts out: 'It's all your fault!', a love-hatred reaching its climax when in the film's final scenes a confrontation takes place between the two men. Here Willems shifts the blame from the father-surrogate to Aissa, and though disowned and struck in the face by Lingard, he cannot bring himself to shoot his paternal assailant.

The displaced father/son relationship is mirrored by the real father/daughter relationship between Babalatchi and Aissa. That union reinforces the tribal and cultural identity of the pair in the face of the colonialist menace, and dramatises the responsibilities of daughters in south Asian societies, allowing Reed to contrast a dysfunctional parent/child relationship with one that in many ways is loving and respectful, in another of the wish fulfilment fantasies of family harmony conjured up by a director with an unconventional childhood.

The fierce loyalty displayed by Aissa to her father is an unmistakable gesture of solidarity with her own culture. Whenever a conflict arises between attendance on Willems or her father she never doubts where duty lies. Beyond that show of defiance, and lifted out of the context of the cultural significance of their relationship, Aissa personifies the conciliatory, dutiful daughter. She is also a motherless child, substituting for her mother in her father's life. And yet, in submission to her father, whom she considers invested with magical powers, Aissa is in other ways an independent powerful spirit. Her forcefulness represents at once the native's defiant anti-colonialism, an affront to the white man whose difference and economic superiority are undeniably attractive, as well as, indirectly – again, beyond the culturally specific boundaries of her role – the European woman's persecution by what Victoria Secunda calls the 'tyranny of femininity' (1993: 269). She is also the deflected expression of tensions arising out of the return to domesticity by women liberated from convention in wartime. When after Aissa abandons him for her ailing father, Willems rages that he, not her father, is now her owner, the comparison he makes between ownership by parent or lover further identifies the two men in Aissa's life, and reinforces the film's interest in processes of displacement. Perhaps, too, Aissa intuits the real nature of Willems's feelings for her, even though, as Willems himself muses in an early close-shot, when the camera focuses on their faces locked in an embrace: 'What a perfect relationship ours is. I wonder what you'd think if you could understand a word of what I said. I could even tell you the truth if I knew what it was – something between loving and hating. Stronger than either.'

The contradictory but related drives of love and hate stem from both local and primordial origins. At one level, Willems's attraction to Aissa is a stereotypical representation of the European male's fascination with the exotic female. Reed, through Conrad, follows in the footsteps of Flaubert in *Salambô* (1862), Gauguin in his South Seas pictures, or Rider Haggard's *She* (1886), in exploring the sexuality of the female other. True to characteristically 'Orientalist' indifference to representation of the reality of Malayan women, where the imperatives of genre and box office glamour over-ride other considerations, Kerima, an Algerian woman, not a Malayan, was cast as Aissa. Conrad's native woman with 'the face of a golden statue with living eyes' (Conrad 1992: 71) is a solemn beauty, whose allure in the script is defined in line with exotic convention:

> She neither speaks nor moves in this scene and for most of it her eyes are lowered to the ground. But even in repose it is impossible not to be aware of the sinuous beauty of her body, the strange compelling strength of her personality. Her face is by no means pretty or even attractive in the Western sense and yet it is startlingly beautiful – deeply savagely beautiful with a suggestion of underlying passion – a beauty that is at once as old as the world and as young as today. This is Aissa, daughter of Badawi – perhaps she is twenty years old but it is impossible to be sure – for another twenty years or so, until her face suddenly withers into that of an old woman, she will retain the agelessness of the East. (Fairchild 1951: 42–3)

Silenced here by an 'Orientalist' script, Aissa remains mute throughout the film, her lowered gaze the sign of submission, especially to her father, a condition that speaks as much of Western fantasy as of Eastern reality. Also tellingly, the script emphasises her sexual aura, stressing her minatory allure, or 'savagery', illustrating Rana Kabbani's argument that the eroticism promised by the East was mystery laced with violence (1994: 68). Aissa's sexuality is the stage for European control, a Western projection onto the Eastern exotic of contradictory desires. But colonisation, as Homi Babha argues, is not one-dimensional. Rather it leads to an ambivalence towards otherness on the part of the coloniser, something that, as Robert Young also notes, indicates that 'colonial discourse is founded in anxiety, and that colonial power itself is subject to the effects of a conflictual economy' (1993: 142). And yet, as in the case of Orientalist paintings, the desirable woman was, as Rana Kabbani further comments, 'hardly ever "foreign" looking ... conformed closely with conventional standards of European beauty' (1994: 80–1). Kerima, a dusky Algerian with European features, combines the uncharted allure of the exotic with the reassuring impact of the familiar. This is the woman whom Willems both loves and hates. Desire offers Willems liberation from himself, and self-discovery through the embrace of the other, but it is also a route to anxiety about loss of autonomy resulting from the fear of feminisation, and perhaps, even more deeply, self-loathing prompted by the white man's horror of miscegenation. A dissolute Dionysus, Willems surrenders through alcohol and sex not to the willing transformation of the self but to despair. The alliance with Aissa , though, also ultimately belongs to the pattern of Willems's rebellion against the law of the father, a law embodied in his real, but absent and never mentioned father, displaced onto Lingard and also, through a further process of displacement, onto Aissa's father, Badawi. A social and cultural protest, the white man's transgression against the taboo of miscegenation is also the cry of an adult still suffering an infant's pain of rejection. Aissa, then, is additionally the absent mother towards whom his deepest, ambivalent, desires are directed.

The white women, who also to some extent belong to this pattern of comparisons and displacements, serve not only to provide insipid contrasts to the fiery sexuality of Aissa, the bad mother chosen above the good mother, Mrs Almayer, but also to expose the restrictions imposed on their own lives by prevailing attitudes. Willems's treatment of his wife as a drudge ('You nag, you must not nag'), a woman instantly forgotten once the fateful voyage with Lingard begins, is eclipsed in pathos only by the ashen portrayal of Almayer's wife. Like Ethan's sister in law in *The Searchers* (Ford, 1956), caught fondly caressing Willems's coat in an unmistakable gesture of undeclared love for her brother in law, Mrs Almayer is drawn to Willems like a moth to a flame. Tired of her infantile husband, whose impatience, sneering remarks about her wardrobe and affection for none but his spoilt daughter (Morley's real life daughter), she is the reluctant epitome of the woman trapped by parenthood, upbringing and perhaps, above all, by economic circumstances in a marriage devoid of love and respect. When Willems, outwardly a man of risk and adventure, wanders into her life she cannot avoid glimmers of envy and desire as she hears him describe his unconquerable fascination for the native girl. Mrs Almayer's muted adulterous *amour fou* for Willems remains undeclared, her death-wish not powerful enough to fall prey to the call of the wild.

She remains a captive in marriage, while Willems is coupled with Aissa, as the rain pours down on both, uniting them, returning them to the destructive forces of nature neither has been able to resist. The revised draft of the script describes the finale in the following way: 'these two can never find peace but only torment – who can never be together and yet must always be together. It is as though each were seeing a vision of their own slow death. They are so still that they might already be as dead as the blank, unseeing, uncaring eyes of the graven images which watch over them.' In a second version of the script, the final description differs: 'she takes up her hair in her hands and inclines her head slowly over her shoulders, wringing out her long black tresses, twisting them persistently. She lets go of her hair [crossed out], it falls scattered over her shoulder like a funeral veil, she squats down suddenly, clasping her ankles, she rests her head on her drawn up knees and remains still, very still in the streaming mourning of her hair' (William Fairchild, Screenplay 2).

Separate shots of Willems and Aissa convey the solitude of these inseparable characters: a close-up of Aissa is followed by one of Willems as he looks out, from his hut, at the departing Lingard. The last image, a subjective shot, is of Lingard in his canoe, being navigated out of the frame by islanders, deserting forever the renegade Crusoe now left to the Oedipal mercy of his female Friday.

Neither this nor the revised script mentions the rain, nature's repossession of the characters, responding to their death-wish return to a state of inanimate being. As in *Heart of Darkness*, the self-destructive urges of the intruder (here Willems, in *Heart of Darkness* Kurtz), are matched by the havoc caused by nature itself, something already hinted at in Aissa's first appearance and already defined in Conrad's text: 'Through the checkered light between them she appeared to him with the impalpable distinctness of a dream. The very spirit of that land of mysterious forests, standing before him like an apparition behind a transparent veil – a veil woven of sunbeams and shadows' (1992: 70). The Eastern equivalent of the African *She*, or the Latin American Rana, the goddess of *Green Mansions* (W. H. Hudson, 1904), Aissa proves to be the nemesis of Willems, the bedraggled Western anti-hero enduring his penitential destiny in a mercilessly hostile paradise, plunging him ever deeper into the treacherous waters of a lost maternal paradise. The father's shadow has been cast off only to be replaced by the equally suffocating presence of the mother, her displaced version, Aissa, in the deadliest regions of Mother Nature, a remote and rain-soaked corner of the South Asian Seas.

The Man Between (1953)

After the mixed reception that greeted *Outcast of the Islands*, Reed reverted to a trusted formula, one that had brought him his greatest critical successes, the thriller format of *Night Train*, *Odd Man out*, *The Fallen Idol*, and, above all, *The Third Man*. But *The Man Between* fared no better than *Outcast*. In its favour was the casting of James Mason and Claire Bloom in key roles, against it, the absence of a script by Graham Greene, photography by Robert Krasker, and music by Anton Karas. Even so, the film has redeeming features, not the least of which is Reed's treatment of a favourite theme, troubled masculinity. As Johnny was torn between loyalty to a political cause and allegiance to a moral law, or Harry between love of self and of others, so Ivo wavers between the demands of opposed political systems. James Mason's Ivo lacks the youthful glamour of his wounded hero in *Odd Man Out*, but he is still charismatic in middle age, especially when at the end he yields to his better nature by helping Susanne (Claire Bloom) escape from the East, a final selfless gesture that makes all the more poignant his previous descent into blackmail and treachery in Cold War East Germany. Like Lime, Ivo is something of a dandy, his hat, snappy overcoat with a fur-trimmed collar, natural charm and *savoir faire* with women confirming disenchantment with the shabby, colourless world of post-war Eastern bloc countries, where streets are overshadowed not by the sexualised advertisements for Western materialism but huge posters of the regime's political masters.

Set in Berlin, with all its potential for East/West tensions following the Berlin airlift in 1948 and the growing hysteria in relations between the USA, UK and the USSR, the collision between Ivo, a victim of experience, the casualty of a defeated country now ruled by ruthless ideologues, and the wide-eyed innocent young woman, the female equivalent of what Robert Moss refers to as the often featured 'naif' of Reed's films, made for an engrossing drama, recalling but also developing areas explored in earlier work.

Susanne's first glimpse of Ivo is of his hat and coat hanging over a bar stool in the restaurant to which she has been taken by her brother Martin and sister in law Bettina (Hildegarde Neff). The suggestion here of mystery is reinforced by an early impression of Ivo's hollow identity, of a man playing a part forced on him by external as well as internal pressures, a character reduced to the trappings of a self. Ivo's self-awareness, even self-loathing, is expressed in words when, much later, Susanne attempts to explain his behaviour through appeal to extenuating circumstances:

> IVO: I took part in the plunder of Holland and France. I saw hostages executed ...
> SUSANNE: So you were ordered!
> IVO: I was ordered. I did not invite you to set yourself up as my judge to say I am innocent ...

The film ran into many difficulties, especially over budget and screenplay. Reed was forced to cut back on location shooting in Germany, eventually succumbing to Korda's orders in increasingly impatient telegrams: 'You may remember how often I tried to impress upon you that to shoot night after night extreme long shots requiring a large organisation was not right and that it would make very little difference in the final picture if this very expensive method of shooting should be economically handled in order to finish in the shortest possible period of time' (Korda 1953).

Well before these difficulties and squabbles with Korda, Reed had had misgivings about the screenplay by Harry Kurnitz, finding it humourless and turgid. His attempts to hire other writers to improve it ended with the appointment of Eric Linklater, after various other writers had been approached, including Graham Greene, who declined the invitation: 'A general criticism I have of the first fifty scenes is that I have no idea what the story is about. Perhaps this would not matter if the events were startling and mysterious enough, but they are neither startling nor mysterious ... It seems to me that the whole story is meaningless and flat without a living character in it. A thriller about Europe today has simply got to have some significance about it and not simply end in long exciting chases ... (Greene n/d a). Even James Mason, after a first reading of the screenplay, complained in a telegram to Reed of its lack of humour: 'Liked shape of script very much but as you say dialogue somewhat dry and humourless enthusiasm unabated [*sic*]' (Mason 1952). The remarks about the humourlessness seem justified, especially when inevitable comparisons would unfavourably be made with *The Third Man*, but Greene's comments about the political shallowness of the narrative seem less persuasive. They hint at a great writer's condescension towards a screenplay written by a rival in a genre he considers his own. The film does, indeed, end, as Greene notes, in a chase, but to claim it has no thematic significance is to do it an injustice.

The toing and froing from East to West not only sets up superficial contrasts between twin settings governed by opposed political systems, but also creates a spatial metaphor for mental processes blurring distinctions between ideologically defined concepts of good and evil. *The Man Between* reflects the pathology of clashing cultures stifled by the paranoid measures of defensive ideologies. The film was made at the height of the Cold War, against a background of spies and mutual suspicion typified by the Burgess/Maclean affair, the arrest of the Rosenbergs, and the case of Alger Hiss, but propaganda on both sides fails to reduce the complexity with which human motivation and behaviour is treated. Ivo lives in the East, but he is also ultimately the film's, admittedly tarnished, hero. Like other Reed figures (Baines, Willems, Mr Kandinsky) he is idolised by a boy, Horst (Dieter Kraus), who follows him around, looking out for his safety, acting as a mercurial messenger and, above all, like the cat whose fondness for humans extends only to Harry Lime, to affirm the redeeming features of a man vilified on both sides of the Iron Curtain.

Partly through desperate circumstances, partly through egotism, Ivo is engaged in blackmail. Blackmailed himself by the East Berlin chief of police, Halender (Ernest Schroeder), he responds by blackmailing Bettina, who lives on the West side, and to whom he is still legally married. Thinking he had died in the war, she has married Martin (Geoffrey Toone), a British official whose sister Susanne eventually becomes infatuated with Ivo. Through these two women the film measures the innocence of the British against the experience of the European. Claire Bloom's fresh English rose plucked from the sheltered environment of the Home Counties is, though, clearly unsuited to the climate of the continent in which Bettina, her more hardened sister in law survives. The heavies, as in *The Third Man*, are all on one side, their totalitarian ideology best represented by Halender, a man of Sidney Greenstreet's girth, but with none of the latter's Falstaffian humour lightening his sinister persona. The one exception is Ivo, the man-between, his shuttles between East and West a measure of the film's interest in political alternatives and provisional forms of national or personal identity. By no stretch of the imagination a politically committed director, Reed makes of Ivo – the agent from the East – another divided character, thus avoiding simplistic contrasts between East and West, or political virtue and vice. In the scene at the restaurant, a dissolve from a close-shot of Bettina's face to a clown's invites reflection on her deception and betrayal by Ivo as well as her identification with the Allied forces in power in West Berlin.

Despite details such as this, as well as memorable scenes in an ice rink, during part of Susanne's guided tour through the underworld of East Berlin by Ivo, her suave and self-motivated Pluto, or in one of the shattered post-war city's street locations, *The Man Between* is no rival to *The Third Man*. But, for all its flaws, including James Mason's implausible German accent, in its explorations of innocence and experience, and the inner tensions of a man torn between rival allegiances, the film bears the hallmarks of Reed's thematic territory. In *The Man Between* the Euripidean touch – a character dies, like Alcestis, so another may live – gives the film even more poignancy.

A Kid for Two Farthings (1955)

Reed's last film for Korda at London Films, *A Kid for Two Farthings*, sees him focusing more directly on aspects of British life before launching himself as an international, Hollywood-backed director. The title, as Robert Moss (1987: 211) points out, refers to a Jewish song, 'One kid, one kid, which my father bought for two farthings', and announces the film's interest in East End Jewry, though other ethnicities are also acknowledged. The screenplay was written by Wolf Mankowitz, the location shooting took place in Petticoat Lane (renamed 'Fashion Street'), and many of the roles given to Jewish actors, above all, David Kossoff, Sidney James, Sidney Tafler and Alfie Bass. Much criticism, both contemporary and subsequent, has centred on the film's eclecticism in its choice of actors and actresses with different backgrounds and accents, but in this it follows Reed tradition (as in *The Stars Look Down* and *Odd Man Out*). The upper-class accents of Celia Johnson as Joanna, and Jonathan Ashmore as Joe, were considered inappropriate for a mother and son scraping a living at the grubby shop of Mr Kandinsky (Kossoff). As ever in a Reed film, hybridity may be regarded a strength, since strict social realism seems to have been relegated here to secondary importance. As well as raising questions about British ethnicity, the film returns to Reed's familiar territory of child psychology. Fed stories by Mr Kandinsky about the magical wish-fulfilment powers of unicorns, Joe buys a kid goat believing it to be, on the evidence of its single crumpled horn, a unicorn. He wishes for many things, such as that Mr Kandinsky gets the steam trouser-press that he cannot afford, and for himself, above all, that his father comes home from Africa.

Christine Geraghty (2000) has drawn attention to the number of child-centred films made in the 1950s, highlighting the relevance to these of work by child psychologists such as John Bowlby and D. W. Winnicott. Screened only two years after the publication of John

Bowlby's hugely influential *Child Care and the Growth of Love* (1953), *A Kid for Two Farthings* complicates the view that, although the father's role in a child's life is clearly important, partial or complete maternal deprivation could lead to the child's serious disturbance: 'Partial deprivation brings in its train an anxiety, excessive need for love, powerful feelings of revenge, and arising from these last, guilt and depression ... complete deprivation ... may entirely cripple the capacity to make relationships with other people' (Bowlby 1953: 14). In *A Kid for Two Farthings*, though, firstly, the mother is not at home attending to the child's needs, but at work, since her husband's absence necessitates her employment. Secondly, the child does not seem wholly contented by the availability of his mother, and is more concerned with mourning the absence of his father. The anxieties of the child are focused on the father, illustrating Winnicott's argument that 'one of the things that a father does for his children is to be alive and stay alive during the children's early years ... Although it is natural for children to idealise their fathers, it is also very valuable for them to have the experience of living with them and getting to know them as human beings, even to the point of finding them out' (1962: 84). Meanwhile, the child's mother (Celia Johnson) reflects the reality of married British women, 41 per cent of whom in 1951 were in employment (Geraghty 1986: 32) and, seemingly, for whatever reason, resisting the arguments of child psychologists to seek fulfilment exclusively in domesticity as mothers and/or seductive companions for their husbands.

The whimsy and lightness of touch of *A Kid for Two Farthings* recall, as fantasy, Ealing comedy and the films of René Clair, but the film guards against over-sentimentalisation of its ethnically diverse Petticoat Lane urban pastoral – what Durgnat unjustly refers to as its 'experiment in local colour' (1971: 168) – through its darker themes of materialism, domesticity and death. As in *The Fallen Idol*, the film privileges the child's view, but in so doing, often by placing the camera at child's eye level, it makes the viewer aware of a paradise of lost innocence. This was Reed's first film in colour and, complementing the sounds of vendors, traders, customers and inhabitants of 'Fashion Street', Edward Scarfe's photography pays tribute to the gaudy sights of the neighbourhood: the open air fruit and vegetable market, indoor bric-a-brac, consumer goods and, above all, the garish costumes of the local citizens no more spectacularly displayed than in the golden hair and various combinations of azure and royal blue outfits into which Diana Dors, the star that commentators have variously defined as the knowing, carnal, strong-headed British Marilyn Monroe (Geraghty 1986; Harper 2000) squeezed her Swindon-born curvaceous frame.

But the daylight sights and sounds of a bustling, noisy, wise-cracking community are not untouched by darkness. The film's awareness of death points to the irretrievable loss of innocence, a melancholy theme signposted at the earliest opportunity. Joe's pets all die, buried in a backyard, leading him to admit, parroting Mr Kandinsky's Yiddish syntax, that he is not a 'born chick-raiser'. Even the unicorn dies, although Joe is assured by Mr Kandinsky that it has merely returned to its African home. In reality it too has fulfilled its role as one of the film's reminders of lost innocence and, as the kindly Mr Kandinsky cradles the expired kid in his arms, humming a doleful Yiddish melody as he takes it out for burial, the night fails to obscure the view in the distance, loyal to its ecumenical agenda, of St Paul's Cathedral, an unrealistic sight from Fashion Street/Petticoat Lane, but an appropriate metaphorical presence as a *memento mori* for all. The last words of the film belong to Mr Kandinsky during this solitary funeral procession: 'Unicorns can't grow up in Fashion Street, but boys, boys have to'. As he heads off in the direction of St Paul's, the more orthodox Jewish character, another of Reed's choric figures, reading from a sacred text, pushing a gramophone, walks towards the camera: the unicorn, or innocence, is silenced by the song of experience.

The sombre conclusion, a fitting climax to the elegiac mood of the film, provides necessary ballast to comic fantasy. Comedy's 'place apart', here represented by Fashion Street, is not Utopian. The very name, 'Fashion Street', points to a more life-affirming celebration of colour, shape and design – instead of the conservatism of British society in the early 1950s – as well as through allusion to the transience and vanities of a secular trade, to the Isaiahan reflection on the perishability of all things. Reed balances fantasy with reality, reaching out for life, while not disavowing death, linking the life-denying instincts of conservative England with the inescapable fate that awaits all. Sandwiched between the Black Shirt attacks on East End Jewry, and the Notting Hill race riots involving the largely Caribbean community, this is a picture of London that cannot help but reflect, however lightly, a deeper national malaise.

Fashion Street's characters are not spared the flaws of those outside the magical boundary of their East End community. Here, as elsewhere, there are also chislers (Sid James, the jewellery salesman, passing off semi-precious stones as invaluable gems), self-seekers (Sidney Tafler, the tailor who objects to the sacred English ritual of the tea-break – 'I'm a tea-break financier?') – and mischief-makers, like the jealous blonde who tries to destroy the romance between the neighbourhood golden couple, Sonia and Sam. These ultimately innocuous egotists live side by side with the cosy, warm-hearted and generous populace of a post-war Arcadia. Partly used as a way of critiquing English reserve through a discourse of Jewish informality, Irene Handl's stolen pinches of Joe's cheek whenever he passes by, as she sits plucking feathers for, one suspects, one of the talismanic recipes of Jewish cuisine, chicken soup, are also, at one end of the spectrum of neighbourhood life, examples of minor irritation and miscalculated affection. At the other end, Blackie Isaacs (Lou Jacobi), the wrestler, 'The Python', and his cronies, are all clearly more intent on lining their own pockets than in contributing to the community ethos. Blackie, the owner of the local gym, encourages Sam (Joe Robinson), a male blond bombshell, to give up body-building for the more lucrative career of wrestling, to become another hero in the East End tradition of locally produced pugilists like Terry Spinks, Terry Downes and Billy Walker, starting with a bout against the Python, the snake in the Edenic grass of the East End, not for the declared altruistic purpose of earning a purse that will enable him to buy his girlfriend Sonia (Diana Dors) an engagement ring, but so that he can make a handsome profit for all concerned. The relationship between Sam and Sonia, and the subsequent confrontation between Sam and the Python, raise questions that further contribute to the process of disillusionment undermining the celebration of the East End ethnic and classless idyll.

Sam and Sonia seem destined for each other, the alliteration of their first names reformulated in their reflected physical shapes. Diana Dors's hourglass contours and shoulder length peroxide hair respect 1950s feminine styles (Geraghty 1986, Harper 2000). But Sam's physique, developed into the bulging, muscle-choked torso of a Steve Reeves or a gay porno magazine pin-up, is also feminised, his Tony Curtis quiff, and narcissistic concern over facial damage in the wrestling ring, making him seem more like an adolescent girl than the 1950s hulks of the day, such as Victor Mature and Charlton Heston. Reed's interest in these jocular references to male vanity includes serious attention to gay under-currents, the paradoxically unmanly world of body-building and, through these reflections, to issues of masculinity, developed in the British cinema (Medhurst 1986: 346–54, and 1996: 117–32), above all through Dirk Bogarde vehicles like *The Spanish Gardener* (Leacock, 1956). The Wolfenden Report was still two years away from publication in 1957, but as Andy Medhurst notes, public debate on homosexuality had been aired ever since the revelations in 1951 of the Burgess/Maclean spying scandal. Sam's subversive or queer masculinity has a knock-on effect on Sonia and, through her impatience with Sam, on the film's meditation on normative heterosexuality and the pressure on couples to legitimise their relationships through marriage.

Not unduly concerned about the damage to Sam's looks, as long as he just buys her that engagement ring, Sonia urges him to wrestle so he can earn the money for the ring and down payments on the furniture for their future home. In no rush to commit himself to marriage (their leisurely courtship has so far improbably lasted four years), Sam perhaps unconsciously uses body-building and its relative penury as a strategy of delay, physical culture his way of resisting the community's almost hysterical endorsement of marriage. It is as if in its desire to see the golden couple settled the neighbourhood uses the fantasy of wedded bliss to compensate for the reality of unhappy marriages. The fantasy triumphs and Sam agrees after all to meet the Python in the ring.

The Python was played by Primo Carnera, a famous Italian heavy-weight boxing champion, a six foot seven inches giant of a man known as the 'Ambling Alp' who, at the end of his career, turned to wrestling. The climactic duel between Sam and the Python seems to typify Barthes's view of wrestling as not sport but spectacle. Whereas boxing is a 'Jansenist sport', a conflict whose outcome is in doubt, a struggle between theoretically well-matched opponents, wrestling is excess, involving combatants whose role is not to win but to represent the spectacle of 'suffering, defeat and justice' (1973: 19). In these dramas the principals are signs of villainy and heroism. The wrestling match in *A Kid for Two Farthings* , though, is also a contest, pitting Sam, the neighbourhood paladin, against an ogre, the projection of repressed or denied otherness. In a community of mixed ethnicities – Jewish, Indian (the perfume vendor), black (a regular at Blackie's gym) – the Python's Italianness counts against him. His aura of gangsterism (attributable in part to well-documented accounts of Primo Carnera's involvement in fight-fixing claims levelled at his gangster manager, Owney Madden), and sexual predatoriness, make him an unfit member of the community. He is Fashion Street's Malvolio, a negative, displaced image of their own treatment – a community of ethnic minorities – by mainstream society.

The match betwen Beauty and the Beast is also the community's hopes for the victory of the boy next door over the foreigner, or even, from Reed's point of view, for the triumph of an alternative masculinity to the hegemonic, violent one represented by the Python. The triumph of Sam is not only that of youth, beauty and – so the community hopes – of marriage over independence (since he now has the money to buy the ring, furniture and the rest) but also of the gentile. Sam works for a Jew (Mr Kandinsky) and, as in the case of Sonia (employed by Sidney Tafler's Madam Rita and Brenda de Banzie's 'Lady' Ruby, both identified ethnically by their Jewishness), is never identified as Jewish. Though both belong to this community, they are held up as an ideal couple devoid of ethnicity, celebrated – above all in the symbolic victory of Sam over the rejected alien, the Python – precisely for their unproblematic Englishness. But the proof that Fashion Street is, beneath the surface of Jewish wit, heart-warming gestures, and childhood fantasies, no real paradise, is given right at the start of the film: Joe's father, Joanna's husband, has left it behind in favour of Africa, as if in search of real otherness, not its slightly laboured version in Bethnal Green. In much the same way, Reed abandoned the world of Korda's London films in search of backing in Hollywood.

An Englishman abroad

6

After the death of Alexander Korda (1956), for whose London Films he had made five films (*The Fallen Idol, The Third Man, Outcast, The Man Between* and *A Kid for Two Farthings*), Reed was keen to try his hand again in Hollywood. His last two films for Korda had been major disappointments both critically and commercially, so it was something of a surprise that he was commissioned by Hecht-Lancaster to direct *Trapeze*. Although the majority of the films he made from 1955 to the end (*Follow Me* (1972)), all Hollywood-financed, were by his standards mediocre, there are three exceptions: *Trapeze, Our Man in Havana* and *Oliver! Our Man* has already been discussed out of chronological order in the chapter on the Graham Greene collaborations; *Oliver!* will provide the focus for the last sustained analysis of a Reed film. While this chapter will conclude, out of chronological sequence, with a detailed commentary of *Trapeze*, which I consider an unjustly neglected film, preliminary remarks on *The Key, The Running Man* and *The Agony and the Ecstasy* will, I hope, demonstrate that even what are on balance rightly considered flawed films contain many remarkable moments. *The Last Warrior* (1970) and *Follow Me* brought his career to an end with a whimper in a final phase that was not without merit.

The Key (1958)

Reed was approached to direct *The Key* by Carl Foreman who, after working on films like *Champion* (Robson, 1949), *Home of the Brave* (Robson, 1949) and *High Noon* (Zinnemann, 1952), all written by him, had fallen foul of HUAC. After moving to England, he had begun to work anonymously on various films (including *Bridge on the River Kwai*, directed by David Lean, 1957). Now writing again under his own name, Foreman turned Jan de Hartog's novel *Stella* into a script, acquired financial backing and became the film's executive producer. The assembled cast included major stars like William Holden, who had just completed *The Bridge on the River Kwai*, and Sophia Loren, who after rising to prominence in the Italian cinema had made two films in Hollywood, *Boy on a Dolphin* (Negulesco, 1957) and *The Pride and the Passion* (Kramer, 1957). While filming *Desire under the Elms* (Mann, 1958) she was approached by Foreman for *The Key*. Other important cast members included, above all, Trevor Howard, Kieron Moore (a last-minute choice as Stanley Baker's replacement), Oscar Homolka and Bernard Lee.

The story concerns the rescue by tugboats – the 'Red Cross of the sea' – during the Second World War of merchant ships under fire in the Atlantic from German U-boats or submarines. Churchill had feared that the real threat to the war effort, and to the lifeline of ships that carried food and ammunition from the USA, came from the U-boats in the Battle of the Atlantic. Against this background of heroism at sea another story develops in which the widow of a tugboat captain gets passed on, along with the key to the dead man's flat, to successive seamen, from Philip to Chris to David to Kane. At the start of the film, following the death of her husband Philip – whose photo she continues to display by her bedside – Stella is living with Chris (Trevor Howard). Before he in turn dies at sea he gives David (William Holden) the key to the flat. Fearing he may not return from a mission, David gives the key he has cut for Stella to Kane (Kieron Moore) instead. But David returns safely from his mission, too late, however, to prevent Kane, who believes David has died in a rescue mission, from using the key. Angered by what she considers David's failure to break free of the cycle in which she herself seems at first listlessly content to find comfort in the company of strangers, and in which men treat women as mere sexual commodities of exchange, Stella leaves the flat. The original ending, released in Europe, sees David setting off in search of Stella. In this version, accompanied by Kane, David reaches the station only in time to see the train, with Stella on board, depart from the platform. A cut to the interior of the compartment shows Stella in close-up, before the camera reverts to a shot of David and Kane leaving the platform together. 'I'll find her when I get back to London. I'll find her', David remarks, but the impression given is that this promise has no more substance than the steam in which both they and the moving train are shrouded. The twinning of David with Kane is interesting: as with Lime and Martins, or various other pairings in Reed's films, Kane is readable as David's shadow or spectre, a visualised projection of his own death, at the very least a reminder of David's mortality. Prior to this scene he is coupled with David in the revolving door of the hotel where they are both billeted, and they cross each other's paths on many other occasions. The film is an elegy, like Milton's *Lycidas*, mourning the loss of heroic young men, something highlighted by Kane when he tells David after Chris's death: 'Have a good time as long as it lasts.' In the USA a happy ending that sees David catching up with her on a train provided a more conventional conclusion.

The film, thus, has two main levels of interest. First, it allows Reed, through Foreman's script, to return to the familiar territory (covered, for instance, through *Easy*, *Pitt*, and all the men in *The Way Ahead*) of a masculinity forged in the crucible of war. The sequences at sea, photographed by Oswald Morris in cinemascope and monochrome, are vivid depictions of individual acts of heroism against a ruthless enemy, in what one of the men calls 'U-Boat Alley', as well as nature itself. As the boat rocks and swerves over the raging tungsten-coloured waves that threaten to swamp the men while steaming towards distressed vessels in inclement weather, the stomachs of even the hardiest men betray them. First Chris, then David, exemplify the courage of those whose work was so essential to the war effort in the Atlantic. But war and nature also brutalise, and religion here is no consolation. Although Stella's prayers in the Church seem to be answered as David returns home safely, the carol singing led by Van Damm appears to have failed to make an impression with a higher authority when an avalanche of bombs demolishes the building. The aftermath of war gives Harry Lime the opportunity, like a carrion crow, to feed off the misfortunes of others; in *Outcast* Willems regresses in the wilderness to a state verging on savagery. In its unambiguously sexualised Freudian *mise-en-scène* of keys, flats, entry and withdrawal (Freud 1982: 471), the brutalisation of the men in *The Key* leads them to treat Stella, who seems resigned to her situation – as if herself defeated by the loss of all values occasioned by war – as no more than an object of sexual gratification to be passed on from one man to another. What does sexual morality matter, she wonders, when killing and death have become routine. Devastated by the loss of her lover Philip, she lives in a dream, her attraction to Chris and David not born of swooning passions but compulsion. Like Anna in *The Third Man*, she is a sleep-walker, her mind filled only with memories of Philip, whose clothes and photograph she has preserved. Later on, she even calls David 'Philip', as Anna called Holly 'Harry'. And yet, in conflict with these contradictory drives to be true to Philip and to punish herself through successive relationships with other men, rival impulses make her yearn for a life that would allow her to break free of this cycle of provisionality. Stella's serial relationships are a form of repetition compulsion prompted by a death instinct, a way of overcoming the trauma of loss caused by Philip's death. Torn between mourning for Philip and a craving for domesticity, she agrees to marry Chris and, after his death, actually proposes to David. The tenant on the ground floor comments that she never leaves the flat ('She's never out, that one'), and it is remarkable how often Stella appears in pyjamas, dressing gown or bathrobe, seen serving, cooking or, when David and Chris are brought together in an early scene at the flat, sitting apart from the men, or remaining at home when they set off together for the pub. But here, the 'lady in a dressing gown' is not the pathetic house-bound, physically unattractive and slovenly impersonation by Yvonne Mitchell in J. Lee Thompson's 1957 version. The domestic uniform of pyjamas, dressing gown or bathrobe confirms Sophia Loren through accoutrement as a woman whose femininity is defined erotically, a dream-like Circe, in an alluring *mise-en-scène* in which her admirers are also hopelessly trapped. Stella's reality is to some extent buried under the fantasies projected on her by the men by whom she is desired. But Sophia Loren's foreignness, the face that launched a thousand tugboats, identifies the exotic as dangerously alluring, her beauty projecting power as well as sensuality.

When difficulties arose over her availability for the role of Stella, Ingrid Bergman agreed to step in. Ingrid Bergman would have brought her own aura of warm but less convulsive sexuality to the role, but Sophia Loren's dusky glamour, her expressive eyes and busty, full-lipped sensuality suited perfectly the fantasy of the Circe or Lorelei, whose lusciousness is believed by some of the men to be the cause of their ruin. The reviewers picked up on the Lorelei associations (e.g. Barker 1958), but avoided mentioning that Stella's role is less that of the mysterious sorceress who lures sailors to their doom than the men's fantasy version. In Heine's poem, the Lorelei's sorcery is responsible for the mariner's death: 'Ich glaube, die wellen verschlingen / Am Ende Schiffer und Kahn; / und das hat mit ihrem Singen / Die Lorelei getan' (In the end, if I remember rightly, the waves swallow up the boatman and his boat. And that is what she has done, the Lorelei and her singing (in Forster 1975: 329)'. In *The Key* she is associated by others with death: by the official at the Ministry of Labour where, in search of work, she is informed that she was reported killed in an air raid almost a year previously, or by seamen like Van Dam (Oscar Homolka), not one of her lovers, who warns David: 'That woman's bad luck – she will kill you.' At one point, as Stella goes down to the pier to bid farewell to Chris before his last mission, the sign behind her reads, significantly, ' Out of Bounds', words that refer not just to government buildings but also to the mysterious presence of the Lorelei herself. The links between desire and death are reinforced after the dissolve from a kiss between David and Stella and a mine waiting to go off at sea. Reed's sea settings – *Outcast, Penny Paradise, Bank Holiday, The Running Man* (1963) – dissolving boundaries, offered him suitable opportunities for reflection on instabilities of self and identity, and even final questions about the mysteries of existence.

The attraction of the men, Chris, David and Kane, to Stella responds in part to her foreignness but also to fatality, drawing them to her aura of sorrow and death and, thus, to the promise of liberation from life itself. In the tradition of all *liebestod* lovers, David is entranced by Stella as if in recognition of the impermanence of all things. David is also heir to what Marcuse calls the 'Great Refusal', a fantasy whose truths are incompatible with reason and the laws by which society – here one in the grip of war – is governed. His fantasy of Stella is part patriarchal, in that it reduces her to an object of sexual exchange, but it is also, more radically, a rejection through her of civilisation and all its discontents.

The Running Man (1963)

Reed's next offer came from MGM, the chance to re-make *Mutiny on the Bounty*, but tensions with Marlon Brando reached such a pitch he was forced to abandon the film, to be replaced by Lewis Milestone. Even so, Columbia thought highly enough of Reed to offer him *The Running Man*. Based on Shelly Smith's novel *Ballad of the Running Man* (1962), Reed's *The Running Man*, scripted by John Mortimer, was a moderate box office success, and a critical failure. *The Times* headline declared 'Sir Carol Reed underrates his audience' (Anon 1963h). Richard Roud (1963) wondered 'Whatever happened?' (i.e. to Carol Reed), in *The Guardian*, Felix Barker (1963) in *The Evening News*, and the reviewers in *The New Statesman* (Anon 1963e), *The Daily Worker* (Anon 1963b) and the *Jewish Chronicle* (Anon 1963d) were all unimpressed. There were more sympathetic notices in *The Tablet* (Anon 1963g). *The People* (Anon 1963f) and *The Daily Mirror* (Anon 1963a). But, on balance, what was considered its repeat of an old formula (only five months earlier the similarly themed *Five Miles to Midnight*, directed by Anatole Litvak, had been screened in London), its lack of true suspense, poor writing and acting failed to rescue Reed's reputation from post-1940s obscurity. Nevertheless, looking back at the film now, there is much to admire in its characteristic touches. In addition to its format as a suspense narrative – with faint echoes also of *Double Indemnity* (Wilder, 1944) – *The Running Man*, as its title suggests, is readable, beyond its formulaic interest in the fraudulent schemes of a fugitive from the law, as being concerned with an individual's desire for release from the limits of self. It is also about the breakdown of marriage and the blossoming of romance in another exoticised environment. Although there are existential implications in Rex Black's (Laurence Harvey) attempts to alter his identity, the focus lies more on questions of desire, the suffocations of marriage, and the protean nature of identity. *The Running Man* reunited Reed with Robert Krasker, allowing him to explore what Robert Moss has described as 'not romanticism that attracts women but self-absorbed worldliness and off-handed sophistication' (1987: 244). Rex Black, in this sense, is a less convincing variant of the Harry Lime type, his romantic foil the straighter, duller and more naïve version of the Holly Martins type Stephen (Alan Bates). The story involves a staged fatal accident by Rex Black, provoked into deceiving the insurance company who had refused to approve his claim – owing to his own failure to renew the policy that had expired by only two days – for a previous accident that had destroyed his business. Rex disappears, first to Paris and then to Malaga, but not before he visits his accomplice, his wife Stella, for a final evening together and last minute discussion about her collection and transfer of the insurance money before they head incognito overseas, their departure recalling the flight of the suburban forger, Mr Redfern, and his family in *Laburnum Grove*. During the course of the evening they are visited by Stephen, the insurance claims man, who checks up on some of the details, enquiring whether Rex had suicidal tendencies. Satisfied that all is in order, Stephen leaves, and Stella asks her husband, 'Rex, when this is all over we'll be ordinary, won't we?'

While the challenge of beating the system and a desire for material gain animate Rex's actions, his fake suicide and re-birth with a new identity point to other complicating psychological factors. The false accident is indeed a form of suicide, enabling him to sever ties with his background, his inefficiency and failure as a business man providing him with an opportunity to re-invent himself and to practise deception on others. Later on, as their relationship begins to flounder, Stella warns Rex: 'In another few days you may have forgotten who you are.' The journey from England to France and from there to Spain offers another spatial metaphor for the destabilisation of fixed identities. The redefinition of the self in foreign lands – as in *Outcast, The Third Man, Easy, The Man Between* – is further nuanced through Rex's acquisition of the passport and identity of a slightly inebriated Australian sheep-farmer in a Paris bar. Rex's transformation as 'Jim Jerome' releases vicious as well as more playful drives. In Laurence Harvey's unrestrained, somewhat camp Australian accent, gaudily dyed buttercup-coloured hair and newly grown gingery moustache (the colour aptly matching the onomatopoeia of 'Jim Jerome'), Rex revels in his new identity as a vulgar, party-going, free-spending antipodean. Harvey's appearance was ridiculed at the time. The anonymous review in *The Evening Standard* (Anon 1963c) is not untypical: 'It [the picture] has only two real surprises. One is the blond hair-do, ginger whiskers and Australian accent that Mr Harvey disguises himself with. That is very funny. The other is that Sir Carol Reed directed the film. That is not.' Even more cruelly, Cecil Wilson in *The Daily Mail* (1963) queried the sense of allowing Laurence Harvey to disguise himself as Leslie Phillips. But his conversion from a free-spirited aviator – his earlier professional identity as Rex Black – into a land-locked 'black' sheep farmer measures his fall in elemental terms from air to earth, and hence, the illusory freedom acquired through deception of the insurance company. The descent into an abyss from which there is ultimately no escape as, first, his relationship with Stella deteriorates and, second, his own authentic, untimely death becomes inevitable once the attempts to foil what he imagines is his pursuit by Stephen, the claims man, spiral out of control. As Stephen, the wry, emotionally restrained Alan Bates provides the right blend of enigma and tenacity, suspicion and infatuation, to terrorise and play on the guilty conscience of the fraudulent couple and on the doubts and uncertainties of the audience. In that sense, Rex's staged death has indeed been suicidal: the destruction of the law-abiding suburban citizen from Croydon, that side of her husband with which Stella had felt more comfortable.

But the ordinariness craved so vehemently by Stella frustrates Rex and, to some extent, provokes his perverse behaviour, driving him towards living out the 1960s fantasy of a Whicker's World life of exoticism, shaken and stirred with a dash of James Bond luxury and danger. Rex delights in shining, in being a success in the company of women, attracting attention and even notoriety, deriving pleasure from making fools of others. He epitomises the narcissism and daring of the bullfighter, a parallel with whom is drawn when two young Spanish boys take him to an empty bullring, persuading him to imitate the gestures of the *matador* as they perform the role of the bull. Though a cliché, this is one of the few acknowledgements of Spanish otherness that connects with the film's primary concerns. Elsewhere, the arbitrary but ill-conceived periodic intrusions of guests attending a local wedding fail entirely to capture the authenticity of Andalusian life, music and customs. The mock bullfight is appropriate in the immediate context of Rex's narcissism as well as, more widely, in Reed's abiding interest in father/son relationships.

Like many other Reed protagonists, Rex inspires the admiration or even devotion of boys who see in the exceptional man inspirational qualities of drive and self-confidence. But Rex's dash and brio are compromised by pride and over-reaching, a sadistic tendency, noted by Stella, that delights in tormenting others: 'You love it, don't you? You love taking risks and teasing him [Stephen] because you think he's trying to catch you ... You think you're far too clever for him and everyone else in the world, don't you? And you like that'. But the over-reacher gets his comeuppance. The twist to the story is that Stephen, who comes across the couple in Malaga, has not pursued them, as they believe, to investigate the insurance claim further, since he later reveals to Stella, but not to Rex, that he no longer works for the Excelsior Insurance Company, and is now an employee of a paints firm, who have granted him holiday leave.

Stephen's presence and his enigmatic remarks tease both audience and characters. Rex and Stella read Stephen's behaviour as suspicious, and as the audience aligns itself with the guilty couple in hoping for their continued evasion of justice, Reed confronts us with our own complicity and moral compromises. Where in *The Fallen Idol* the audience was made to see the action through the innocent eye of childhood, in *The Running Man* events are viewed through the per-spectives of maturity, fraud and guilt. While fraud provides the turning point in Rex's life as he abandons security for risk, for Stella it represents initially little more than an opportunity for obliging her dominant husband. Her desire for change and risk-taking is far more subdued than her husband's. Admittedly, in early scenes in Malaga, her willing-ness to wear the brightly coloured summer clothes bought for her by Rex indicates freedom as well as pleasure in fashion and colour, but she soon grows weary of this masquerade of affluence and becomes increasingly disappointed by Rex's refusal to return to the 'ordinariness' that predates their new-found prosperity.

Rex's complaint is significant: 'Two days and you've hardly said a word ... I mean, after all, I brought you to this beautiful place. There's a sun out there, fresh air, flowers and a bit of sea that actually wouldn't freeze you to death if you put your bottom in it. These clothes I bought you, these exquisite dresses which you could at least ... Well, can't you be just a little bit grateful?'. Up to this point Stella has been the unques-tioning, submissive partner, ready to fit in with her husband's fantasy of femininity. The revolt of the complaisant lover is therefore all the more disappointing to a man hitherto accustomed to getting his own way, and heir to the 1960s culture of Jean Shrimpton dolly birds, jet-setting film heroes, oblivious to the imminent arrival of the century's second wave of feminism.

Hitchcock blonde look-alike, Lee Remick, who resisted conversion into a regressive 50s dumb blonde stereotype, is Reed's Grace Kelly, but without the latter's hidden steel, cast in the role of a mainly domesticated heroine, only towards the end finding the courage to challenge her controlling husband. We assume Stella is initially attracted to him on account of his masterful personality. She is the precursor of the surrendered wife posing no threat to a man's identity, docile and unwilling or unable to question his authority. Not even when Rex is no longer the man she thought she married does she truly betray him, only sleeping with Stephen in a pretence of desire, in order to buy his complicity through sex. She only loosens the ties that bind them together as a last resort when Rex attempts to strangle her.

As ever in a Reed film, the consequences of crime – the initial fraud – cannot be confined to its perpetrators. Its ripple effect involves others and, in creating its own momentum, becomes, as in Greek tragedy, an infernal machine that, once set in motion, is predictable in outcome. Rex dies, Stella betrays, Stephen is humiliated.

The Agony and the Ecstasy (1965)

Of all Reed's later films none has attracted as much patronising commentary and laboured humour as *The Agony and the Ecstasy*. Reviewers over-dosed on jokes about interior decorators and ceilings, the abundance of agony and the rationing of ecstasy (Samuels 1972: 179). Despite its critical dismissal, it made reasonable money, taking $185,000 in advance sales, the highest ever recorded for any film within three months of opening. Reed accounts for its critical failure through the refusal by Twentieth Century Fox to provide sufficient funds for the bigger-scale production originally envisaged for the film: 'That was supposed to have been much bigger. Darryl Zanuck's trouble with Twentieth Century Fox led to a cut in the budget. We were prepared for big action sequences, and all we had was the Sistine Chapel' (in Samuels 1972: 178). It is doubtful whether, even with a bigger budget, mere expansion of the epic scenes would have substantially improved the film.

Reed was offered *The Agony and the Ecstasy* after first choice Fred Zinnemann turned it down. Adapted from the novel by Irving Stone, the script was written by Philip Dunne, one of Hollywood's most respected writers (whose other work included *The Robe*). According to the pressbook, Dunne's prodigious research – complementing the epic scale of the film – included consultation of many authorities, including

Giorgio Vasari's *Lives of the Artists*, John Addington Symonds's *Renaissance in Italy*, Giovanni Papini's *Michelangelo*, Marcel Brion's *Michelangelo Buonarroti*, and Ludwig von Pastor's *Saints and Sinners: a History of the Popes* for his screenplay. In fact, the film relies most heavily on Vasari's 'life' of Michelangelo. It follows the early part of the 1568 biography in its reference to Michelangelo's origins, patronage by Lorenzo 'il Magnifico' in Florence, rise to prominence as a sculptor, move to Rome where eventually, on his accession to the Papacy in 1503, Julius contracted him to build his tomb, a sojourn that led to the envious rivalry with Cardinal Bramante and his favourites (the most prominent of whom was the young Raphael), and the eventual commission for the Sistine Chapel. The constant exchanges in the film between Michelangelo and Julius ('when will you make an end?') are found in Vasari: 'for His Holiness was always asking him importunately when it would be ready. On one of these occasions Michelangelo retorted that the ceiling would be finished "when it satisfies me as an artist". And to this the Pope replied: "And we want you to satisfy us and to finish it soon"' (1983: 353). The reference to Julius as a 'wilful man by nature' (1983: 350) perfectly fits Rex Harrison's Julius. Perhaps even more significantly for the film, Vasari begins his essay with a long paragraph outlining what he sees as Michelangelo's divine inspiration, something that most obviously led to the scene of his vision of the Creation before returning to Rome to begin work on the ceiling: 'Meanwhile, the benign ruler of heaven graciously looked down to earth, saw the worthlessness of what was being done, the intense but utterly fruitless studies and the presumption of men who were farther from true art than night is from day, and resolved to save us from our errors. So he decided to send into the world an artist who would be skilled in each and every craft' (1983: 325).

Heston's monumental persona was ideal for the role and in keeping with contemporary taste for film epics (e.g. *El Cid* (Mann, 1961), *The Fall of the Roman Empire* (Mann, 1964), *Ben Hur* (Wyler, 1959)). Early in 1964 locations were found in Italy, at Querceta, Todi, Montero, Florence, the Orsini Castle at Lake Bracciano, the Villa Giulia, Rome and Cinecittá and De Laurentiis studios, for shooting to begin. The Sistine Chapel, the focal point of the film, was rebuilt at Cinecittá studios, for although permission was granted by the Vatican for filming in the original, the dilapidated state of the ceiling eventually made that impossible.

Following his usual practice, Reed worked closely with the screenwriter. Asked whether he substantially influenced his writers, Reed once replied: 'Yes. I work with the author from the original conception right through to the finished script. You've got to be willing to sit with him, to say, you know "We could do this with a book rather than dialogue ...". You know, letting an inexperienced screenwriter – even when he is an experienced novelist – or playwright – work alone won't do. I don't write, though I have written a few stories, some of which were filmed by other men. But I think I can be of help in interpreting the writer's ideas' (Samuels 1972: 164). Reed's influence on the script is unmistakable, allowing him to shape the Stone/Dunne material into a film that once more draws on his perennial parent/child theme and perhaps, above all, to reflect, through meditation on art, on his own life as a film director. Reed is on record as saying in the programme of the Royal Premier Screening on 27 October 1965, at the Astoria Theatre, London: 'I see this as a study of a genius and not a hero, at least in the conventional sense. What interests me most is that Michelangelo was a man tormented by self-criticism ... anxious about the work still left to do ... who thought of his art as an act of self-confession' (Twentieth Century Fox 1965). The autobiographical element of *The Agony and the Ecstasy* is unmistakable.

Like other biopics of artists (e.g. *Rembrandt* (Korda, 1936) and *The Naked Maja* (Koster, 1959)), *The Agony and the Ecstasy* is to some extent guilty, in common with films like *Lust for Life* (Minnelli, 1955), as Griselda Pollock argues, of making art 'neither public, social, nor a product of work. Art and the artist become reflexive, mystically bound into an unbreakable circuit which produces the artist as subject of the art work and the art work as the means of contemplative access to that subject's "transcendent" and "creative subjectivity"' (1980–81: 58–9). *The Agony and the Ecstasy* makes some effort to contextualise Michelangelo's life and work through references to his early days in Florence, his relations with contemporaries – though it censors his homosexuality – his awareness of art history and reliance on assistants both in the Sistine Chapel itself and in the quarries. But this film, like *Lust for Life*, is not interested in a 'catalogue raisonnée' of an artist's *oeuvre*, and makes its impact through concentration, via one work, the fresco in the Sistine Chapel, on the relationship of two men, and the motives that drive each of them to pursue his own ambitions.

Even so, the tension between Reed's own preoccupations and the generic or other demands of the biopic are noticeable. Though not made at the peak of the genre's Hollywood popularity (1930s–40s), the film still adheres to key premises. Focusing on the four years that Michelangelo took to complete the frescoes in the Sistine Chapel – rather than the entire life of Michelangelo – *The Agony and the Ecstasy* nevertheless bears out Carlyle's dictum that the history of the world is the biography of great men. But the film's view of its great men – Michelangelo and

Julius II – presents 'a world view that naturalises certain lives and specific values over alternative ones' (Custen 1992: 4). The availability of Heston – complete, according to the Press Book, with a short piece of plastic tube inserted in his nostril to give it the broken look of Daniele da Volterra's Michelangelo death mask – as an actor suited to epic roles, a time in the mid 1960s when American power was again flexing its muscle overseas (Cuba, Vietnam), highlights the provisionality of the biopic's truths, a mediation rather than an irrefutably accurate document of individual acts or historical events. Indeed, the film's concentration on the agonies of the artist, painting and sculpting against a background of wars waged by the Pope himself, reflects Reed's own attempts to make sense of reality in the context of wars in the Middle East as well as in Vietnam and elsewhere across the world in the 1960s.

The appropriate irascibility on screen between Julius and Michelangelo developed from mutual off-screen hostility: 'Heston very politely and very nicely made me feel that it was extremely kind of me to be supporting him. Carol did very little to disabuse him of this notion, so I did everything I could to make myself believe that the picture was about Pope Julius rather than about Michelangelo' (quoted by Wapshott 1991: 252). The struggle between Heston and Harrison now looks like one of the highlights in what at other levels remains an uneven film. Harrison – Professor Higgins, the King of Siam, Julius Caesar and, above all, the exponent of light but also arrogant, even acidic comedy, such as in his portrayal of the jealous husband in *Unfaithfully Yours* (Sturges, 1948) – seemed like a strange choice for the Vicar of Christ. But the real Pope Julius was a man of many parts: warrior, politician, patron of the arts and father of three daughters, all plausibly contained within Harrison's persona.

War provides an apt background for a drama of personal conflict. Throughout Michelangelo's ordeal to finish the frescoes on time, an increasingly irate Pope addresses his genius employee as 'my son', a variant for plain 'Buonarroti', a term routinely used by Catholic priests of male members of their congregation, but here delivered as invective, aimed at a prodigal offspring whose waywardness has incurred the wrath of an impatient father. Julius was twice the age of Michelangelo, and Rex Harrison (born 1908) sixteen years older than Charlton Heston (born 1924).

When Julius appears to dismiss the infirm Michelangelo from the project, claiming he has employed the younger Raphael to complete the ceiling, he relies on basic child psychology to force Michelangelo out of his bed and back on to the scaffolding to continue his work. The ruse is prompted by the frustration of an employer eager to have his commission finally completed but, less discernibly, it also reveals the affection of a father for a faltering son in danger of failing his greatest challenge. Earlier, Julius's tests of endurance for his 'son' take the shape of appeals to his courage. When, initially, Michelangelo refuses the commission, insisting he is no painter but a sculptor, Julius asks, 'are you afraid then?'. His mission is to release the mature genius in Michelangelo, a father recognising and seeking to develop the potential in his son, in just the same way as Michelangelo liberates the forms and patterns of the shapeless material with which he works, already placed there by divine intervention, in the slabs of marble hewn from the Italian countryside: 'God sets them in there. The sculptor sets them loose.' Michelangelo's explanation of the origins of creativity highlights, once again, the pressures of genre and authorship. As often in the biopic, especially in the Biblical epic, the hero retreats in solitude to the wilderness and, also in line with earlier biopic artist heroes, goes in search of authenticity. Just as Al Jolson in The Jolson films, Eddie Duchin in *The Eddie Duchin Story* (Sidney, 1956), or Glenn Miller in *The Glenn Miller Story* (Anthony Mann, 1953) search for a special sound to their music, so Michelangelo looks for his own visual form. 'Doesn't he ever stop worrying?', someone asks. 'No, not until he finds what he's looking for,' answers someone else. Through a subjective shot the audience shares Michelangelo's view of nature. Over-awed by the mountains and clouds, this 'son' of the Pope, imbued with religious feeling, imposes on the mute and inchoate forms of the wilderness his subjective vision of divine creation, in much the same way as the makers of the film mediate their own notions of history through the bare facts of an artist's commission to paint frescoes for a sixteenth-century Pope.

When Raphael advises Michelangelo to sacrifice pride to the completion of his masterpiece the self-consciousness of this scene becomes even more incontrovertible: 'For what is an artist in this world but a servant? A lackey for the rich and powerful. Before we ever begin to work to feed this craving of ours we must find a patron. A rich man of affairs, or a merchant, or a prince, or a Pope. We must bow, fawn, kiss hands to be able to do the things we must do or die. We are harlots always peddling beauty at the doorsteps of the mighty.' Even though written by Dunne, the sentiment seems to come, with his own varied experiences of modern patrons and potentates like Rank, Korda, Zanuck and others, straight from Reed's heart. This moment of self-assessment draws attention to the need for patrons as well as to the inevitable difficulties in remaining true to the artist's own vision.

In his study of Leonardo da Vinci, Freud (1984b) emphasises the importance for the artist of ignoring models of authority – which in Michelangelo's case would be the revered figures in the history of painting and sculpture – who represent symbolically the authority of the parent: 'Only Leonardo could dispense with that support; he would not have been able to do so had he not learnt in the first years of his life to do without his father. His later scientific research, with all its boldness and independence, presupposed the existence of infantile sexual researches uninhibited by his father, and was a prolongation of them with the sexual element excluded' (1984b: 73). When the Cardinals object to the nudity of some of the figures in the frescoes they are contemptuous of Michelangelo's need to redefine his relationship to authority – Christian or otherwise – through appeal to earlier traditions that enable him to assert his own identity:

> CARAFFA: [to Julius] Shameful. Obscene and shameful. This artist takes his inspiration from the Greeks, who glorified the human body. He has turned Your Holiness' own chapel into a pagan temple.
> BEMBO: No, no. Forgive me, Cardinal. Rather his fault lies in having strayed too far from the Greeks ... Those twisted masses of flesh! Those tormented muscles! Surely no Greek would have painted so. Barbarous.

Michelangelo attempts to remain both faithful to and distanced from the authority of the father. In the five scenes of the Creation, the fall and expulsion from Eden, and the story of Noah, the central figure is Man, placed at the apex of the ceiling, brought to life through the touch of divinity. Adam is made in God's image, perfect, beautiful, not tainted by original sin. Elsewhere, other figures, like the Titans, represent the age's celebration of human power and achievement. Vasari describes the ceiling in this way:

> Then he went on to the Creation of Adam, where he showed God being borne by a group of nude angels of tender age who appear to be bearing up not one figure alone but the weight of the world; and this effect is achieved by the venerable majesty of the Divine Form and the way in which he moves, embracing some of the putti with one arm, as if to support himself, while with the other he stretches out his right hand towards Adam, a figure whose beauty, pose, and contours are such that it seems to have been fashioned that very moment by the first and supreme creator rather than by the drawing and brush of a mortal man.
> (1983: 354)

They are the visual equivalents of Hamlet's eulogy, 'What a piece of work is a man,' inspired by the supreme father-figure (Freud 1984b: 73), a personal God, psychologically nothing other than the exalted father, created by the usurper of his authority, the Promethean son who challenges as well as obeys the will of the father. At this level Michelangelo's art is the narrativisation of the self, the visualisation on the Sistine Chapel ceiling of the relationship with his father, displaced on to the figure of Pope Julius II, a drama that in pictorial terms, far from being pure invention is dredged from the memories of his own childhood, defined by Freud, in his analysis of Leonardo's sources of creativity, as the 'secret mental impulses, which are hidden even from himself, by means of the work that he creates' (Freud 1984b: 57). The relationship between Michelangelo and Pope Julius allowed Reed, via Freud, to explore the ways in which an artist's work discloses the enduring bonds between parents and offspring. Michelangelo's art, like Reed's, is a survey of observable reality, but in both cases art is also the artist's way of understanding himself, above all, in his relationship with an absent (Beerbohm Tree) or surrogate (Pope Julius) father.

Trapeze (1965)

Reed's attempts to make a film on its publication of Max Catto's The Killing Frost (1959, first published in 1950) were shelved. While considering instead the possibility of a film on the legendary circus owner Barnum, he was contacted in 1955 by Lancaster and Hecht, who by now were also interested in filming The Killing Frost, retitled Trapeze, and scripted by Liam O'Brien, James Webb and Wolf Mankowitz. Reed was offered a cut of the profits, artistic control and independence in direction (Wapshott 1990: 276). As a former acrobat, Lancaster had wanted to do for the circus what Powell and Pressburger had done for ballet in The Red Shoes (1948): to dramatise the reality of rehearsal, performance and offstage life in the 'Greatest Show on Earth'. As dance is the dominant metaphor for The Red Shoes, so the high wire is the figurative landscape for the characters in Trapeze. Reed was delighted by this opportunity to continue to work for a Hollywood outfit, and production duly began in the autumn of 1955, on an eventual budget of $4million, with filming taking place principally at the Cirque d'Hiver, as well as at the Billancourt studios in Paris. Far from the 'standard Hollywoodian' fare, derogatively referred to by Durgnat (1971: 168), the result was one of Reed's most powerful films. Lancaster was joined by Tony Curtis from Universal and by Gina Lollobrigida who, along with Anna Magnani and Sophia Loren, was already a major star of the Italian cinema. Two circus films – a genre that includes examples as grandiose as De Mille's The Greatest Show on Earth (1952) and as voyeuristic as Tod

Browning's *Freaks* (1932) – had recently appeared, and with which *Trapeze* had much in common: Renoir's *The Golden Coach* (1953), a story about a forceful leading lady (Magnani) in an Italian circus that travels to Mexico, and *Carnival Story* (Neumann, 1954), with Anne Baxter in the Magnani role of the assertive female. The Magnani and Baxter roles invite comparison with Lollobrigida's in *Trapeze*.

Gina Lollobrigida's credentials for the film were driven by the box office. She was paid $160,000, a huge salary for a foreign film star. Her casting in her previous film as the world's most beautiful woman, *La donna più bella del mondo* (Leonard, 1954), as well as in earlier ones where she appears as a faithless wife (*La infidele* (Monicelli, 1953)) and a prostitute (*Woman of Rome* (Zampa, 1954)), confirmed her status as one of the cinema's sex goddesses. She was thus the focus of the reviewers of *Trapeze*: the headlines announcing the making of the film in *The Star* proclaim 'La Lollo's return' (Anon 1955b); *The Daily Sketch* refers to 'La Lollo on the trapeze' (Anon 1955a); *The Daily Telegraph* exclaims: 'Lollobrigida Enchantress' (Dixon 1956), and *The Daily Express* is even less ambiguous: 'La Lollo Speaks English – I Wasn't Listening' (Mosley 1956). And yet, for all the undoubted impact of La Lollo's concupiscent physique, her other attributes do not go by entirely unnoticed. Leonard Mosley in *The Daily Express* pays tribute to them: '... a short scene in which she tells Lancaster what she thinks of him. All she is wearing by this time – for she has been at work with her zip fastener – is a towel wrapping. And I think it is a tribute to Lollo's skill that suddenly her inner talent triumphs over her outer shape – and you forget the curves and the covering and pay attention to the words and the expression in the eyes' (1956). The second edition (1959) of the novel exploits the casting of Gina Lollobrigida in the film. It shows her in close-up, shoulders bared seductively, against a background of miniscule flying male trapezists, the contrasts in size between Gina and the men a measure of the power she holds over them.

Gina Lollobrigida clearly does not belong to Reed's repertoire of what Sue Harper would classify as Anglo-Saxon 'nice girls', the Jessie Matthews of *Climbing High*, the Shani Wallis of *Oliver!* or the Phyllis Calvert of *Kipps*. Less sinister than Aissa in *Outcast*, less bitter than Anna in *The Third Man*, she nevertheless belongs to a list of dark-haired and darkly motivated *belles dames sans merci* exotics ruled by passion or self-interest. Her Italianness links her to the meanings associated with the film's continental setting. Italy and France are routinely associated in the Anglo-Saxon imagination with sex. One of the major differences between the two is that Paris usually connotes libertinage, *liaisons* – often *dangereuses* – that ultimately resist moral judgement, whereas Italy

– more Mediterranean, more family-orientated, more governed by notions of family honour, vendetta and matriarchal power – offers sex with domesticity.

While Gina signed her contract without difficulties, the accounts of Tony Curtis's involvement are contradictory. In his autobiography Curtis claims Universal were not reluctant to loan him out, adding that Lew Wasserman re-drafted his contract precisely in order to allow him to work outside the studio. But, in her biography of Burt Lancaster, Kate Buford (2000) argues that Lancaster exerted considerable pressure on Universal to get Curtis. Whatever the truth, Curtis himself described the role as 'the most important of my career' (Curtis and Paris 1994: 127), not least perhaps because of its commercial success. The film grossed $7.5 million in the USA alone and, even though initially faring less well critically, prompted revised opinion when Lancaster won the best actor award at the Berlin Film Festival in 1956.

The novel, *The Killing Frost*, starts out, beyond its eulogy of the balletic grace of the trapeze artists, as a description of the rivalry between two men for the love of a woman, but ends up as a narrative of frustrated gay desire in which one of the lovers, Ribble, kills the woman who has come between him and the man he loves. His libido is satisfied by women, but more fulfilling desires are sparked by men: 'They [women]'re out to get hold of you, body and soul. They don't know that a man's got to have his freedom, sex is just one of his appetites – but with women it's everything, the beginning and the end. They try to smother you with love. Love? It's just possession. They squeeze the life out of you. They won't let a man have any interests but them ... Women! They make me sick' (Catto 1959: 74). Ribble seduces the woman – in the novel, an Anglo-French *femme fatale* – away from Tino, only to murder her for having destroyed his relationship with him, before himself committing suicide after Tino's execution for the crime of which he is innocent. In *The Killing Frost*, misogyny is Ribble's driving force; in the film, other issues are drawn into the delineaments of his personality. But while the film is unable to make direct reference to gay desire, it suffers from no coyness in eulogising the body of the male through the balletic grace of the male trapeze artists in their skimpy vests on sculpted torsos.

Treated more indirectly in the film, homosexuality remains an interest. The eroticisation of Burt Lancaster as Ribble and Tony Curtis as Tino clearly works on two levels, appealing both to heterosexual and homosexual audiences. Lancaster's evolution from Noir-related, damaged proletarian loser (e.g. *The Killers* (Siodmak, 1946), *Criss Cross* (Siodmak, 1948), *Brute Force* (Dassin, 1947)) to matinee idol pin up (e.g. *The Flame*

and the Arrow (Tourneur, 1950), *The Crimson Pirate* (Siodmak, 1952))
where his torso routinely suffered shameless exposure, is allowed to
progress in this film, though even here the anguished persona of his
Noir roles is nuanced in early shots by irresistible delight in the display
of his magnificent swashbuckler physique. The opening shots of
Trapeze recall those of *The Crimson Pirate*. In the latter, Lancaster's Vallo
swings into view from a rope tied to a ship's mast to address his
audience: 'Gather round lads and lasses! Gather round!'. The words are
uttered through lips stretched to form Hollywood's most recognisable,
orthodontically near perfect, slightly minatory, six-inch wide Pepsodent-
white grin. The smile aims for friendliness but seems also, narcissis-
tically, to honour its owner's manly beauty. It illuminates a body sheathed
in crimson tights, its bared torso's modesty protected only by a sash,
also crimson, draped over the right shoulder to cover a manly breast.
Burt Lancaster's honey-tinted flowing locks (darker and shorter in the
Noir films) add to the theatricality and specularisation of the persona in
this and subsequent scenes (at one point mutating into outright, though
comic, femininity when Vallo's schemes require cross-dressing). Traced
over with these as well as some of the darker tendencies, *Trapeze*
gestures to the Burt Lancaster of *The Crimson Pirate*, and has Ribble, the
doomed trapeze artist, also swing into view at the top of a (circus) mast.
Gone here, though, are the flowing bottle-blond locks and narcissistic
grin; the aerial acrobatics lead in this film not to unblemished heroic
feats, but to disaster, for before the credits vanish Ribble falls from the
grip of his catcher to become the misanthropic rigger, eventually rescued
from bitter reclusiveness by Lola and Tino.

This panegyric of male beauty through Lancaster's athletic form is
matched at another level by Tony Curtis. To Lancaster's Zeus Curtis is
Gannymede, the 'daring young man on the flying trapeze, flying through
the air with the greatest of ease', the boyish beauty (Lancaster born in
1913, Curtis in 1925), whose equally gym-toned body is lit up by large
periwinkle eyes and thick dark lashes the envy of any budding female
starlet on the Universal lot from which for his role as Tino he was
plucked. Lancaster and Curtis are the perfect male couple (teaming up
again in McKendrick's *Sweet Smell of Success*, 1957), a marriage between
equal paragons of male beauty. Once Ribble agrees to be Tino's catcher,
and to act as tutor to the younger, uncrippled man's quest for the triple
somersault on the trapeze, the transformation of men into gods of the
air is complete. In *Carnival Story* the audience comes to see 'gods in
action', as Bill (George Nader), one of her admirers puts it to 'Willie'
(Anne Baxter), hoping for accidents and death. But, with or without its
mortal dangers, the trapeze in *Trapeze*, where in a deliberate pattern of

onomatopoeia 'triples' by 'Ribble' lead to 'cripples', is also here what Hitchcock would have called a 'MacGuffin', an excuse for a story about human desire. When Tino, casually dressed in leather jacket and slacks, bounds up the stairs of a Paris Metro station in search of fame, Reed's elaborate allegory of love-hatred begins.

The budding relationship between the pair is threatened when they are joined by Lola to form a female-complicated triple act that threatens the male-only 'triple' somersault that binds Tino and Ribble to each other. The 'triple', though, already points towards a lack, a skill in three movements played out by only two men, a pairing ready for expansion through Lola's intervention in a dangerous triangle of desire. No sooner does Lola join the act than trouble begins. The trio stand behind the curtain, awaiting the fanfare announcing to the crowd their entry into the ring. For a moment Lola (by now attracted to Ribble, even though Tino had been her earlier target) and Tino squabble, but Ribble utters a command of patriarchal authority: 'Tino!', a single word sufficient to restore, even though only temporarily, the male order jeopardised by a designing woman. Ribble calls the troupe to attention, one arm raised aloft, their statuesque pose prefacing ascent to their heavenly perches. These Olympians shame the lesser mortals of the circus, the overweight owner, the dwarf, the bit players, all of whom are a sort of composite reality principle to offset the ideal fantasy figures of the fliers who, in the air, gliding to the tune of the Blue Danube waltz (replacing the novel's 'Libiano' waltz from *La Traviata*), look at life from lofty heights, making sense of the world from distant horizons. The men are dressed in trousers and vests; their trousers failing to conceal the contours of their manhood, their vests, cut to a décolleté, revealing sufficiently their pectorals and sculpted shoulders to gratify the desires of all sexual orientations. The taut, he-man outlines of these 1950s icons are set off by the curvaceous figure of Gina Lollobrigida, her allure further embroidered through the more colourful patterns of her costume. While her corset-shaped uniform, squeezing her wasp-waisted upper body into a voluptuous shape is flecked with a variety of colours, the men's vests and trousers are snowy-white. Their belts, though, as if now indelibly stamped by her pervasive influence, mirror the colours of Lola's costume, their white capes signifying a virile purity soon to be violated by the woman in their midst.

Not uncommonly for a film made by Carol Reed, Tino's quest for Ribble, before distraction by Lola, is a search for an absent father and, through him, a lost identity. This slightly reverses the pattern in the novel where, though we are informed Tino is 25 and Ribble 40, it is Tino who is described as having a protective feeling for Mike and his childish ways (Catto 1959: 152). Here Tino's quest for his father surrogate Ribble carries double-edged Oedipal significance: first, the journey from New York to Paris, that parallels Ribble's, many years earlier, along the same route, focuses on the son's need for a role model and guidance from a man of experience, a quest given metaphorical expression through the desire to learn the 'triple' that only Ribble can teach; second, once in Paris, another journey begins. When Tino suspects Lola of deception, he makes for the maestro's home, to return his mislaid walking stick. This journey within a journey culminates in Tino's witnessing of Lola's betrayal, a discovery readable as Tino's spectatorship of the primal scene. Tino returns the walking stick,or phallus, to the father, forced to prevent his own castration at his hands through denial of his passion for Lola, the mother-figure in their triangle of desire. The triangulation of these adult relationships points to the displaced wishes and frustrations of childhood, but, seen from the perspectives of the two men, it is also suffused with homosexual meaning, the rivalry for Lola motivated partly by undeclared or unconscious same-sex desire.

As the film explores these interlocking passions, Tino's quest becomes, at the very least, a mediation, in social and political terms, of the period's growing uncertainty about dominant models of masculinity. The novel's frame of reference is late 1940s America; the film's, while clearly continuing to draw on post-war, post-Korean and post-McCarthy American realities, is further complicated by its director's Britishness. *Trapeze* is caught between the more war-damaged roles – including Reed's own Johnny McQueen or Harry Lime – of 1940s British and Hollywood males, and the more questioning ones of 60s anti-heroes. The fifties saw in England, perhaps more than in the USA, a spate of films, like *The Dam Busters* (Anderson, 1954) or *The Colditz Story* (Hamilton, 1954), that endorsed more comfortable definitions of masculinity. Even so, films like *The Browning Version* (Asquith, 1951), the Ealing comedies, or the rise of the Hammer Horror film, allowed room for less mainstream versions of masculinity, as Alec Guinness or Christopher Lee or feminised stars like Dirk Bogarde launched their own idiosyncratic assaults on dominant trends. The more direct address of homosexuality of a film like *Victim* (Dearden, 1961), and the full impact of the Angry Young Men in the theatre and their 1960s variants in the 'Free cinema' and beyond, were yet to be felt. Nevertheless, British films of the 1950s, in keeping with the agendas of those made in Hollywood by, say, Lang, Ray or Sirk, are also imbued with the contradictions and ambiguities of male identity that later decades tackled more robustly.

In many 1950s Hollywood films disorientated individuals, confused by the demands of the social order, seek out patriarchal figures in vain attempts to cure their own insecurities. In some films, for instance *Rebel without a Cause* (Ray, 1953), or *Written on the Wind* (Sirk, 1956), these men have feet of clay. The pattern is reproduced in *Trapeze*, where Ribble, the father-figure, is not only absent (he is in Paris, not America), but also crippled, his damaged leg the outward sign, like L. B. Jefferies's broken leg in *Rear Window* (Hitchcock, 1954), made only a year previously, of a wounded inner self. The setting of the film, Paris, the Cirque d'Hiver, the bar, Ribble's flat, connotes exotic, slightly menacing, sexual revelry. This blend of elements, both positive and negative, is crystallised in Ribble, his patriarchal authority confirmed by a history of sexual adventures, and undermined by his down-at-heel, even alcoholic, demeanour and moral and physical abasement signified by physical injury.

Exoticism (the world of the circus), sex (Katy Jurado and Gina Lollobrigida), and danger (the caged animals, the trapeze itself) are the film's defining features of Paris. Catto's Paris is a city 'that stirred your blood. He (the Detective on Ribble's trail) didn't care much for the French – cynical lot, no substance to 'em – but you couldn't help feeling they got the devil of a lot of pleasure out of just breathing and walking about. Vivacious! They gave you the sensation that it was good to be alive' (1959: 254). It had already been the *mise-en-scène* of desire in a Reed collaboration, *It Happened in Paris*. There it repeats a traditional view of the city, illustrated by the intertitle of *A Woman of Paris* (Chaplin, 1923), 'where fortune is fickle and a woman gambles with life'. In *Trapeze*, Paris is an appropriate setting for a drama concerned with victims of desire, where through their obscure idols of love men and women unconsciously seek regression to the securities of parental authority.

But the bonds between Ribble and Tino reach beyond the complications of father/son relations to reflection on the contrast between what might be called closed and open personalities. Adam Phillips's discussion on narcissism (2000) provides a useful point of entry to this further dimension in the relations between Ribble and Tino: 'Narcissism, broadly speaking, becomes one of the keywords in psychoanalysis for those forms of life that, in various ways, have tried to escape from all those things that are assumed, by the different psychoanalytical theorists, to make a life worth living. A good life is one in which one has been able to escape from the right things' (2000: 204). In going on to discuss the patient suffering from narcissism, Phillips writes of an infant who has been too open, 'too receptive to the mother's messages' (2000: 205), needing perhaps to find ways of closure. Inspired by Laplanche, he writes of the personality as having systolic and diastolic impulses (2000: 205). For the patient who seeks in analysis release from narcissism, Philips refers to Laplanche's stress on a deconstruction of the old, a subversion of the coherent story of the self constructed by the patient. Deconstruction prepares the ground for a new construction. Most importantly, according to Laplanche, in his or her creation of a sense of self, the infant is especially prone to messages from the mother:

> And it is finally inevitable that the messages should be enigmatic, and so in need of translation ... For Laplanche this is what might once have been called the given, the foundational experience, from which escape is not possible, of being the recipient of the mother's unconscious messages. Escape, one can say, is not an option here; it is not a question of how to get away, but of what can be done by way of continuing retranslation ... that which the subject wishes to escape from but cannot is considered to be his essence. (2000: 207)

Ribble, not a case history of the narcissistic patient, nevertheless displays a narcissistic tendency. After his fall, he becomes a man locked within himself, his lowly status as a rigger leading to a shabby existence that excludes him from the ranks of the admired *dramatis personae* of the circus, forcing him into solitary retreat, to life as a malcontent whose acquired narcissism has found no one to deconstruct it. The most obvious cause of this condition is his injury, a fall from the catcher's grip and from grace in a profession in which he seems condemned to be a menial rigger. But the dependency of Ribble on the circus, as well as a chance remark by a former lover, Rosa (Katy Jurado), point to perhaps the more than literal causes of his condition. By refusing initially Tino's requests to come out of retirement and to teach his eager pupil the triple, Ribble seeks forlornly, to escape from his past. By remaining in the circus, albeit in the lowly capacity of a rigger, he has, however, epitomised the futility of this ambition. Additionally, Ribble is at first alone, disavowing his need for a partner – male or female – for companionship or love, for otherness. At first, too, having eventually agreed to work on the triple with Tino, thus loosening up his narcissism to make room for male companionship, he hurls abuse at Lola before feigning affection as part of a strategy to discredit her in Tino's eyes. During his phase of hostility towards Lola, one definable as a continued narcissistic escape from women, his angry remark to Rosa – a former lover, now married to another circus performer – about her unwelcome maternal attentions reveals the deeper causes of his malaise. His failure to escape from the world of the circus represents an inability to distance himself from an excessive 'receptive openness to ... the mother's messages'

(Phillips 2000: 206). His apparent transformation from narcissistic misogynist to loving partner for Lola satisfies studio preference for happy endings, but does little to contradict the notion that the whole cycle of escape, narcissism and need will be set in motion once more. Nevertheless, the emergence – however temporary – of Ribble from narcissistic seclusion to reconciliation with otherness through companionship and love for Tino and Lola provides a life-affirming antidote to a traumatic condition through the potentially healing power of human contact.

Lola's function is partly to serve as an important channel through which Ribble confronts and unlocks his isolation, but although the film pairs Lola and Ribble in its happy ending enough has been exposed through the ambiguity of Reed's assertive, sexually self-conscious opportunist to raise questions about the durability or even desirability of this relationship. There are moments when the film's deep suspicions about women develop into caricature. At one point Lola appears, decked out in another of her figure-hugging costumes, in black tights and glistening corset-shaped top, her hair crowned with pink wing-like adornments that, like the silver jewel-studded and moon-shaped tiara from another scene, create the impression she has sprouted diabolical horns, of a piece with her fleeting association with the circus snake. Lola's sexual devilry is, however, given plausible and qualifying social contexts that explain the root causes of her self-centredness. Her poor origins are the spur to ruthless acts of survival: 'I don't want to love you,' she tells Ribble, a remark that, while acknowledging the strength of her feelings for him, sees them as obstacles to her triumph through career over poverty. When, at first, Ribble assaults her verbally – 'For your sake Lola get out, or one day these hands won't be there to catch you!' – and when, also, one of the members of the act she abandons delivers a blow to her face, the film exposes the prejudices of men threatened by assertive women.

The equivocal imagery that surrounds Lola is mirrored by the ambivalent treatment of Ribble. Often photographed through nets, he too seems in need of rescue from captivity. An early low angle shot, looking up at the flyers, includes a clown at the bottom right hand edge of the frame, a mute ironic commentator on characters whose aerial acrobatics are also flights of ultimately earth-bound fantasies. When, finally, Ribble surrenders to Lola, the film recognises the power of love for good as well as ill, affirming that the all-male space of the trapeze benefits from the intrusion of the female. When the circus-owner exclaims that Lola is what the audience wants to see his remark stretches beyond the usual appeal to the objectification of the female to the view that the female belongs with the male, and vice versa, that the contribution of the female is essential both in relation to the feminisation of the male and to the balance and variety in the spectacle of life. Like Johnny in *Odd-Man Out*, Ribble is forced to soften his rigid masculinity through assimilation of femininity, here given unambiguous expression through the Lola, or 'La Lollo', as she was known to her tabloid scribes and fans, of Gina Lollobrigida.

The last hurrah

7

Oliver! (1968)

Although *The Last Warrior* (1970) and *Follow Me* (1972) are not without merit, both films were relative flops, with *The Last Warrior*, the story of an inebriated Indian stirring up trouble on a reservation, eventually withdrawn from circulation. The film that gave a boost to Reed's flagging reputation was *Oliver!*, by any standards an impressive musical, and true epilogue to a long and distinguished, though variable, career. In retrospect *Oliver!* seems like an incongruous film for the times. The end of the 1960s, the decade of so-called sexual liberation, was also one of political upheaval. Vietnam and the Paris riots of May 1968 are perhaps the two most dramatic episodes of the period's turbulence, anticipated or reflected in films like *Weekend* (Godard, 1967), *Z* (Costa-Gavras, 1968), and *If* (Anderson, 1968). This was the context in which *Oliver!* was made, seven years after its first night on the London stage, a film version that, while recognising the box office potential of a smash hit, became in Reed's hands a mediation of the age's radicalism into a predominantly escapist genre that additionally found sources in the Dickens original, and the earlier film versions, for commentary on gender and the relations between the sexes. Although Reed had made one musical early on, *A Girl Must Live*, and had included musical interludes in other films, such as in *Climbing High* and *The Third Man*, he was a director identified with less idealistic genres. Columbia, who owned the rights to the film, offered it to Reed on the back of his work for them on *The Key*, *Our Man in Havana*, and *The Running Man*, and perhaps also in acknowledgement of his sensitive handling of child actors. His Britishness was also considered an important factor for a film carved out of a novel by one of the most quintessential of British cultural icons, Charles Dickens. The offer, even to a director uncomfortable in musicals, was too good to refuse.

While some British actors and actresses appeared in Hollywood musicals – e.g. Jack Buchanan, Peter Lawford – and while some British musicals achieved a measure of success – above all, Jessie Matthews films such as *Evergreen* (Saville, 1934) or *First a Girl* (Saville, 1935), the Gracie Fields (*Sing As We Go* [Dean, 1934]) and George Formby (*It's in the Air* (Kimmins, 1938)) or Anna Neagle films like *Spring in Park Lane* (Wilcox, 1948) – the genre has a relatively poor history both in the careers of British stars in Hollywood, and in the British cinema in general. Immediately prior to *Oliver!*, the genre flickered into life with *Half a Sixpence* (Sidney, 1967), the musical version of *Kipps*.

As ever, a film musical that owes its origins to a stage version, especially one that was a smash hit on both sides of the Atlantic, runs the risk of unfavourable comparison with other productions. Often the film version is regarded as too respectful of the stage original. The Rodgers and Hammerstein musicals, for instance, have sometimes been undervalued for that reason. The further weight under which the fame and relative neglect that *Oliver!* has laboured are issues concerned with fidelity to one of the most well-known stories in the history of English literature, one that, additionally, had spawned non-musical versions, perhaps the most famous of which was David Lean's *Oliver Twist* (1948).

Like most musicals, *Oliver!* is, to use Dyer's term, largely 'utopian' (1977a). The very last scene, as the credits roll, reprises one of the big production numbers, 'Consider Yourself', sung by the chorus of East End Londoners celebrating Oliver's finally successful attempts to find love and a family. More than that, the number, as in many musicals, affirms the importance of community. This choice, not any of the more reflective, solitary recitatives or individual *tours de force*, such as 'Where is Love?', or 'I'm Reviewing the Situation', highlights the social more than the personal, sending the audience back home to its own various communities with optimism and renewed energy. The closure's celebration of community, though, and the temptation to read the reunification of the Dodger and Fagin routine, as they cheekily dance out of the frame to continue their pick-pocketing careers as a sort of Panglossian comment on human affairs, do not entirely drown out the minor chords of a film that in some respects bring *Oliver!* into line with musicals like *West Side Story* (Wise, 1961) and *Cabaret* (Fosse, 1972), that are not squeamish about emphasising what in a description of downbeat musicals Michael Wood (1975) has referred to as the darkness in the dance. *Oliver!* makes a virtue of the narrative's inescapable inclusion of Nancy's death, drawing on it to provide its own commentary, in its own formal way, on violence. In this film brutality and kindness are constant companions, their fusion a topic developed in the preparation and structure of the musical numbers. Reed's *Oliver!*, though, is the least sombre of the four most famous versions: in the original novel Fagin is hanged; in the silent (Lloyd Bacon, 1922), and Lean (1948), films he is arrested by the police; here he escapes justice. There is no shot to match the drawing by Cruickshank – the illustrator of the Dickens first edition – of Shylock sitting alone in the condemned man's cell – included in the Lloyd Bacon version – his face contorted by terror as he awaits execution.

Like the best musicals, *Oliver!* gives its audiences intense pleasures through narrative, character, star performers, as well as through its array of formal effects: music, dance, colour, décor, camera movement and so on. The characters and narrative are well enough known but unlike, say, Donen/Kelly or Astair/Rogers, or Jessie Matthews musicals, *Oliver!* boasts no big name stars, something that initially worried Columbia. While Harry Secombe and Shani Wallis had minor reputations, Ron Moody, on whom so much depended as Fagin, was unknown. Making up for the stars' relative obscurity is the film's exuberant form. The numbers in *Oliver!*, with their multiple layers of fantasy, provide spectacular effects. Benefiting from Hollywood expertise – choreography by Onna White, orchestration by John Green and Eric Rogers – the film was in no danger of being compromised by the more cramped style of the British musical. The combination of these talents allowed Reed, with his professionalism and sure handling of child actors, to rise to the challenge of directing a film in a genre with which he had only a passing acquaintance, and succeeded in making *Oliver!* that rare commodity, a first-rate British musical.

The last thirty years or so have seen much critical commentary on the musical that removes it from coffee table or high camp discussion. The links between number and narrative are now taken for granted. Even in the most banal examples – say Betty Grable's number 'O'Brien has gone Hawaian' in *Song of the Islands* (alter Lang, 1942) – numbers are seen to emerge from the narrative, to have some connection with it (very loose in *The Jolson Story* (Green and Lewis, 1949), very tight in *Meet Me in St Louis* (Minnelli, 1942)), moments of even more poetic licence to embroider, tease out, showcase or comment on matters raised in the narrative. There are, strictly speaking, ten numbers in *Oliver!*, though one or two of these are reprised, and the orchestral music of some of them is used non-diegetically to accompany different scenes, usually to provide perspective. For instance, 'Where Is Love?' is often used to underscore Oliver's search for affection and perhaps, above all, maternal love, such as when Nancy sets out to inform on Fagin and Sikes, after the latter takes Oliver – recaptured while on his way to pay Mr

Brownlow's book bill – on a house-breaking mission. The background music 'Where Is Love?' positions Nancy as a surrogate mother figure, a forerunner of Mr Brownlow's housekeeper at the end of the film when Oliver returns home. These are the Good Mother figures who are the wish-fulfilment alternatives to the Bad Mother figures at the workhouse and at the undertaker's.

For the first few minutes there is no dialogue, only music as, taking full advantage through all the resources of the medium, the film presents its generic credentials. The opening number, 'Food, Glorious Food', choreographically recalls *Metropolis* (Lang, 1926). Like the down-trodden workers in one of the late German Expressionist cinema's greatest dystopias, the workhouse children in *Oliver!* are regimented captives, seen at first on a treadmill, then descending in columns into an ever deeper abyss of underworld enslavement, the sign 'God of Love' and the contrasted meals of gruel for the children, and sumptuous menus for their masters, no consolation for children whose spiritual needs are eclipsed by those of their famished stomachs.

'Food glorious food / Hot sausage and mustard / While we're in the mood / Cold jelly and custard' they sing. The opening lines, though, are not just a cry for any type of food, they are a schoolboy's dream menu, the 1950s lyrics written by a song-writer/composer whose East End and pre-Macdonald's era origins reflect the popular taste of the day. The parallels between spiritual and bodily forms of sustenance continue as 'Food, Glorious Food' gives way seamlessly to the Beadle's 'For what we are about to receive ...' operatically delivered Grace, followed by the boys' sung reply, 'Amen', and another shot of the 'God is Love' sign. The Rabelaisian figure of Harry Secombe, his benignly comic Goonish associations, mitigating the negative aura of his role as the Beadle, to some extent counteracts the equally overblown size of the horse-faced workhouse mistress (Peggy Mount) and the sybaritic governors.

While the over-fed privileged few are rotund, and move naturally, the children are skeletal, their movements – even when eating – stiff and mechanical, responding to the commands of the Beadle. The meagre repast completed, Oliver draws the short straw. After he pronounces the immortal words, 'Please sir! I want some more!', the response is again musical as the Beadle issues instructions to stop the fleeing culprit who has dared ask for a second helping. The music's allegro rhythm is accompanied by the frantic camera work and editing that record Oliver's attempts at flight, before the pace slackens and the Beadle takes up the song 'Oliver! Oliver! Never before has a boy wanted more.' Like the juvenile protagonists of the picaresque novel, Oliver must liberate himself from the physical and moral squalor into which he was born, before being re-born, released from the underworlds of the workhouse and the undertaker's that are his unwelcome birthright.

The theme of captivity in an underworld continues in the film's subsequent number, 'Where Is Love?'. Punished for daring to defend his dead mother's honour, Oliver finds himself more desperately alone, surrounded by coffins, as he launches into the affecting lyrics, set to a plangent, slow-moving melody: 'Where is love? / Does it fall from skies above? / Is it underneath the willow tree / That I've been dreaming of? / Where is she / Whom I close my eyes to see? / Will I ever know the sweet hello / That is meant for only me?'. The lyrics pick up the earlier ironic reference to the divine origins of love: true love is divine, or natural (the willow tree) but hidden, its revelation secret and available only to the initiate. Oliver's role typifies not only the yearning of all human beings for love but also the special quality of the relations between mother and child, as well as the operations of a secular form of grace, making him the representative of the wish-fulfilment fantasy of the rewards of love to those who are prepared to look for it. The rewards are his miraculous release from his prison-like cell when the bars of his window come away in his hands, enabling him to escape from the underworld of the undertaker's.

Mark Lester's Oliver is made to endure further ordeals before this figure of grace, of almost unearthly angelic looks and manner – with his blond locks, trusting expression, and fragile, barely audible voice, more innocent than in the impersonations by Jackie Coogan or John Howard Davies – can 'consider himself' rescued by the upper world. Reed's *Oliver!* is a study in the violation of purity by evil. The exaggerated softness of the child is designed to stir the audience's protective instincts. The camerawork of the 'Where is Love' number, with its slow movement, alternate shots of Oliver in medium and close-up contributing to the effect of the character's lamb-like softness and vulnerability, is abandoned in 'Consider Yourself', one of the big production number set pieces. Here, what Robert Moss refers to as the 'Hogarthian ambience' of a London swarming with individuals and groups from seemingly every walk of life, celebrates the teeming vitality of the capital, a world of tumblers, newspaper boys, chimney sweeps, policemen, all going about their business, from which the Artful Dodger emerges to lead Oliver away to an alternative, darker world whose superficial differences fail to obliterate obvious similarities: the sunlit world of the Covent Garden community provides a contrast to the shady world inhabited by Fagin and his boys. But, as in the outer world, so in its dark underside, there is music. The legitimate businesses of the upper world, celebrated in song and dance, are immediately contrasted with the illegitimate pursuits of the criminal underworld, led by Fagin in the 'You Got to Pick a Pocket or Two' number. The number in honour of thievery, defined as merely a game ('just a game, Oliver, just a game') points to a truth about the gang's activities. As the criminals are almost entirely children – the exceptions, along with Fagin, being Nancy and Sikes – thieving is to some extent a children's game, Fagin a kind of Pied Piper figure, avenging himself on a community that has spurned him – on social or even racial grounds – by leading some of its children astray.

When Fagin goes into his 'You Got to Pick a Pocket or Two' routine, he dresses up for the occasion, putting on a black hat, green overcoat, cane and handkerchiefs, as if for a show, or a game of deceit. This spirit of ludic, Bakhtinian marginalisation – the Jewish East Ender – is later seen watching over the sleeping, exhausted Oliver. The revelry of the number is replaced by a change of mood, as Fagin's absurd antics give way to dramatic gravitas, a fatherly concern invested with tragic pathos, reaching out to the lost boy, and through him, to his own mislaid fatherhood, the fugitive from justice but also the father-figure to the Barrie-esque lost boys in his criminal care. As he watches over the slumbering Oliver, Fagin begins to hum, slowly and softly, almost as a lullaby the melody of 'You Got to Pick a Pocket or Two', its Hebraic chords of melancholy mixing in with the sound of a distant church bell tolling to form a hybridised anthem for all outcasts.

The counter family into which Oliver is welcomed shares features with the straight family, caricaturing to some extent the latter's strategies – especially in its more dysfunctional aspects – by providing an exaggerated parental presence that inhibits the child's independence. The children in Fagin's gang are brought up to be terrified of independence, their criminality and fear of captivity and punishment by the law the seal that prevents the drive towards separation.

So, as Fagin watches over Oliver, he combines the straight parent's genuine concern as well as that over-protectiveness for a child that undermines conflict and independence. The next two numbers, 'It's a Fine Life' and 'I'd Do Anything' serve partially to flesh out the counter-family ambience of Fagin's world, something that acquires its most moving expression through the construction of Nancy as a mother-surrogate for the boys. In another evocation of *Metropolis*, Nancy is a flashback to the Good Mother figure, first seen drawing the under-privileged children to her skirts in one of the film's earliest scenes. 'It's a Fine Life', as later, also, 'Oom pah-pah', her last number before death at Sikes's hands, stresses the normality of the Cockney-with-a-heart-of-gold, toast of the local community, whose life-affirming attributes are summarised in the opening line, 'It's a Fine Life!'. The second number, with Nancy now at Fagin's, shows the extent of the children's devotion to their mother-substitute, the Wendy to this community of lost boys: 'I'd Do Anything for You!'.

Fagin, though, is the more controlling parent, and his authority is reclaimed in the next number: 'If You Go, But Be Back Soon'. The children go, as if to school, not to study but to work, sent on their way with a wave by a possessive parent. This latest of the miserable counter-family underworlds to which Oliver is in his early life condemned is contrasted, finally, with the Utopian family, Oliver's rightful world, presided over by his grandfather, Mr Brownlow. The darker hues of Fagin's world are replaced by John Box's art work of brightly lit white façade décor in the Regency-style crescent inhabited by Mr Brownlow and neighbours. This is the setting for 'Who Will Buy My Sweet Red Roses?'. Long shots of the sweep of the crescent, and its invasion by milkmaids, knife-sharpeners, morning horse-riders, road-sweepers and many other law-abiding citizens reformulate the hustle and bustle of the 'Consider Yourself' number, stressing again the value of community, once more setting the criminal or undesirable activities of workhouse, undertaker's or thieves' den against the law-abiding and community-spirited activity of the conventional world. As the number develops, the sequence includes reaction and subjective shots of Oliver who marvels at this world's hitherto only dreamt-of alternatives unfolding before him.

The dream temporarily vanishes when, fearing Oliver's betrayal, Fagin and Sikes compel Nancy to renounce her surrogate-mother status by helping them recover the boy. When, at first, she refuses, urging Sikes to give the boy a chance in life, Sikes puts his hand on Nancy's neck before manhandling and striking her. Here the film cuts to a shot of Dodger and others of Fagin's delinquent band, all shocked by this act of brutality against their saintly madonna. The next shot is of Nancy, hurt, in close-up, her hand held up to her bruised cheek. Sikes departs. Shaken by Sikes's explosion of violence, Fagin offers to help Nancy, but perhaps the greater shock is reserved for the audience as, despite suffering at the hands of Sikes's brutality, Nancy picks herself up and launches into her East End love-song. Weeping, face cupped in her hand, positioned against a dark background, she watches Bill and his dog disappear in the distance, and then, in close-up, tearfully begins to sing 'As Long As He Needs Me'. The camera is quite still. Nancy's voice grows steadily stronger. The camera starts to move, following her in medium shot, as, outside Fagin's den, she walks along the rickety bridge on which Sikes will eventually meet his doom. In this at least the couple, Nancy and Sikes, are united, fatally attracted to each other. With

Sikes's departure, Nancy is left alone in the darkness to deliver her hymn to unconditional love. In no other musical is the link between love and violence so poignantly treated. Sikes's violence speaks less of sadism, the pleasure that arises from cruelty, than from some ill-defined instinct of self-preservation. Sykes is Reed's most extreme portrayal of what R. W. Connell has defined as hegemonic masculinity. Other milder examples include Rex in *The Running Man*, Joe Gowlam in *The Stars Look Down*, the Chief of Police in *Odd Man Out*; even Harry Lime. Drawing on Gramsci, Connell argues that, in relation to gender issues, hegemony refers to models of masculinity that both endorse unequal relations between men and women and promote a dominant, unique and "natural" concept of being a man (Connell 1995).

Characterised throughout the film by an almost permanent attitude of glum hostility, Oliver Reed, Carol Reed's nephew, perfectly captures the character's uncontrollable violence, born of inner turmoil and a damaged psyche that feeds off the unappeased aggression all around. In an East End underworld culture of machismo and fear of feminisation, Sikes acts in accordance with the demands of a perverse social law, perfectly illustrated by the lyrics of Nancy's 'As Long as He Needs Me': 'He doesn't say the things that he should / He acts the way he thinks he should,' a masculinity predicated on violence and denial.

In contrast, Nancy's attraction to Sikes confirms the law of love as a force that heeds neither moral imperative nor rational justification. Like *Carousel*'s (King, 1956) Julie, Nancy is another woman with no logical explanation for her helpless desire, refusing to wonder why reason plays no part in love. Julie's comments on the irrationality of love in *Carousel* could serve to define Nancy's desire: 'What's the use of wonderin' if he's good or if he's bad / Or if you like the way he wears his hat / What's the use of wonderin' if he's good or if he's bad / He's your fella and you love him, and that's all there is to that.' Like Julie's in *Show Boat* who 'can't help lovin' dat man of mine', Nancy's love for Sikes illustrates Freud's concept of 'overvaluation' (1985b: 142–3), the hypnotic process by which the lover is exempted from criticism, becoming in part a substitute for 'an unattained ego ideal of one's own'. Like Anna's fascination by Lime, Nancy's attraction is to a man of strength, whose attributes fill her own void. The problematic relationship between Nancy and Sikes acquires even more poignancy when viewed from the perspectives of the growing feminist literature of the time when the film was made. *The Female Eunuch* was yet to be published, but the novels of Doris Lessing, Fay Weldon, Margaret Drabble, Sylvia Plath and others touch either directly or indirectly on the abuse of women by violent men. Nancy needs to be needed, her masochistic dependence on Sikes, to be controlled, to be maltreated, is attributable to no clear impulse. As the song, 'As Long As He Needs Me' ends, she exits in long shot, the camera remaining behind barriers of wood, in darkness, to suggest that Nancy too is trapped by social circumstances as well as by a self-destructive notion of love, preventing her from 'reviewing the situation' of relations with an abusive lover.

Initially content to define herself through association with a man, she eventually finds her own strength and courage in attempting to foil Sikes's plan to recapture Oliver, a moment when the actions of a Dickensian character turn her into a heroine for the emerging feminism of late 1960s Britain. Fagin, however, ever the survivor, does review the situation. In a series of close and medium shots, he appears like some agonising figure from an El Greco painting, reconsidering his friend-ship, to the accompaniment of Hebraic strains, as if digging deep into his racial identity to find the traditional resources of the Jew's knack for survival in a hostile world.

Oliver! is a film about not only the survival instincts of outsider figures like Fagin and the Dodger, skipping away into the sunset like Chaplin and the little boy in *The Kid* (1921), but also the triumph of innocence. In the decade of Vietnam and the glorification of hegemonic masculinity in films like *The Green Berets* (Wayne, 1968), made in the same year as *Oliver!*, Reed's film offers alternative models: the ludic, regressive, reformable qualities of outsider figures like Fagin and the Dodger, and the innocent, feminised qualities of an Oliver. The film's hyperbole of conformist male violence and hegemonic masculinity, Sikes, denounced by Dickens, Lloyd and Lean in different circum-stances, is also condemned by Reed in the Vietnam years.

Conclusion

8

By any standards, Reed's achievements are considerable, but his often self-deprecating remarks have not helped his reputation. His attitude to his films seems in some ways to parallel the approach to art associated with one of his protagonists, Michelangelo. Reed liberates his films from raw material provided not by divine inspiration, but by a host of collaborators. In producing the finished article from inchoate form, he nevertheless managed to stamp on it his unmistakable personality. In saying this, I am not attempting to re-write the history of auteurism, by forcing Reed into the pantheon of art movie directors. Nevertheless, while recognising and emphasising the collective nature of his art – noting in preceding chapters the contribution of all his collaborators, highlighting the impact of national or transnational traditions, genre, intertextuality, and so on – I have also been struck by unmistakable idiosyncrasies of form and content.

Reed's eye for detail and for creating atmosphere through photography or editing is unsurpassed in the British cinema. In relation to the former, one thinks of the sudden conversion of Havana in the later stages of *Our Man in Havana* from its tourist-brochure representation to a darker alternative when Robert Krasker's slanted camera, also a feature of Reed films not photographed by him, begins to reveal the compromises and betrayals of the vacuum-cleaner salesman tempted by the offer of the Foreign Office shilling. As regards the latter, to cite only one example, the editing of Harry Lime's pursuit by Martins and the police through the Vienna sewers is a lesson in cinematic suspense as Harry's increasingly desperate sprints leading only to deadends climax in the famous shots of his fingers slipping back through the grille once Martins's fatal bullet finds its target.

But content as well as form makes these films undeniably Reed's. Although relying on a wide variety of protagonists, milieux and social classes, their theme is invariably rootlessness or human isolation: a woman suspected of murder in *The Girl in the News*, an abandoned boy in *The Fallen Idol*, a foreigner in *Outcast*, a fraudster in *The Running Man*, an Oedipally fixated artist in *The Agony and the Ecstasy*, a disaffected gunman in *Odd Man Out*, a charismatic racketeer in *The Third Man*. In all these films, but in a way that avoids the narrower constraints of social realism or sexual politics, Reed's discriminating eye sees the shared predicaments of suffering humanity. His characters are often outsiders, individuals excluded either through external or internal circumstances, caught 'between' transgression and conformity whether in aristocratic (e.g. *Climbing High*), working-class (*Penny Paradise*), military (*The Way Ahead*) or any other milieu. The settings of the films – often urban – emphasise the atmosphere of alienation: Havana, Vienna, Belfast, Newcastle, London, are all 'uncanny' spaces offering little or no comfort to their troubled men or women, projecting the inner torments of their marginalised inhabitants. Often, too, the setting is foreign: Cuba (*Our Man in Havana*), the Far East (*Outcast*), Austria (*The Third Man*), Switzerland (*Climbing High*), North Africa (*The Way Ahead*), Spain (*The Running Man*), the Atlantic Ocean (*The Key*), shifting spaces that provide an appropriate background to narratives about displacement and destabilised identity. No film of Reed's, however ultimately unsatisfactory in form or content, is denied some of these characteristic flourishes. Even *Follow Me* is never less than interesting in its dramatisation of the clash between a conformist husband and a free-spirited, rootless American woman (Mia Farrow), in what to her is the alien milieu of London. In *Follow Me*, right at the very end of his career, Reed is still the poet of alienation.

In this respect, although many films concentrate on the shadow of the father over the son, they also include scrutiny of the son's quest for the mother. While the preponderance of father/son narratives may indeed be partly attributable, as some have argued, to feelings prompted by his illegitimacy, Reed's closeness to his mother is an equally significant contributory factor to the films' representation of personal and family relationships. So, for instance, Oliver, Ribble, Willems, Kipps, and the men in *The Way Ahead*, all characters who are asked to measure up to various forms of the masculine paternal ideal, are also to some extent either inspired or compromised by feelings towards real or absent mothers. Seen in this light, Nancy, Lola, Aissa, Ann Pornick, and Mrs Gillingham are, beyond all their other roles as women in search of their own real or absent mothers, mother-surrogates for lost boys, perhaps for Reed himself, weaving around all of them the displaced reparative fictions, inspired by the memories of a broken childhood, through which he sought to know himself.

In addressing issues like these, sometimes through brilliant handling of film form, Reed stakes a legitimate claim to be considered one of the truly outstanding figures of the British cinema. As the old woman remarks to Kathy in *Odd Man Out*, 'That wasn't a bad fella as them fellas go ..., and what he said was true, darling.'

Filmography

It Happened in Paris, 1935, 68 mins, b/w

Directors: Carol Reed and Robert Wyler
Production company: Associated Talking Pictures
Producer: Bray Wyndham
Script: John Huston and H. F. Maltby (from the play *L'Arpete* by Yves Mirande)
Cast: John Loder (Paul), Nancy Burne (Jacqueline), Edward H. Robins (Knight), Dorothy Boyd (Patricia), Esme Percy (Pommier), Minnie Rayner (Concierge), Lawrence Grossmith (Bernard), Paul Sheridan (Baptiste), Bill Shine (Albert), Warren Jenkins (Raymond), Val Norton (Roger), Kyrle Bellew (Elvira), Nancy Pawley (Ernestine)

Midshipman Easy (AKA: Men of the Sea), 1935, 70 mins, b/w

Director: Carol Reed
Production company: Associated Talking Pictures
Producer: Basil Dean and Thorold Dickinson
Script: Anthony Kimmins (from novel by Capt. Frederick Marryat)
Cinematography: John W. Boyle
Film Editing: Sidney Cole
Art Direction: Edward Carrick
Musical Director: Ernest Irving
Cast: Hughie Green (Midshipman Easy), Margaret Lockwood (Donna Agnes), Roger Livesey (Captain), Robert Adams (Mesty), Harry Tate (Mr Biggs), Dennis Wyndham (Don Silvio), Tom Gill (Gascoine), Lewis Casson (Mr Easy), Dorothy Holmes-Gore (Mrs Easy), Frederick Burtwell (Mr Easthupp), Arnold Lucy (John Rebiera), Esme Church (Donna Rebiera)

Laburnum Grove, 1936, 73 mins, b/w

Director: Carol Reed
Production company: Associated Talking Pictures
Producer: Basil Dean

Script: Anthony Kimmins and Gordon Wellesley (from a play by J. B. Priestley)
Cinematography: John W. Boyle
Film Editing: Jack Kitchen
Art Direction: Edward Carrick and Denis Wreford
Music: Ernest Irving
Cast: Edmund Gwenn (Mr Redfern), Cedric Hardwicke (Mr Baxley), Victoria Hopper (Elsie Radfern), Ethel Coleridge (Mrs Baxley), Katie Johnson (Mrs Radfern), Francis James (Harold Russ), James Harcourt (Joe Fletten), Norman Walker (Man with glasses), David Hawthorne (Inspector Stack), Frederick Burtwell (Simpson), Terence Conlin (Police Sergeant)

Talk of the Devil, 1937, 76 mins, b/w

Director: Carol Reed
Production company: British and Dominions
Producer: Jack Raymond
Script: Anthony Kimmins, Carol Reed and George Barraud
Cinematography: Francis Carver
Film Editing: Merrill White, John Morris and Helen Lewis
Art Direction: C. Wilfred Arnold
Music: Percival Mackey
Cast: Ricardo Cortez (Ray Allen), Sally Eilers (Ann Marlow), Randle Ayrton (John Findlay), Basil Sydney (Stephen Findlay), Frederick Culley (Mr Alderson), Charles Carson (Lord Dymchurch), Gordon McLeod (The Inspector), Margaret Rutherford (Housekeeper)

Who's Your Lady Friend?, 1937, 73 mins, b/w

Director: Carol Reed
Production company: Dorian
Producer: Martin Sabine
Script: Anthony Kimmins and Julius Hoerst (from the play *Der Herr Ohne Wohnung* by Oesterreicher and Jenbach)
Cinematography: Jan Stallach
Film Editing: Merrill White, John Morris and Helen Lewis
Art Direction: Erwin Scharf
Music: Richard Stolz, Ernest Irving and Vivian Ellis
Cast: Frances Day (Lulu), Vic Oliver (Dr Mangold), Betty Stockfeld (Mrs Mangold), Romney Brent (Fred), Margaret Lockwood (Mimi), Frederick Ranalow (The Cabby), Sarah Churchill (Maid)

Bank Holiday (AKA: Three on a Weekend), 1938, 86 mins, b/w

Director: Carol Reed
Production company: Gainsborough
Producer: Edward Black
Script: Rodney Ackland, Roger Burford and Hans Wilhelm
Cinematography: Arthur Crabtree
Film Editing: R. E. Dearing
Art Direction: Vetchinsky
Cast: John Lodge (Stephen Howard), Margaret Lockwood (Catherine Law-
    rence), Hugh Williams (Geoffrey), René Ray (Doreen Richards), Merle
    Tottenham (Milly), Linden Travers (Ann Howard), Wally Patch (Arthur),
    Kathleen Harrison (May), Garry Marsh ('Follies' manager), Jeanne Stuart
    (Miss Mayfair), Wilfrid Lawson (Police Sergeant), Felix Aylmer (Surgeon),
    Michael Rennie (Guardsman)

Penny Paradise, 1938, 72 mins, b/w

Director: Carol Reed
Asst Director: Basil Dearden
Production company: Associated Talking Pictures
Producer: Basil Dean
Script: Thomas Thompson, W. L. Meade and Thomas Browne (from a story
    by Basil Dean)
Cinematography: Ronald Neame and Gordon Dimes
Film Editing: Ernest Aldridge
Art Direction: Wilfred Shingleton
Sound: Eric Williams
Music Score: Harry Davies and Harry O'Donovan
Cast: Edmund Gwenn (Joe Higgins), Jimmy O'Dea (Pat), Betty Driver (Betty
    Higgins), Ethel Coleridge (Aunt Agnes), Syd Crossley (Uncle Lancelot),
    James Harcourt (Amos Cook), Jack Livesey (Bert), Maire O'Neill (Widow
    Clegg)

Climbing High, 1938, 78 mins, b/w

Director: Carol Reed
Production company: Gaumont-British
Producer: Michael Balcon
Script: Marion Dix, Lesser Samuels and Stephen Clarkson
Cinematography: Mutz Greenbaum
Art Direction: Alfred Junge and W. W. Murton
Editing: A. Barnes and Michael Gordon
Sound: Alex Fisher
Costume Design: Norman Hartnell
Music Direction: Louis Levy

Cast: Michael Redgrave (Nicky Brooke), Jessie Matthews (Diana Castle), Margaret Vyner (Lady Constance), Alastair Sim (Max), Noel Madison (Gibson), Mary Clare (Lady Emily), Basil Radford (Reggie), Francis L. Sullivan (Madman), Enid Stamp-Taylor (Winnie), Torin Thatcher (Jim), Tucker McGuire (Patsey), Athole Stewart (Uncle)

A Girl Must Live, 1939, 89 mins, b/w

Director: Carol Reed
Production company: Gainsborough
Producer: Edward Black
Script: Frank Launder and Austin Melford
Cinematography: Jack Cox
Film Editing: R. E. Dearing
Art Direction: Vetchinsky
Music: Louis Levy
Cast: Margaret Lockwood (Leslie James), Renee Houston (Gloria Lind), Lilli Palmer (Clytie Devine), George Robey (Horace Blount), Hugh Sinclair (Earl of Pangborough), Naunton Wayne (Hugo Smythe Parkinson), David Burns (Joe Gold), Mary Clare (Mrs Wallis), Kathleen Harrison (Penelope), Drusilla Wills (Miss Pokinghorn), Wilson Coleman (Mr Joliffe), Kathleen Boutall (Mrs Blount), Muriel Aked (Mesdames Dupont), Martita Hunt (Mesdames Dupont)

The Stars Look Down, 1939, 110 mins, b/w

Director: Carol Reed
Production company: Grafton
Producer: Isadore Goldsmith
Script: J. B. Williams (from the novel by A. J. Cronin)
Cinematography: Mutz Greenbaum and Henry Harris
Film Editing: Reginald Black
Art Direction: James Carter
Music: Hans May
Cast: Michael Redgrave (Davey Fenwick), Margaret Lockwood (Jenny Sunley), Emlyn Williams (Joe Gowlan), Nancy Price (Martha Fenwick), Edward Rigby (Robert Fenwick), Allan Jeayes (Richard Barras), Cecil Parker (Stanley Millington), Milton Rosmer (Harry Nugent), Olga Lindo (Mrs Sunley), Desmond Tester (Hughie Fenwick), David Markham (Arthur Barras), Frederick Burtwell (Heddon), Edmund Willard (Ramage)

Night Train to Munich (AKA: Gestapo/Night Train), 1940, 93 mins, b/w

Director: Carol Reed
Production company: Twentieth Century Fox

Producer: Edward Black
Script: Sidney Gilliat and Frank Launder (from a story by Gordon Wellesley)
Cinematography: Otto Kanturek
Film Editing: R. E. Dearing
Art Direction: Vetchinsky
Sound Department: B. C. Sewell
Music: Louis Levy
Cast: Rex Harrison (Gus Bennett), Margaret Lockwood (Anna Bomasch), Paul Henreid (Karl Marsen), Basil Radford (Charters), Naunton Wayne (Caldicott), James Harcourt (Axel Bomasch), Felix Aylmer (Dr John Fredericks), Roland Culver (Roberts), Eliot Makeham (Schwab), Raymond Huntley (Kampenfeldt)

The Girl in the News, 1941, 78 mins, b/w

Director: Carol Reed
Production company: Twentieth Century Fox
Producer: Edward Black
Script: Sidney Gilliat (from the novel by Roy Vickers)
Cinematography: Otto Kanturek
Film Editing: R. E. Dearing
Art Direction: Vetchinsky
Sound Department: B. C. Sewell
Music: Louis Levy
Cast: Margaret Lockwood (Anne Graham), Barry Barnes (Stephen Garringdon), Emlyn Williams (Tracy), Roger Livesey (Bill Mather), Margaretta Scott (Judith Bentley), Basil Radford (Dr Treadgrove), Irene Handl (Miss Baker), Wyndham Goldie (Edward Bentley), Mervyn Johns (James Fetherwood), Betty Jardine (Elsie), Felix Aylmer (Prosecuting Counsel)

Kipps (AKA: The Remarkable Mr Kipps), 1941, 95 mins, b/w

Director: Carol Reed
Production company: Twentieth Century Fox
Producer: Edward Black
Script: Sidney Gilliat (from a story by H. G. Wells)
Cinematography: Arthur Crabtree
Film Editing: Alfred Roome
Art Direction: Vetchinsky
Costumes: Cecil Beaton
Original Music: Charles Williams
Music Direction: Louis Levy
Cast: Michael Redgrave (Arthur Kipps), Diana Wynyard (Helen Walshingham), Arthur Riscoe (Chitterlow), Phyllis Calvert (Ann Pornick), Max Adrian (Chester Coote), Helen Haye (Mrs Walshingham), Lloyd Pearson

(Shalford), Michael Wilding (Ronnie Walshingham), Edward Rigby (Buggins), Mackenzie Ward (Pearce), Hermione Baddeley (Miss Mergle), Betty Ann Davies (Flo Bates), Irene Browne (Mrs Bindon-Botting)

A Letter from Home, 1941, 17 mins, b/w

Director: Carol Reed
Production company: Twentieth Century Fox
Producer: Edward Black
Script: Rodney Ackland and Arthur Boys
Cinematography: Jack Cox
Cast: Celia Johnson

The Young Mr Pitt, 1942, 118 mins, b/w

Director: Carol Reed
Production company: Twentieth Century Fox
Producer: Edward Black
Script: Sidney Gilliat and Frank Launder (from a story by Viscount Castlerosse)
Cinematography: Freddie Young
Film Editing: R. E. Dearing
Art Direction: Vetchinsky
Sound Department: B. C. Sewell
Costume Design: Cecil Beaton and Elizabeth Haffenden
Music: Louis Levy
Cast: Robert Donat (William Pitt), Robert Morley (Charles James Fox), Jean Cadell (Mrs Sparry), Phyllis Calvert (Eleanor Eden), John Mills (William Wilberforce), Raymond Lovell (George the Third), Max Adrian (Sheridan), Felix Aylmer (Lord North), Albert Lieven (Talleyrand), Stephen Haggard (Lord Nelson), Geoffrey Atkins (William Pitt (as a boy)), Henry Hewitt (Addington), Herbert Lom (Napoleon)

The New Lot, 1942, 44 mins, b/w

Director: Carol Reed
Production company: Army Kinematographic Service

The Way Ahead (AKA: The Immortal Battalion), 1944, 115 mins, b/w

Director: Carol Reed
Asst Director: Frank Bevis
Production company: Two Cities
Producer: John Sutro and Norman Walker

Associate Producer: Stanley Haynes
Script: Peter Ustinov (from a story Eric Ambler)
Cinematography: Guy Green and Derick Williams
Special Effects: Henry Harris and Bill Warrington
Art Direction: David Rawnsley
Asst Art Direction: Arthur Lawson
Editing: Fergus McDonell
Sound: Desmond Dew, Harry Miller and C. C. Stevens
Original Music: William Alwyn
Music Direction: Muir Mathieson
Cast: David Niven (Lieutenant Jim Perry), Stanley Holloway (Brewer), James
    Donald (Lloyd), John Laurie (Luke), Jimmy Hanley (Stainer), William
    Hartnell (Sergeant Fletcher), Raymond Huntley (Davenport), Leslie
    Dwyer (Beck), Hugh Burden (Parsons), Reginald Tate (CO), Leo Genn
    (Captain Edwards), Renée Asherson (Marjorie Gillingham), Mary Jerrold
    (Mrs Gillingham), Tessie O'Shea (herself), Raymond Lovell (Mr Jackson),
    A. E. Matthews (Colonel Walmsley), Peter Ustinov (Rispoli, the cafe-
    owner), Jack Watling (Marjorie's boyfriend), Penelope Dudley-Ward
    (Mrs Perry), Trevor Howard (Officer on ship), George Merritt (Sergeant),
    Alfred Goddard (Instructor)

The True Glory, 1945, 87 mins, b/w

Director: Carol Reed and Garson Kanin
Production company: Ministry of Information, Britain; Office of War
    Information, USA
Script: Private Peter Ustinov, Gerald Kersh, Private Harry Brown, Staff Sgt
    Guy Trosper, Sgt Saul Levitt, Major Eric Maschwitz, Captain Frank
    Harvey, Flt Lt Arthur Macrae, Flt Officer Jenny Nicholson
Cinematography: Army Film Unit, American Army Pictorial Service, Camera-
    men of Britain, USA, Canada, France, Belgium, Poland, Holland, Czecho-
    slavakia and Norway
Editing: Lt Robert Verrell, Sgt Lieberwitz, Sgt Bob Farrell, Sgt Jerry Cowen,
    Sgt Bob Carrick, Sgt Bob Clark
Music: William Alwyn

Odd Man Out (AKA: Gang War), 1946, 111 mins, b/w

Director: Carol Reed
Asst Director: Mark Evans
Production company: Two Cities
Producers: Carol Reed and F. Del Giudice
Associate Producer: Phil C. Samuel
Script: F. L. Green and R. C. Sherriff (from the novel *Odd Man Out* by F. L.
    Green)

Cinematography: Robert Krasker
Special Effects: Stanley Grant and Bill Warrington
Art Direction: Ralph W. Brinton
Editing: Fergus McDonell
Sound: Desmond Dew and Harry Mille
Music Score: William Alwyn
Music Direction: Muir Mathieson (played by the London Symphony Orchestra)
Cast: James Mason (Johnny McQueen), Robert Beatty (Dennis), Robert
    Newton (Lukey), F. J. McCormick (Shell), Fay Compton (Rosie), Beryl
    Measor (Maudie), Cyril Cusack (Pat), Dan O'Herlihy (Nolan), Roy Irving
    (Murphy), Joseph Tomelty (Cabby), W. G. Fay (Father Tom), Arthur
    Hambling (Alfie), Kathleen Ryan (Kathleen), William Hartnell (Fencie),
    Denis O'Dea (Head Constable)

The Fallen Idol (AKA: Lost Illusion), 1948, 92 mins, b/w

Director: Carol Reed
Asst Director: Guy Hamilton
Production company: London Films
Producer: Carol Reed
Associate Producer: Phil Brandon
Script: Graham Greene. Additional dialogue by Lesley Storm and William
    Templeton (from the story *The Basement Room* by Graham Greene)
Cinematography: Georges Périnal
Special Effects: W. Percy Day
Art Direction: Vincent Korda and James Sawyer
Editing: Oswald Hafenrichter
Sound: Bert Ross
Music Score: William Alwyn
Music Direction: Dr Hubert Clifford
Cast: Ralph Richardson (Baines), Michèle Morgan (Julie), Jack Hawkins
    (Detective Ames), Bernard Lee (Detective Hart), Sonia Dresdel (Mrs
    Baines), Dora Bryan (Rose), Denis O'Dea (Inspector Crowe), Walter
    Fitzgerald (Dr Fenton), Karel Stepanek (First Secretary), Joan Young
    (Mrs Barrow), Dandy Nichols (Mrs Patterson), Geoffrey Keen (Detective
    Davis), Bobby Henrey (Philippe), Gerard Heinz (Ambassador), James
    Hayter (Perry), Hay Petrie (Clockwinder), John Ruddock (Dr Wilson)

The Third Man, 1949, 104 mins, b/w

Director: Carol Reed
Asst Director: Guy Hamilton
Production company: London Films

Producer: Carol Reed, Alexander Korda and David O. Selznick
Associate Producer: Hugh Perceval
Script: Graham Greene, Alexander Korda, Carol Reed and Orson Welles
(from the story *The Third Man* by Graham Greene)
Cinematography: Robert Krasker
Art Direction: John Hawkesworth, Joseph Bato and Vincent Korda
Asst Art Direction: Fernand Bellan
Editing: Oswald Hafenrichter
Costume Design: Ivy Baker and James Sawyer
Makeup: George Frost
Sound: John Cox
Music Direction: Anton Karas
Cast: Joseph Cotten (Holly Martins), Orson Welles (Harry Lime), Alida Valli
(Anna Schmidt), Trevor Howard (Major Calloway), Bernard Lee (Sergeant
Paine), Wilfrid Hyde White (Crabbin), Paul Hoerbiger (Porter), Ernst
Deutsch (Baron Kurtz), Herbeil Halbik (Hansel), Paul Hardtmuth (Hall
Porter), Alexis Chesnakov (Brodsky), Martin Boddey (Man), Nelly Arno
(Kurtz's Mother), Geoffrey Keen (British Policeman), Siegfried Breuer
(Popescu), Erich Ponto (Dr Winkel), Paul Smith (MP), Hedwig Bleibtreu
(Old Woman)

Outcast of the Islands, 1952, 102 mins, b/w

Director: Carol Reed
Production company: London Films
Producer: Carol Reed
Script: William Fairchild (from the novel by Joseph Conrad)
Cinematography: John Wilcox
Film Editing: Bert Bates
Art Direction: Vincent Korda
Music: Brian Easdale
Cast: Trevor Howard (Peter Willems), Ralph Richardson (Captain Lingard),
Robert Morley (Almayer), Wendy Hiller (Mrs Almayer), Kerima (Aissa),
George Coulouris (Babalatchi), A. V. Bramble (Badavi), Wilfrid Hyde
White (Vinck), Dharma Emmanuel (Ali), Annabel Morley (Nina), Betty
Ann Davies (Mrs Williams)

The Man Between, 1953, 100 mins, b/w

Director: Carol Reed
Production company: London Films
Producer: Carol Reed
Script: Harry Kurnitz (from the novel by Walter Ebert *Susanne in Berlin*)
Cinematography: Desmond Dickinson
Film Editing: A. S. Bates

Art Direction: Andre Andrejew
Sound Department: A. G. Ambler, John Cox and Red Law
Costume Design: Bridget Sellers
Music: John Addison
Music Direction: Muir Mathieson
Cast: James Mason (Ivo Kern), Claire Bloom (Susanne Mallison), Hildegard Neff (Bettina Mallison), Geoffrey Toone (Martin Mallison), Aribert Waescher (Halendar), Ernst Schroeder (Olaf Kastner), Dieter Krause (Horst), Hilde Sessak (Lizzi), Karl John (Inspector Kleiber)

A Kid for Two Farthings (AKA: The Unicorn), 1955, 96 mins, col.

Director: Carol Reed
Production company: London Films
Producer: Carol Reed
Script: Wolf Mankowitz (from his novel of the same name)
Cinematography: Edward Scaife
Film Editing: A. S. Bates
Art Direction: Wilfred Shingleton
Costume Design: Anna Duse
Music: Benjamin Frankel
Cast: Celia Johnson (Joanna), Diana Dors (Sonia), David Kossoff (Kandinsky), Brenda De Banzie ('Lady' Ruby), Joe Robinson (Sam), Jonathan Ashmore (Joe), Sidney Tafler (Madame Rita), Primo Carnera (Python Macklin), Lou Jacobi (Blackie Isaacs), Sid James (Ice Berg), Meier Leibovitch (Mendel), Irene Handl (Mrs Abramowitz), Danny Green (Bason), Alfie Bass (Alf)

Trapeze, 1956, 105 mins, col.

Director: Carol Reed
Production company: Hecht-Lancaster/Susan
Producers: Harold Hecht, James Hill and Burt Lancaster
Script: James R. Webb, Ben Hecht and Wolf Mankowitz (adaptation by Liam O'Brien) (from the Max Catto novel *The Killing Frost*)
Cinematography: Robert Krasker
Film Editing: Bert Bates
Production Design: Rino Mondellini
Costume Design: Veniero Colasanti
Makeup Department: Louis Bonnemaison, Iole Cecchini and Sarnelli Trieste
Sound Department: Jacques Carrère
Music: Malcolm Arnold
Music Direction: Muir Mathieson
Cast: Burt Lancaster (Mike Ribble), Tony Curtis (Tino Orsini), Gina Lollobrigida (Lola), Katy Jurado (Rosa), Thomas Gomez (Bouglione), Johnny

Puleo (Max the Dwarf), Minor Watson (John Ringling North), Gérard Landry (Chikki), Jean-Pierre Kérien (Otto), Gabrielle Fontan (Old Woman)

The Key, 1958, 134 mins, b/w

Director: Carol Reed
Production company: Open Road
Producer: Carl Foreman
Script: Carl Foreman (from the novel *Stella* by Jan de Hartog)
Cinematography: Oswald Morris
Film Editing: Bert Bates
Art Direction: Geoffrey Drake
Music: Malcolm Arnold
Cast: William Holden (David Ross), Sophia Loren (Stella), Trevor Howard (Chris Ford), Oskar Homolka (Van Dam), Kieron Moore (Kane), Bernard Lee (Wadlow), Beatrix Lehmann (Housekeeper), Noel Purcell (Porter), Bryan Forbes (Weaver), Russell Waters (Sparks)

Our Man in Havana, 1959, 111 mins, b/w

Director: Carol Reed
Production company: Columbia
Producer: Carol Reed
Associate Producer: Raymond Anzarut
Script: Graham Greene (from his novel *Our Man in Havana*)
Cinematography: Oswald Morris
Film Editing: Bert Bates
Art Direction: John Box
Costume Design: Phyllis Dalton
Makeup Department: Gordon Bond and Harry Frampton
Sound Department: John Cox, Red Law, Edward McQueen-Mason and John W. Mitchell
Music: Hermanos Deniz Cuban Rhythm Band
Cast: Alec Guinness (Jim Wormold), Maureen O'Hara (Beatrice Severn), Burl Ives (Doctor Hasselbacher), Ernie Kovacs (Captain Segura), Noel Coward (Hawthorne), Ralph Richardson ('C'), Jo Morrow (Milly), Paul Rogers (Hubert Carter), Grégoire Aslan (Cifuentes), Jose Prieto (Lopez), Duncan Macrae (MacDougal), Maurice Denham (Admiral), Raymond Huntley (General)

Mutiny on the Bounty, 1962, 178 mins, col.

Director: Lewis Milestone (uncredited Carol Reed)
Production company: MGM/Arcola
Producer: Aaron Rosenberg

Script: Charles Lederer, Eric Ambler, William L. Driscoll, Borden Chase, John Gay and Ben Hecht (from the novel by Charles Nordhoff and James Norman Hall)
Cinematography: Robert Surtees
Film Editing: John McSweeney Jr
Art Direction: George W. Davis and J. McMillan Johnson
Production Design: George W. Davis, Henry Grace, J. McMillan Johnson and Hugh Hunt
Costume Design: Moss Mabry
Makeup Department: Mary Keats and William Tuttle
Sound Department: Milo B. Lory
Music: Bronislau Kaper
Cast: Marlon Brando (Fletcher Christian), Trevor Howard (Capt. William Bligh), Richard Harris (John Mills), Hugh Griffith (Alexander Smith), Richard Haydn (William Brown), Tarita (Maimiti), Percy Herbert (Matthew Quintal), Duncan Lamont (John Williams), Chips Rafferty (Michael Byrne), Noel Purcell (William McCoy), Ashley Cowan (Samuel Mack)

The Running Man, 1963, 103 mins, col.

Director: Carol Reed
Production company: Columbia
Producer: Carol Reed
Script: John Mortimer (from the Shelly Smith novel *The Ballad of the Running Man*)
Cinematography: Robert Krasker
Film Editing: Bert Bates
Art Direction: John Stoll
Makeup Department: George Frost and George Scott
Sound Department: Claude Hitchcock, Bob Jones and Peter Thornton
Music: William Alwyn
Music Direction: Muir Mathieson
Cast: Laurence Harvey (Rex Black), Lee Remick (Stella Black), Alan Bates (Stephen), Felix Aylmer (Parson), Eleanor Summerfield (Hilda Tanner), Allan Cuthbertson (Jenkins), Harold Goldblatt (Tom Webster), Noel Purcell (Miles Bleeker), Ramsay Ames (Madge Penderby), Fernando Rey (Police Official), Juan José Menéndez (Roberto), Eddie Byrne (Sam Crewdson), Colin Gordon (Solicitor), John Meillon (Jim Jerome), Roger Delgado (Spanish Doctor)

The Agony and the Ecstasy, 1965, 138 mins, col.

Director: Carol Reed
Production company: Twentieth Century Fox
Producer: Carol Reed

Script: Philip Dunne (from the Irving Stone novel *The Agony and the Ecstasy*)
Cinematography: Leon Shamroy
Film Editing: Samuel Beetley
Art Direction: Jack Martin Smith
Production Design: John DeCuir
Costume Design: Vittorio Nino Novarese
Makeup Department: Grazia De Rossi and Amato Garbini
Sound Department: Carlton W. Faulkner and Douglas O. Williams
Music: Alex North
Music Direction: Alexander Courage
Cast: Charlton Heston (Michelangelo), Rex Harrison (Pope Julius II), Diane
    Cilento (Contessina de Medici), Harry Andrews (Bramante), Alberto
    Lupo (Duke of Urbino), Adolfo Celi (Giovanni de Medici), Venantino
    Venantini (Paris De Grassis), John Stacy (Sangallo), Fausto Tozzi
    (Foreman), Maxine Audley (Woman), Tomas Milian (Raphael)

Oliver!, 1968, 133 mins, col.

Director: Carol Reed
Production company: Romulus/Warwick/Columbia
Producer: Donald Albery and John Woolf
Script: Vernon Harris and Lionel Bart (from the Charles Dickens novel
    Oliver Twist)
Cinematography: Oswald Morris
Film Editing: Ralph Kemplen
Art Direction: Terence Marsh
Production Design: John Box
Costume Design: Phyllis Dalton
Makeup Department: George Frost and Bobbie Smith
Sound Department: Buster Ambler, John Cox, Jim Groom and Bob Jones
Music: Lionel Bart and Johnny Green
Cast: Ron Moody (Fagin), Shani Wallis (Nancy), Oliver Reed (Bill Sikes),
    Harry Secombe (Mr Bumble), Mark Lester (Oliver Twist), Jack Wild (The
    Artful Dodger), Hugh Griffith (The Magistrate), Joseph O'Conor (Mr
    Brownlow), Peggy Mount (Mrs Bumble), Leonard Rossiter (Mr Sower-
    berry), Hylda Baker (Mrs Sowerberry), Kenneth Cranham (Noah
    Claypole), Megs Jenkins (Mrs Bedwin), Sheila White (Bet), Wensley
    Pithey (Dr Grimwig), James Hayter (Mr Jessop), Elizabeth Knight
    (Charlotte), Fred Emney (Workhouse Chairman)

The Last Warrior (AKA: Flap), 1970, 107 mins, col.

Director: Carol Reed
Production company: Warner Brothers
Producer: Jerry Adler
Script: Clair Huffaker (from her novel *Nobody Loves a Drunken Indian*)
Cinematography: Fred J. Koenekamp
Film Editing: Frank Bracht
Art Direction: Mort Rabinowitz
Music: Marvin Hamlisch
Cast: Anthony Quinn (Flapping Eagle), Shelley Winters (Dorothy Bluebell), Claude Akins (Lobo Jackson), Tony Bill (Eleven Snowflake), Victor Jory (Wounded Bear), Victor French (Rafferty), Rodolfo Acosta (Storekeeper), Anthony Caruso (Silver Dollar), Don Collier (Mike Lyons), Susanna Miranda (Ann Locking)

Follow Me (AKA: The Public Eye), 1972, 95 mins, col.

Director: Carol Reed
Production company: Universal
Producer: Hal B. Wallis
Associate Producer: Paul Nathan
Script: Peter Shaffer (adapted from his play of the same name)
Cinematography: Christopher Challis
Film Editing: Anne V. Coates
Art Direction: Robert Cartwright
Production Design: Terence Marsh
Costume Design: Julie Harris
Makeup Department: Ronnie Cogan and Hugh Richards
Sound Department: John Aldred, Bob Bones and Don Sharpe
Music: John Barry
Cast: Mia Farrow (Belinda), Topol (Julian Cristoforou), Michael Jayston (Charles), Margaret Rawlings (Mrs Sidley), Annette Crosbie (Miss Framer), Dudley Foster (Mr Mayhew), Michael Aldridge (Sir Philip Crouch), Michael Barrington (Mr Scrampton), Neil McCarthy (Parkinson)

References

Agate, James (1941), 'Myself at the Pictures. Kipps and not Kipps', *Tatler*, 4 June.

Ambler, Eric and Peter Ustinov (n/d) *The Way Ahead*. Draft script 3, BFI Carol Reed special collection.

Anderson, Benedict (1991 [1983]), *Imagined Communities. Reflections on the Origin and Spread of Nationalism*, London: Verso.

Anon (1939a), 'Climbing High', *Glasgow Bulletin*, 5 June.

Anon (1939b), 'Climbing High', *News Chronicle*, 25 February.

Anon (1939c), 'Climbing High', *News Review*, 2 March.

Anon (1940a), 'The Stars Look Down', *The Manchester Guardian*, 27 March.

Anon (1940b), 'The New Films: *The Stars Look Down*', *Newcastle Evening Chronicle*, 6 March.

Anon (1941a), 'The Week's New Films (*Kipps*)', *News Chronicle*, 23 May.

Anon (1941b), 'The Cinema. British Films in 1941', *The Scotsman*, 21 January.

Anon (1948), 'October releases. A Graham Greene Screenplay', *The Tablet*, 16 October.

Anon (1952), 'Outcast of the Islands', *The Daily Mail*, 18 January,

Anon (1955a), 'La Lollo on the Trapeze', *The Daily Sketch*, 7 May.

Anon (1955b), 'La Lollo's Return', *The Star*, 24 January.

Anon (1959), 'Our Man in Havana', *The Daily Telegraph*, 16 April.

Anon (1963a), 'What Makes Larry Run?', *The Daily Mirror*, 2 August.

Anon (1963b), 'The Running Man', *The Daily Worker*, 3 August.

Anon (1963c), 'Look, It's Harvey in Ginger Whiskers!', *The Evening Standard*, 1 August.

Anon (1963d), 'The Running Man', *The Jewish Chronicle*, 2 August.

Anon (1963e), 'The Running Man', *The New Statesman*, 2 August.

Anon (1963f), 'The Running Man', *The People*, 11 August.

Anon (1963g), 'The Running Man', *The Tablet*, 7 August.

Anon (1963h), 'Sir Carol Reed Underrates his Audience', *The Times*, 1 August.

Anstey, Edgar (1941), 'The Cinema', *The Spectator*, 16 May.

Babington, Bruce, ed. (2001), *British Stars and Stardom from Alma Taylor to Sean Connery*, Manchester: Manchester University Press.

Babington, Bruce (2001), '"Queen of British Hearts": Margaret Lockwood revisited', in Babington, ed. (2001): pp. 94–107)
Babington, Bruce (2002), *Launder and Gilliat*, Manchester and New York: Manchester University Press.
Babington, Bruce and Peter William Evans (1985), *Blue Skies and Silver Linings. Aspects of the Hollywood Musical*, Manchester and New York: Manchester University Press.
Babington, Bruce and Peter William Evans (1989), *Affairs to Remember. The Hollywood Comedy of the Sexes*, Manchester and New York; Manchester University Press.
Barker, Felix (1958), 'Two Hours and I Knew...', *The Evening News*, 29 May.
Barker, Felix (1963), 'Snap', *Evening News*, 1 August.
Barr, Charles, ed. (1986), *All Our Yesterdays. 90 Years of British Cinema*, London: British Film Institute.
Barthes, Roland (1970), *S/Z*, Paris: Seuil.
Barthes, Roland (1973 [1953]), 'Wrestling', in *Mythologies*, London: Paladin: pp. 15–25.
Bell, David, ed. (1999), *Psychoanalysis and Culture. A Kleinian Perspective*, London: Duckworth.
Bloom, Harold (1973), *The Anxiety of Influence. A Theory of Poetry*, New York and London: Oxford University Press.
Borossa, Julia (2001), *Hysteria*, Cambridge: Icon Books.
Bowlby, John (1953), *Child Care and the Growth of Love*, Harmondsworth: Penguin.
Bowra, C. M. (1952), *Heroic Poetry*, London: Macmillan.
Britton, Andrew (1983), *Cary Grant: Comedy and Male Desire*, Newcastle: Tyneside Cinema.
Brown, Geoff (1977), *Launder and Gilliat*, London: British Film Institute.
Bruzzi, Stella (1997), *Undressing Cinema. Clothes and Identity in the Movies*, London: Routledge.
Buford, Kate (2000), *Burt Lancaster. An American Life*, London: Aurum Press.
Campbell, Joseph (1988 [1972]), *The Hero with a Thousand Faces*, Princeton, New Jersey: Princeton University Press.
Catto, Max (1959 [1950]), *Trapeze (The Killing Frost)*, London: Four Square Books.
Cavell, Stanley (1981), *Pursuits of Happiness: the Hollywood Comedy of Remarriage*, Cambridge, Massachusetts and London: Harvard University Press.
Chapman, James (1998), *The British at War. Cinema, State and Propaganda, 1939–1945*, London: I. B. Tauris.
Connell, R. W. (1995), *Masculinities*, Cambridge: Polity Press.
Connolly, Kate (1999), 'Harry in the Shadow', *The Guardian*, Saturday Review, 10 July: 5.
Conrad, Joseph (1992 [1895]), *An Outcast of the Islands*, Oxford: Oxford University Press.

Creed, Barbara (1993), *The Monstruous Feminine. Film, Feminism and Psychoanalysis*, London: Routledge.

Cronin, A. J. (1997 [1935]), *The Stars Look Down*, London: Vista.

Curtis, Tony and Barry Paris (1994), *Tony Curtis. The Autobiography*. London: Heinemann.

Custen, George F. (1992), *Bio/Pics. How Hollywood Constructed Public History*, New Brunswick, New Jersey: Rutgers University Press.

Dehn, Paul (1948), 'Greatest Kid since Coogan', *Sunday Chronicle*, 3 October.

Dixon, Campbell (1956), 'Lollobrigida Enchantress', *The Daily Telegraph*, 30 June.

Drazin, Charles (1998), *The Finest Years. British Cinema of the 1940s*, London: André Deutsch.

Drazin, Charles (1999), *In Search of the Third Man*, London: Methuen.

Durgnat, Raymond (1971 [1970]), *A Mirror for England. British Movies from Austerity to Affluence*, New York and Washington, DC: Praeger.

Dyer, Richard (1977a), 'Entertainment and Utopia', *Movie*, 24: 1–13.

Dyer, Richard (1977b), 'Stereotyping', in Dyer, ed. *Gays and Film*, London: British Film Institute, pp. 27–39.

Evans, Peter W. (2001), 'James Mason: the Man Between', in Babington, ed. (2001): pp. 108–19.

Eyles, Allen (1985), *Rex Harrison*, London: W. H. Allen.

Fairchild, William (1951), *Outcast of the Islands*. Revised draft-script, with Carol Reed's corrections, 2nd Roneo Version, BFI Carol Reed Special Collections.

Falk, Quentin (1990 [1984], *Travels in Greeneland. The Cinema of Graham Greene*, London and New York: Quartet Books.

Forrester, C. S. (1949 [1943]), *The Ship*, Harmondsworth: Penguin.

Forster, Leonard, ed. (1975 [1957]), *Oxford Book of German Verse*, Oxford: Oxford University Press.

Freud, Sigmund (1982 [1953]), *The Interpretation of Dreams* (Penguin Freud Library, vol. 4), Harmondsworth: Penguin Books.

Freud, Sigmund (1983 [1905]), *Jokes and Their Relation to the Unconscious*, Harmondsworth: Penguin.

Freud, Sigmund (1984a), 'Instincts and their Vicissitudes (1915)', in *On Metapsychology. The Theory of Psychoanalysis*, Harmondsworth: Penguin, pp. 105–38.

Freud, Sigmund (1984b [1957]), *Leonardo da Vinci. A Memory of His Childhood*, London, Melbourne and Henley: Ark Paperbacks.

Freud, Sigmund (1985a [1955]), 'Civilization and Its Discontents (1929)', in *Civilization, Society and Religion, Group Psychology*, in *Civilization and Its Discontents and Other Works* (Penguin Freud Library, vol. 12), Harmondsworth: Penguin Books, pp. 251–340.

Freud, Sigmund (1985b [1955]), 'Group Psychology and the Analysis of the Ego (1921)', in *Civilization, Society and Religion, Group Psychology*, in *Civilization and Its Discontents and Other Works* (Penguin Freud Library, vol. 12), Harmondsworth: Penguin Books, pp. 91–178.

Freud, Sigmund (1985c), 'Thoughts for the Times. On War and Death (1915)' and 'Group Psychology and the Analysis of the Ego (1921)', in *Civilization, Society and Religion, Group Psychology, Civilization and Its Discontents and Other Works*, Harmondsworth: Penguin, pp. 57–89 and 93–178.

Freud, Sigmund (1990 [1953]), 'The "Uncanny" (1919)', in *Art and Literature* (Penguin Freud Library, vol. 14), Harmondsworth: Penguin Books, pp. 339–76.

Freud, Sigmund and Joseph Breuer (1991 [1893]), *Studies on Hysteria* (Penguin Freud Library, vol. 3), Harmondsworth: Penguin.

Frye, Northrop (1969 [1957]), *Anatomy of Criticism. Four Essays*, New York: Atheneum.

Geraghty, Christine (1984), 'Masculinity', in Geoff Hurd, ed., *National Fictions. World War II in British Film and Television*, London: British Film Institute, pp. 63–8.

Geraghty, Christine (1986), 'Diana Dors', in Barr, ed. (1986): pp. 341–5.

Geraghty, Christine (2000), *British Cinema in the Fifties. Gender, Genre and the 'New Look'*, London and New York: Routledge.

Gledhill, Christine and Gillian Swanson, (1996), 'Introduction', in Christine Gledhill and Gillian Swanson, eds., *Nationalising Femininity. Culture, Sexuality and British Cinema in the Second World War*, Manchester: Manchester University Press, pp. 1–12.

Green, F. L. and R. C. Sherriff (1948 [1945]), *Odd Man Out*, London: Penguin.

Greene, Graham (1971 [1958]), *Our Man in Havana*, Harmondsworth: Penguin.

Greene, Graham (1980 [1972]), *The Pleasure-Dome. Graham Greene. The Collected Film Criticism 1935–40*, edited by John Russell Taylor, Oxford, New York, Toronto, Melbourne: Oxford University Press.

Greene, Graham (1982 [1935 and 1950]), *The Third Man and The Fallen Idol*, Harmondsworth: Penguin.

Greene, Graham (2001 [1948]), *The Heart of the Matter*, London: Vintage.

Greene, Graham (2001 [1955]), *The Quiet American*, London: Vintage.

Greene, Graham (n/da), 'Letter to Carol Reed', BFI Special Collections.

Greene, Graham (n/d b) *The Third Man*. Script, BFI Carol Reed Special Collection.

Greer, Germaine (1971), *The Female Eunuch*, London: Paladin.

Grinberg, León and Rebeca Grinberg (1999), 'Psychoanalytic Perspectives on Migration', in David Bell, ed., *Psychoanalysis and Culture. A Kleinian Perspective*, London: Duckworth, pp. 154–69.

Guest, Val (2001), *So You Want to Be in Pictures. From Will Hay to Hammer Horror*, London: Reynolds & Hearn.

Haining, Peter (1984), *The Last Gentleman. A Tribute to David Niven*, London: W. H. Allen.

Harman, J. (1959), 'Sorry, Alec. You're not the Best Man in Havana', *The Evening News*, 31 December.

Harper, Sue (2000), *Women in British Cinema. Mad, Bad and Dangerous to Know*, London: Continuum.

Henderson, Joseph L. (1978 [1964]), 'Ancient Myths and Modern Men', in Jung, ed. (1978 [1964]): pp. 97–156.

Hennessy, Peter (1992), *Never Again. Britain 1945–51*, London: Jonathan Cape.

Hornung, E. W. (2003 [1899]), *Raffles: The Amateur Cracksman*, Harmondsworth: Penguin Books.

Hylton, Stuart (2003), *Their Darkest Hour. The Hidden History of the Home Front, 1939–1945*, Stroud: Sutton Publishing Ltd.

Jung, Carl (1978 [1964]), 'Approaching the Unconscious', in Jung, ed. (1978 [1964]): pp. 1–94.

Jung, Carl (1983), *Jung. Selected Writings*, intr. by Anthony Storr, London: Fontana.

Jung, Carl, ed. (1978 [1964]), *Man and His Symbols*, London: Picador.

Kabbani, Rana (1994 [1986]), *Imperial Fictions. Europe's Myth of Orient*, London: Pandora.

Kael, Pauline (1968), 'The Concealed Art of Carol Reed', *The New Yorker*, 44, 14 December: 193–6.

Kirwan, Patrick (1947), 'James Mason Vindicates Himself', *The Evening Standard*, 1 February.

Klein, Melanie and Joan Riviere (1964), *Love, Hate and Reparation*, New York and London: W. W. Norton.

Korda, Alexander (1953), 'Telegram to Carol Reed', 26 February, BFI Special Collections.

Kristeva, Julia (1969), *Semiotike. Recherches pour une sémantique*, Paris: Seuil.

Landy, Marcia (1991), *British Genres. British Cinema and Society, 1930–1960*, Princeton, New Jersey: Princeton University Press.

Lejeune, C. A. (1941), 'Kipps', *The Observer*, 25 May.

Lejeune, C. A. (1960), 'Our Man in Havana', *The Observer*, 3 January.

Lewin, David (1959), 'Our Man in Havana', *The Daily Express*, 16 April.

Light, Alison (1991), *Forever England. Femininity, Literature and Conservatism Between the Wars*, London: Routledge.

Lockwood, Margaret (1955), *Lucky Star. The Autobiography of Margaret Lockwood*, London: Odhams Press.

Loughlin, James (1995), *Ulster Unionism and British National Identity*, London and New York: Pinter.

Mackillop, Ian and Neil Sinyard (2003a), 'Celebrating British Cinema of the 1950s', in Mackillop and Sinyard, eds (2003): pp. 1–10.

Mackillop, Ian and Neil Sinyard, eds (2003b), *British Cinema of the 1950s. A Celebration*, Manchester: Manchester University Press.

Mason, James (1952), 'Letter to Carol Reed', 13 December, BFI Special Collections.

Mason, James (1982 [1981]), *Before I Forget. An Autobiography*, London: Sphere.

Matthews, Jessie (1974), *Over My Shoulder. An Autobiography as Told to Muriel Burgess*, London: W. H. Allen.

Medhurst, Andy (1986), 'Dirk Bogarde', in Barr, ed. (1986): pp. 346–54.

Medhurst, Andy (1996), 'Victim: Text as Context', in Andrew Higson, ed., *Dissolving Views. Key Writings on British Cinema*, London: Cassell, pp. 117–32.

Modleski, Tania (1988), *The Women Who Knew Too Much. Hitchcock and Feminist Theory*, London and New York: Methuen.

Morley, Sheridan (1985), *The Other Side of the Moon. The Life of David Niven*, London: Weidenfeld & Nicolson.

Mosley, Leonard (1956), 'La Lollo Speaks English – I Wasn't Listening', *The Daily Express*, 27 June.

Moss, Robert F. (1987), *The Films of Carol Reed*, New York: Columbia University Press.

Muller, Robert (1959), 'Our Man in Havana', *The Daily Mail*, 30 December.

Mulvey, Laura (1989), *Visual and Other Pleasures*, Basingstoke: Macmillan.

Murphy, Robert (1986), 'Riff-raff: British cinema and the Underworld', in Barr, ed. (1986): pp. 286–305.

Murphy, Robert (2000), *British Cinema and the Second World War*, London: Continuum.

Nietzsche, F. (1984 [1885]), *Beyond Good and Evil. Prelude to a Mythology of the Future*, trans. and intr. by R. J. Hollingdale. Harmondsworth: Penguin.

Niven, David (1971), *The Moon's a Balloon. Reminiscences*, London: Hamish Hamilton.

Orwell, George (1988 [1941]), 'England Your England', *The Lion and the Unicorn. Socialism and the English Genius*, Harmondsworth: Penguin, pp. 33–70.

Phillips, Adam (2000), *Promises, Promises*, London: Faber & Faber.

Pollock, Griselda (1980–81), 'Artists, Mythologies and Media Genius. Madness and Art History', *Screen*, 21: 57–96.

Powell, Dilys (1941), 'Kipps on the Screen', *Sunday Times*, 25 May.

Priestley, J.B. (1934), *English Journey*, London: William Heinemann.

Priestley, J. B. (1935), *Laburnum Grove. A Play*, London: Samuel French.

Raymond, Moore (1940), 'There is a New Spirit in Britain's Film Studies', *Sunday Despatch*, 27 October.

Redgrave, Michael (1983), *In My Mind's Eye. An Autobiography*, London: Weidenfeld and Nicolson.

Reid, David and Jayne L. Walker (1993), 'Strange Pursuits: Cornell Woolrich and the Abandoned City of the Forties', in Joan Copec, ed., *Shades of Noir. A Reader*, London and New York: Verso, pp. 57–96.

Reisz, Karel and Gavin Millar (1999 [1953]), *The Technique of Film Editing*, Oxford: Focal Press.

Richards, Jeffrey (1997), *Films and British National Identity. From Dickens to Dad's Army*, Manchester: Manchester University Press.

Richardson, Michael (1994), *Georges Bataille*, London and New York: Routledge.

Rodó, José Enrique (1967 [1900]), *Ariel*, Cambridge: Cambridge University Press.

Roth, Mark (1981), 'Some Warner's Musicals and the Spirit of the New Deal', in Rick Altman, ed., *Genre. The Musical*, London: RKP/BFI, pp. 41–56.

Roud, Richard (1963), 'Whatever Happened', *The Guardian*, 2 August.

Samuels, Charles Thomas (1972), *Encountering Directors. Interviews*, New York: Capricorn Books.

Sapper (2001 [1920]), *Bulldog Drummond*, Thirsk: House of Stratus.

Sarris, Andrew (1957a), 'First of the Realists', *Films and Filming*, September: 10–11 and 32.

Sarris, Andrew (1957b), 'The Stylist Goes to Hollywood', *Films and Filming*, October: 11–12 and 30.

Schmitt, Richard (1996), 'Racism and Objectification: Reflections on Themes from Fanon', in Lewis R. Gordon, T. Denean Sharplye-Whiting and Renée T. White, eds, *Fanon: A Critical Reader*, Oxford: Blackwell Publishers, pp. 35–50.

Secunda, Victoria (1993), *Women and Their Father. The Sexual and Romantic Impact of the First Man in Your Life*, London: Cedar.

Sedgwick, Eve Kosofsky (1985), *Between Men. English Literature and Male Homosocial Desire*, New York: Columbia University Press.

Shohat, Ella and Robert Stam (1994), *Unthinking Eurocentrism. Multiculturalism and the Media*, London: Routledge.

Sinyard, Neil (2001), 'Sir Alec Guinness: The Self-Effacing Star', in Babington, ed. (2001): pp. 143–54.

Sinyard, Neil (2003), *Graham Greene. A Literary Life*, London: Macmillan.

Sontag, Susan (1980 [1974]), *Under the Sign of Saturn*, New York: Farrar, Strauss and Giroux.

Spicer, Andrew (2003 [2001]), *Typical Men. The Representation of Masculinity in Popular British Cinema*, London and New York: I. B. Tauris.

St Paul (1983), 'The First Epistle of Paul the Apostle to the Corinthians', *The Holy Bible*, London: Eyre and Spottiswoode Limited.

Storr, Anthony (1982 [1968]), *Human Aggression*, Harmondsworth: Penguin.

Strachan, Alan (2004), *Sweet Dreams: A Biography of Michael Redgrave*, London: Weidenfeld and Nicolson.

Street, Sarah (2001), *Costume and Cinema. Dress Code in Popular Film*, London and New York: Wallflower Press.

Theweleit, Klaus (1987), *Male Fantasies*, Cambridge: Polity Press.

Twentieth Century Fox (1965), *The Agony and the Ecstasy. Royal Premiere Screening Programme*, 27 October.

Vasari, Giorgio (1983 [1568]), *Lives of the Artists*, Harmondsworth: Penguin.

Vaughan, Dai (1995), *Odd Man Out*, London: BFI.

Wapshott, Nicholas (1990), *The Man Between. A Biography of Carol Reed*, London: Chatto & Windus.

Wapshott, Nicholas (1991), *Rex Harrison: a Biography*, London: Chatto and Windus.

Watts, Stephen (1950), 'The Fourth Man...', *Picturegoer*, 4 March: 7–8.

Welldon, Estela V. (1980), *Mother, Madonna, Whore. The Idealization and Degradation of Motherhood*, New York and London: The Guilford Press.

Welles, Orson (n/d) 'Letter to Carol Reed', BFI Carol Reed Special Collections, Item 55.

Wells, H. G. (1995 [1909]), *Ann Veronica*, London: J. M. Dent.

Wells, H. G. (1999 [1905]), *Kipps. The Story of a Simple Soul*, London: J. M. Dent.

White, Gordon S. (1948), 'Letter to Carol Reed', 9 November, BFI Special Collection.

White, Rob (2003), *The Third Man*, London: British Film Institute.

Whitebait, W. (1940), 'Night Train to Munich', *New Statesman*, 3 August.

Whitehall, Richard (1962), 'The Stars Look Down', *Films and Filming*, 4 January: 22–3 and 45–6.

Whiteley, Reg (1946), 'Mason Can Take It', *Daily Mirror*, 31 May.

Williams, J. B. and Carol Reed (1939), *The Stars Look Down* (Screenplay), BFI Special Collections.

Wilson, Cecil (1963), 'Up from the Mire to Martinis in Malaga', *The Daily Mail*, 2 August.

Winnicott, D. W. (1962 [1957]), *The Child and the Family. First Relationships*, ed. Janet Hardenberg, London: Tavistock.

Wood, Michael (1975), *America in the Movies; or 'Santa Maria It Had Slipped My Mind'*, London: Secker and Warburg.

Young, Robert (1993 [1990)], *White Mythologies. Writing History and the West*, London: Routledge.

Index